Lace
One-Skein
Wonders

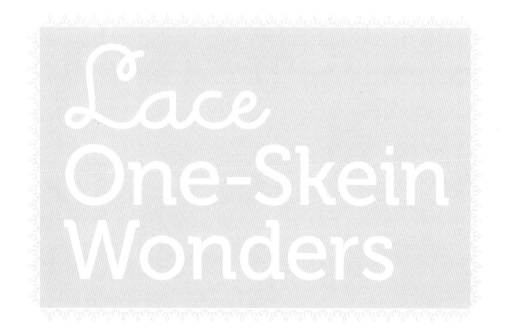

Lace One-Skein Wonders

Edited by
Judith Durant

Photography by Geneve Hoffman

The mission of Storey Publishing is to serve our customers by publishing practical information that encourages personal independence in harmony with the environment.

Edited by Melinda A. Sheehan, Pam Thompson, and Gwen Steege
Art direction and book design by Mary Winkelman Velgos

Photography by © Geneve Hoffman
Photo styling by Wendy Freedman
Set design by Geneve Hoffman
Illustrations by Alison Kolesar
Charts and diagrams by Lori Gayle

Indexed by Nancy D. Wood
Tech edit by Lori Gayle

Storey Publishing
210 MASS MoCA Way
North Adams, MA 01247
www.storey.com

Printed in China by R.R. Donnelley
10 9 8 7 6 5 4 3 2 1

Library of Congress Cataloging-in-Publication Data

Lace one-skein wonders / edited by Judith Durant.
pages cm
Includes index.
ISBN 978-1-61212-058-4 (pbk. : alk. paper)
ISBN 978-1-60342-843-9 (ebook)
1. Knitted lace—Patterns. I. Durant, Judith, 1955– editor.
TT805.K54L33 2013
746.2—dc23

2013012523

Storey Publishing is committed to making environmentally responsible manufacturing decisions. This book was printed on paper made from sustainably harvested fiber.

contents

introduction............. 8

from head to toe 9

Hats & Caps

Etta Hat 10
Tredegar Hat 12
Lacy Liberty Wool Hat 14
Pine Needle Toque 16
Very Pretty Lace Beret 18
Twig Lace Cap 21
Alexandra Hat. 23
Hepatica Hats 25
Nicole's Angora Beanie 27
Ellie's Orange Tam 29
Flutter Toque. 31
Tilting Ladders Hat 33

Mitts, Gloves & Cuffs

Sweet Pea Mitts. 36
Lacy Hand Warmers 39
Trellis Mitts 43
Vine Lace Fingerless Gloves 46
Travel-Worthy Mitts. 48
Pine Needle Mittens. 51
Flutter Mitts 54
Damask Lace Gloves 56
Spicy Lace Cuffs 60

Socks

Downy Buffalo Socks. 62
Tribute Socks. 64
Galvez Socks 68
Buckhorn Socks .71
Vesta Socks 74
Flemish Lace Socks 79
Small Falls Socks. 82

knits for kids 85

Baby & Toddler Wear

Coral Reef Hat 86
Sea Mist Baby Hat 88
Bunny Check Baby Hat 90
Little Leg Warmers 92
Kaya Baby Sweater 95
Lace Baby Top 100
Baby Twist Pullover 103
Three-Button Baby Sweater 105
Hana 109
Haru 112
I Heart You Dress 115

To Have and To Hold

Welcome Home Baby Blanket 120
Granny's Little Diamond
 Lace Blankie 122
Lacy Pig Buddy 124
Meg's Doll Ensemble 126

it's a wrap 129

Scarves

Spring Leaves Scarf 130
Christine's Alpaca Lace Scarf 132
Beaded Lace Scarf 134
Mezzaluna Scarf 136
Luxe Möbius Scarf 139
Emerald Lace Scarf 141
River Rapids 143
Butterflies Are Free 145
Lake Effect Scarf 148
Menat Scarf 150
Raindrops Scarf 152
Paper Lanterns Scarf 154
Chantilly Lace Scarf 155
Broomstick Lace Scarf 157
Cleopatra Scarf 158
A Spray of Lace 164
Ostrich Plumes Scarf 166
Choose Your Look Scarf 167
Symmetria Scarf 169

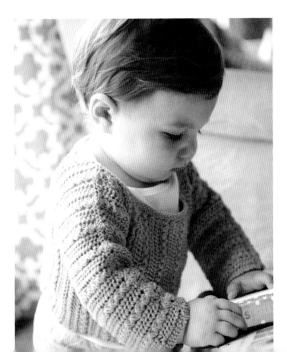

Cowls

April Showers Cowl 173
Mari Lace Cowl 174
Silver Lamé Cowl 176
Jade Sapphire Cowl. 177
Flying Gulls Cowl 180
Violeta Cowl. 181
Islandwood Cowl 183
Pitched Cowl 186
Absolu Lace Cowl 187

Shawls & Stoles

Mirabel Shawl 188
Mary's Shawl 192
Isobel Shawl 193
Crashing Waves Shawl 200
Indian Paintbrush Shawl 204
Julep's Beaded Shawl. 207
Cortona Kerchief 211
Snowdrop Shawlette. 214
Grapevine Shawl. 218
Simply Sweet Shawl 224
Melifera Shawl 226
Trellis Leaf Stole 230
Moss and Leaves Stole 233
Magenta Mohair Lace Stole 240
Red Sky at Night Capelet 242

lacy accessories 245

Drooping Elm Headband 246
Lucy Steele's Fancywork Bags. 248
Wavelet Hair Tie 251
Linen Lace Belt 254
Lacy Legs! 256
Gabriella Bracelet and Choker 257
Lace Headbands 259
Lattice Frost Purse 261

for the home 265

The Iloise Lace Bath Set 266
Lace Bottle Cozy 270
The Alka Dishcloth Set 273
Firefly Table Mat 275
New Wave Sachets 277
Tilting Blocks Pillow 279
Circular Magic Trivet Set 281

appendix 283

About the Designers 284
Abbreviations 290
Glossary. 290
Index 299

introduction

Lace. Beautiful, airy, delicate,
feminine lace. Well, sometimes it's that, and sometimes it can be something quite different! There's
plenty of the former offered here, especially in
the form of scarves, cowls, shawls, and stoles.
Check out Ostrich Plumes Scarf by Jenise Reid on
page 166, Symmetria Scarf by Henna Markkanen
on page 169, Mirabel Shawl by Rae Blackledge on
page 188, and Snowdrop Shawlette by Amanda
Carrigan on page 214 for a few examples of light
and lovely "traditional" lace. Some of our designers
went beyond thin yarn and small needles for this
collection, and we offer lace in heavier weights, too.
If you like worsted weight yarn, look at Etta Hat by
Kim Whelan on page 10, Flutter Mitts by Jenise Reid
on page 54, Hana and Haru by Cheryl Oberle on
pages 109 and 112 respectively, and Welcome Home
Baby Blanket by Ellen Harvey on page 120. And of
course there are projects done with yarns of other
weights, including the ever-popular sock yarn:
Sweet Pea Mitts by Lisa Swanson on page 36, Spicy
Lace Cuffs by Rebecca Mercier on page 60, Baby
Twist Pullover by Liz Nields on page 103, and Indian
Paintbrush Shawl by Vera Sanon on page 204.

Speaking of sock yarn, it's used here for socks,
too — seven pairs, one for every day of the week.
In these pages you'll find plenty of hats and gloves,
garments and accessories for babies, loads of
scarves and shawls, a couple of purses, and even
a lace bottle cozy.

So what makes lace lace? A very basic descrip-
tion is that knitted lace uses yarnovers to create
holes in the fabric and combines these yarnovers
with decreases to maintain a steady (well, some-
what steady) stitch count. By strategically placing
these yarnovers and decreases, you can create
anything from simple repeating designs to wildly
elaborate pictorial patterns. Some define true lace
knitting as only that which requires patterning
on every row, but since most of us like to take a

break with every other row being a "vacation" row
of all knit stitches or all purl stitches, we include
both types here. In fact, we've broadened the
scope even further to allow other methods for
making openwork patterns with yarn. You'll find
three crochet "lace" projects including Cortona
Kerchief by Julie Blagojevich on page 211, Simply
Sweet Shawl by Sharon Ballsmith on page 224,
and Lattice Frost Purse by Sara Delaney on page
261. Also included are Galvez Socks by Debbie
Haymark on page 68 that achieve an openwork
design using dropped stitches and Broomstick
Lace Scarf by Karlie Robinson on page 157 that
uses no yarnovers, but creates a very openwork
pattern by introducing a large (well, huge) needle
on one of four pattern rows.

Wherever practical, we've included patterns
in both written and charted forms. If you're new
to working with charts, choose a pattern presented this way, such as Lacy Liberty Wool Hat
by Meg Myers on page 14, and try working from
the chart — you'll have the written instructions
to refer to if there's something you're not sure
about. Some of the patterns are presented in chart
form only for practicality — row-by-row written
instructions for a project such as Isobel Shawl by
Rae Blackledge on page 193 would fill a book of its
own! You'll find tips for knitting lace, including
working with charts, scattered throughout the
pages. These are indexed separately on page 303
so you can easily find them when you need them.

Once again, our designers have provided
lovely and varied projects, and I hope you find just
the right one — or thirty-one or one hundred and
one — for you or someone on your gift list.

Knit on!

Judith Durant

from head to toe

Hats & Caps ∼ Mitts, Gloves & Cuffs ∼ Socks

Etta Hat

Designed by Kim Whelan

A great beginning knitter's project, Etta is a slouchy hat with a touch of lace.
You'll be surprised how quickly this one knits up!

Finished Measurements

Approximately 18"/45.5 cm circumference at the bottom and 9½"/24 cm deep

Yarn

Brown Sheep Company Nature Spun Worsted Weight, 100% wool, 245 yds (224 m)/3.5 oz (100 g), Color 142W Spiced Plum

Needles

US 6 (4 mm) circular needle 16"/40 cm long and set of four US 6 (4 mm) double-point needles *or size you need to obtain correct gauge*

Gauge

18 stitches and 26 rounds = 4"/10 cm in stockinette stitch

Other Supplies

Stitch marker, yarn needle, form for blocking

Knitting the Hat

- Using the circular needle, cast on 80 stitches. Place marker and join into a round, being careful not to twist the stitches.
- **ROUNDS 1–6:** *K1, p1; repeat from * to end of round.
- **ROUND 7:** Knit, increasing 25 stitches evenly spaced. *You now have* 105 stitches.
- **ROUNDS 8–16:** Knit.
- **ROUND 17:** Purl.
- **ROUND 18:** *P1, yo, ssk; repeat from * to end of round.
- **ROUND 19:** *P1, k2; repeat from * to end of round.
- **ROUND 20:** *P1, k2tog, yo; repeat from * to end of round.
- **ROUND 21:** *P1, k2; repeat from * to end of round.
- **ROUNDS 22 AND 23:** Repeat Rounds 18 and 19.
- **ROUND 24:** Purl.
- Repeat Rounds 8–24 two more times (58 rounds completed).

Decreasing for the Crown

Note: Change to double-point needles when necessary.

- **ROUND 1:** Knit, decreasing 25 stitches evenly spaced. *You now have* 80 stitches.
- **ROUND 2:** *K14, k2tog; repeat from * to end of round. *You now have* 75 stitches.
- **ROUND 3:** *K13, k2tog; repeat from * to end of round. *You now have* 70 stitches.
- **ROUND 4:** *K12, k2tog; repeat from * to end of round. *You now have* 65 stitches.
- Continue in the manner, knitting 1 fewer stitch between the decreases on every round, until 10 stitches remain.
- **NEXT ROUND:** *K2tog; repeat from * to end of round. *You now have* 5 stitches.

Finishing

- Cut yarn, leaving an 8"/20.5 cm tail. Thread tail onto yarn needle and draw through remaining stitches; pull up snugly and secure. Weave in ends. Block. *Note:* This hat was blocked on a combination of a dinner plate, bowl, and saucer — use whatever it takes to get the shape you desire!

Tredegar Hat

DESIGNED BY MICHAELA MOORES

Tredegar is a lovely beret-style hat that begins with a tubular cast on. The decreases for the crown flow beautifully from the main pattern; for a more slouchy hat, work an extra repeat of the lace chart before decreasing for the crown.

Finished Measurements

Approximately 20"/51 cm circumference, unstretched

Yarn

Rowan Tapestry, 70% wool/30% soybean fiber, 131 yds (120 m)/1.75 oz (50 g), Color 171 Rainbow

Needles

US 3 (3.25 mm) circular needle 16"/40 cm long, US 5 (3.75 mm) circular needle 32"/80 cm long, and set of four US 5 (3.75 mm) double-point needles *or size you need to obtain correct gauge*

Gauge

22 stitches and 34 rounds = 4"/10 cm in Tredegar Lace pattern on larger needles

Other Supplies

Stitch marker, yarn needle, dinner plate for blocking

Knitting the Hat

- Using the smaller circular needle and the tubular method (see page 299), cast on 110 stitches. Place marker and join into a round, being careful not to twist the stitches. Work in k1, p1 rib until piece measures 1"/2.5 cm from cast on.

Knitting the Lace

- Change to larger circular needle and knit 1 round. Work Rounds 1–8 of Tredegar Lace chart, working the chart five times in each round. At the end of Round 8, remove marker, k3, replace marker. This is the new start of the round.

- Work Rounds 9–28 of Tredegar Lace chart once, then work Rounds 1–14 once more, repositioning the marker at the end of Round 8 as before.

Decreasing for the Crown

Note: Change to double-point needles when necessary.

- Work Rounds 1–20 of Tredegar Crown chart. *You now have 10 stitches.*

Finishing

- Cut yarn, leaving a 10"/25.5 cm tail. Thread tail onto yarn needle and draw through remaining stitches twice; pull up snugly and secure. Weave in all ends. Block on a dinner plate.

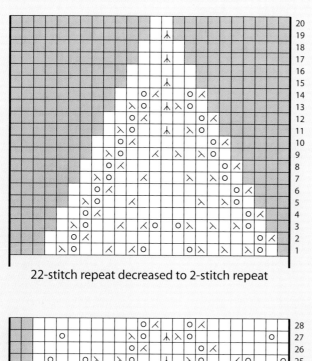

20
19
18
17
16
15
14
13
12
11
10
9
8
7
6
5
4
3
2
1

Tredegar Crown

Work pattern repeat 5 times.

22-stitch repeat decreased to 2-stitch repeat

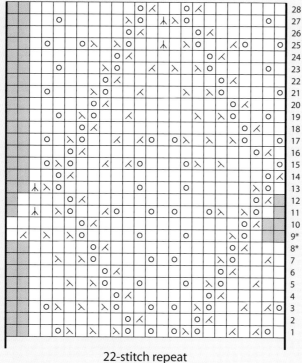

28
27
26
25
24
23
22
21
20
19
18
17
16
15
14
13
12
11
10
9*
8*
7
6
5
4
3
2
1

Tredegar Lace

Work pattern repeat 5 times.
*See instructions for end of Rnd 8 before working Rnd 9.

22-stitch repeat

☐	knit
⟋	k2tog
⟍	ssk
◯	yo
⟁	s2kp
▓	no stitch

13

Lacy Liberty Wool Hat

DESIGNED BY MEG MYERS

This fitted ribbed hat is worked in a simple lace pattern from the bottom up with well-incorporated decreases for the crown. It will stretch to fit many sizes.

Finished Measurements
Approximately 17½"/44.5 cm circumference and 7"/18 cm deep, unstretched

Yarn
Classic Elite Yarns Liberty Wool, 100% washable wool, 122 yds (111 m)/1.75 oz (50 g), Color 7815 Bright Olive

Needles
US 6 (4 mm) circular needle 16"/40 cm long and set of US 6 (4 mm) double-point needles *or size you need to obtain correct gauge*

Gauge
25 stitches and 32 rounds = 4"/10 cm in Lacy Rib pattern, unstretched

Other Supplies
Stitch marker

Knitting the Hat

- With circular needle, cast on 110 stitches. Place marker and join into a round, being careful not to twist the stitches.

- Following the chart or written instructions, work Rounds 1–8 of Lacy Rib five times.

Decreasing for the Crown

- Following the chart or written instructions, work Rounds 1–17 of Lacy Rib Crown Decrease, switching to double-point needles when necessary.

- **ROUND 1:** *K7, p3, repeat from * to end of round.

- **ROUND 2:** *K1, k2tog, yo, k1, yo, ssk, k1, p1, p2tog; repeat from * to end of round. *You now have* a multiple of 9 stitches.

- **ROUND 3:** *K7, p2; repeat from * to end of round.

- **ROUND 4:** *K2tog, yo, k3, yo, ssk, p2; repeat from * to end of round.

- **ROUND 5:** Repeat Round 3.

- **ROUND 6:** *K1, yo, ssk, k1, k2tog, yo, k1, p2tog; repeat from * to end of round. *You now have* a multiple of 8 stitches.

- **ROUND 7:** *K7, p1; repeat from * to end of round.

- **ROUND 8:** *K2, yo, sk2p, yo, k1, ssk; repeat from * to end of round. *You now have* a multiple of 7 stitches.

- **ROUND 9 AND ALL ODD-NUMBERED ROUNDS TO ROUND 15:** Knit.

- **ROUND 10:** *K2tog, yo, k3, yo, ssk; repeat from * to end of round.

- **ROUND 12:** *Ssk, yo, sk2p, yo, k2tog; repeat from * to end of round. *You now have* a multiple of 5 stitches.

- **ROUND 14:** *Ssk, k1, k2tog; repeat from * to end of round. *You now have* a multiple of 3 stitches.

- **ROUND 16:** *Sk2p; repeat from * to end of round. *You now have* 1 stitch in each repeat.

- **ROUND 17:** Knit. *You now have* 11 stitches.

- Cut yarn, leaving an 8"/20.5 cm tail. Thread tail onto yarn needle and draw through remaining stitches twice; pull up snugly and secure on inside.

Finishing

- Weave in all ends. Block.

PATTERN ESSENTIALS

Lacy Rib (multiple of 10 stitches)

- **Round 1 and all odd-numbered rounds:** *K7, p3; repeat from * to end of round.
- **Round 2:** *K1, k2tog, yo, k1, yo, ssk, k1, p3; repeat from * to end of round.
- **Round 4:** *K2tog, yo, k3, yo, ssk, p3; repeat from * to end of round.
- **Round 6:** *K1, yo, ssk, k1, k2tog, yo, k1, p3; repeat from * to end of round.
- **Round 8:** *K2, yo, sk2p, yo, k2, p3; repeat from * to end of round.
- Repeat Rounds 1–8 for pattern.

Lacy Rib Crown Decrease

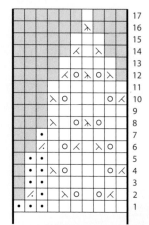

10-stitch repeat
decreased to 1-stitch repeat

Work pattern repeat 11 times.

Lacy Rib

10-stitch repeat

Work pattern repeat 11 times.

	knit		ssk
•	purl		p2tog
o	yo		sk2p
	k2tog		no stitch

Pine Needle Toque

DESIGNED BY JENISE REID

Comfortable and attractive, this topper features an easy-to-work lace pattern. The crown decreases form a lovely eight-point star at the top. (See page 51 for the matching mittens.)

Finished Measurements

Approximately 19½"/49.5 cm circumference and 9"/23 cm deep

Yarn

Knit Picks Palette, 100% Peruvian Highland wool, 231 yds (211 m)/1.75 oz (50 g), Bittersweet Heather

Needles

US 3 (3.25 mm) circular needle 16"/40 cm long and set of four US 3 (3.25 mm) double-point needles *or size you need to obtain correct gauge*

Gauge

23 stitches and 34 rounds = 4"/10 cm in Pine Needle Lace pattern, blocked

Other Supplies

Stitch marker, yarn needle

Knitting the Toque

• Using circular needle, cast on 112 stitches. Place marker and join into a round, being careful not to twist the stitches.

Note: Work the 28-stitch repeat of the Pine Needle Lace chart four times for each round.

• Work Rounds 1–15 of the Pine Needle Lace chart once.

• Work Rounds 16–23 of the chart six times.

Decreasing for the Crown

• Work Rounds 24–38 of the chart once. *You now have* 16 stitches.

Finishing

• Cut yarn, leaving an 8"/20.5 cm tail. Thread tail onto yarn needle and draw through remaining stitches; pull up snugly and secure. Weave in ends. Block.

PATTERN ESSENTIALS

For the rounds on the chart where the pattern repeat begins with sk2p (indicated by *), the beginning of the round must be moved by 1 stitch in order to keep the pattern aligned. End the round *before* each * round 1 stitch before the marker: temporarily slip the last stitch to the right-hand needle, remove the marker, return the slipped stitch to the left-hand needle, and replace the marker on the right-hand needle. When you work the sk2p at the beginning of the * round, the transferred stitch will be the first of the 3 stitches used in the sk2p. The completed sk2p becomes the new first stitch of the round.

Pine Needle Lace

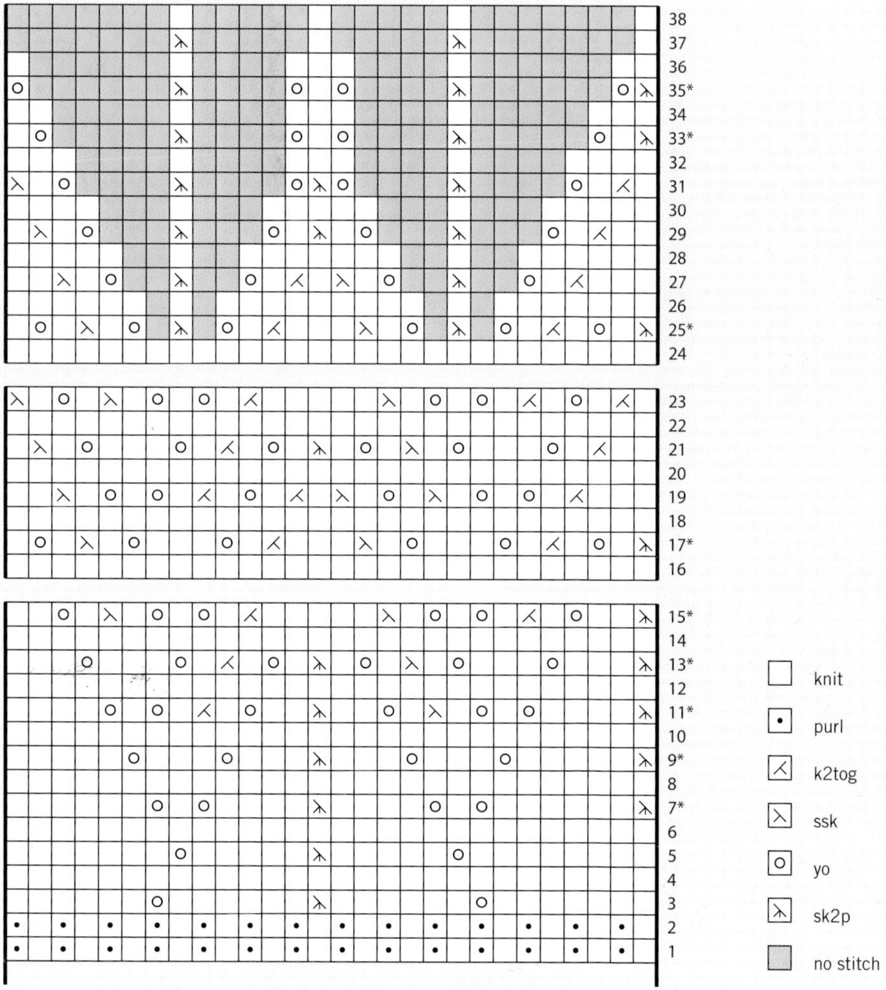

28-stitch repeat decreased to 4-stitch repeat

Work pattern repeat 4 times.
See Pattern Essentials for * rounds.

Legend:
- ☐ knit
- • purl
- ⊼ k2tog
- ⋋ ssk
- ○ yo
- ⋋ sk2p
- ▨ no stitch

Very Pretty Lace Beret

DESIGNED BY VERA SANON

This lace beret, worked in fingering-weight yarn, features an intricate and beautiful lace pattern. The decreases for the crown flow seamlessly from the leafy lace design into an eight-point star pattern.

Sizes and Finished Measurements

To fit 19"–23"/48.5–58.5 cm head, approximately 18"/45.5 cm brim circumference

Yarn

Classic Elite Yarns Mountaintop Collection Vail, 70% alpaca/30% bamboo, 236 yds (216 m)/1.75 oz (50 g), Color 6416 Parchment

Needles

US 3 (3.25 mm) circular needle 16"/40 cm long and set of four US 3 (3.25 mm) double-point needles *or size you need to obtain correct gauge*
Circular needle 16"/40 cm long one size smaller than gauge needle

Gauge

28 stitches = 4"/10 cm in stockinette stitch on larger needle

Other Supplies

Stitch markers, yarn needle, dinner plate for blocking

Knitting the Beret

- Using the smaller needle, cast on 140 stitches. Place marker and join into a round, being careful not to twist the stitches.

- **ROUNDS 1–10:** *K1 tbl, p1; repeat from * to end of round.

- **NEXT ROUND:** Knit, increasing 20 stitches evenly spaced and placing a marker every 20 stitches. *You now have* 160 stitches.

Knitting the Lace

- Change to larger circular needle and follow the text or chart (see page 20) to work Rounds 1–32 of Very Pretty Lace, then work Rounds 1–24 once more (56 lace rounds worked).

- **ROUND 1:** *K2tog, yo, p1, k2tog, k4, yo, p1, yo, k4, ssk, p1, yo, ssk, p1; repeat from * to end of round.

- **ROUND 2:** *K2, k2tog, k4, yo, k1, p1, k1, yo, k4, ssk, k2, p1; repeat from * to end of round.

- **ROUND 3:** *K1, k2tog, k4, yo, k2, p1, k2, yo, k4, ssk, k1, p1; repeat from * to end of round.

- **ROUND 4:** *K2tog, k4, yo, k3, p1, k3, yo, k4, ssk, p1; repeat from * to end of round.

- **ROUND 5:** *K3, k2tog, k4, yo, p1, yo, k4, ssk, k3, p1; repeat from * to end of round.

- **ROUND 6:** *K2, k2tog, k4, yo, k1, p1, k1, yo, k4, ssk, k2, p1; repeat from * to end of round.

- **ROUND 7:** *K1, k2tog, k4, yo, k2tog, yo, p1, yo, ssk, yo, k4, ssk, k1, p1; repeat from * to end of round.

- **ROUND 8:** *K2tog, k4, yo, p1, k2, p1, k2, p1, yo, k4, ssk, p1; repeat from * to end of round.

- **ROUND 9:** *Yo, ssk, k1, k2tog, yo, k1, p1, yo, ssk, p1, k2tog, yo, p1, k1, yo, ssk, k1, k2tog, yo, p1; repeat from * to end of round.

- **ROUND 10:** *K6, (p1, k2) twice, p1, k6, p1; repeat from * to end of round.

- **ROUND 11:** *K1, yo, s2kp, yo, k2, p1, k2tog, yo, p1, yo, ssk, p1, k2, yo, s2kp, yo, k1, p1; repeat from * to end of round.

- **ROUND 12:** Repeat Round 10.

- **ROUND 13:** *K2, yo, ssk, k2, p1, yo, ssk, p1, k2tog, yo, p1, k2, k2tog, yo, k2, p1; repeat from * to end of round.

- **ROUND 14:** Repeat Round 10.

- **ROUND 15:** *K3, yo, ssk, k1, p1, k2tog, yo, p1, yo, ssk, p1, k1, k2tog, yo, k3, p1; repeat from * to end of round.

- **ROUND 16:** Repeat Round 10.

- **ROUND 17:** *Yo, k4, ssk, p1, yo, ssk, p1, k2tog, yo, p1, k2tog, k4, yo, p1; repeat from * to end of round.

- **ROUND 18:** *K1, yo, k4, ssk, k2, p1, k2, k2tog, k4, yo, k1, p1; repeat from * to end of round.

- **ROUND 19:** *K2, yo, k4, ssk, k1, p1, k1, k2tog, k4, yo, k2, p1; repeat from * to end of round.

- **ROUND 20:** *K3, yo, k4, ssk, p1, k2tog, k4, yo, k3, p1; repeat from * to end of round.

- **ROUND 21:** *Yo, k4, ssk, k3, p1, k3, k2tog, k4, yo, p1; repeat from * to end of round.

- **ROUND 22:** *K1, yo, k4, ssk, k2, p1, k2, k2tog, k4, yo, k1, p1; repeat from * to end of round.

- **ROUND 23:** *Yo, ssk, yo, k4, ssk, k1, p1, k1, k2tog, k4, yo, k2tog, yo, p1; repeat from * to end of round.

- **ROUND 24:** *K2, p1, yo, k4, ssk, p1, k2tog, k4, yo, p1, k2, p1; repeat from * to end of round.

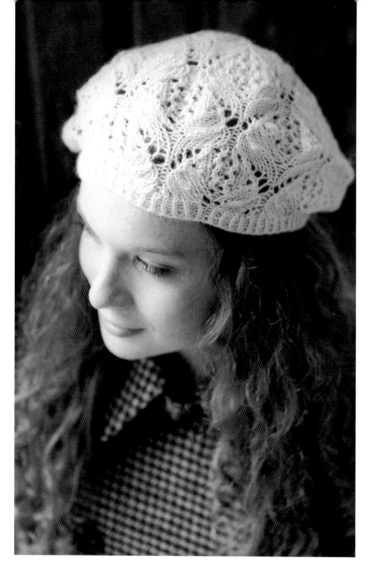

- **ROUND 25:** *K2tog, yo, p1, k1, yo, ssk, k1, k2tog, yo, p1, yo, ssk, k1, k2tog, yo, k1, p1, yo, ssk, p1; repeat from * to end of round.

- **ROUND 26:** *K2, p1, k6, p1, k6, p1, k2, p1; repeat from * to end of round.

- **ROUND 27:** *Yo, ssk, p1, k2, yo, s2kp, yo, k1, p1, k1, yo, s2kp, yo, k2, p1, k2tog, yo, p1; repeat from * to end of round.

- **ROUND 28:** Repeat Round 26.

- **ROUND 29:** *K2tog, yo, p1, k2, k2tog, yo, k2, p1, k2, yo, ssk, k2, p1, yo, ssk, p1; repeat from * to end of round.

19

- **ROUND 30:** Repeat Round 26.
- **ROUND 31:** *Yo, ssk, p1, k1, k2tog, yo, k3, p1, k3, yo, ssk, k1, p1, k2tog, yo, p1; repeat from * to end of round.
- **ROUND 32:** Repeat Round 26.

Decreasing for the Crown

Note: Change to double-point needles when necessary.

- Follow the text or chart to work Rounds 1–12 of Crown pattern. *You now have* 8 stitches total.

Note: Shaping begins with 20 stitches between markers.

- **ROUND 1:** *K2tog, yo, p1, k4, k2tog, s2kp, k4, p1, yo, ssk, p1; repeat from * to end of round. *You now have* 17 stitches between the markers.
- **ROUND 2:** *K2, p1, k10, p1, k2, p1; repeat from * to end of round.
- **ROUND 3:** *Yo, ssk, p1, k3, k2tog, ssk, k3, p1, k2tog, yo, p1; repeat from * to end of round. *You now have* 15 stitches between the markers.
- **ROUND 4:** *K2, p1, k8, p1, k2, p1; repeat from * to end of round.

Very Pretty Lace

20-stitch repeat

Work pattern repeat 8 times.

Crown

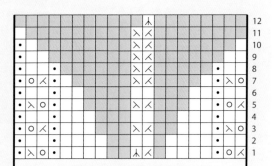

20-stitch repeat
decreased to 1-stitch repeat

Work pattern repeat 8 times.

☐	knit
•	purl
╱	k2tog
╲	ssk
○	yo
⅄	s2kp
▨	no stitch

- **ROUND 5:** *K2tog, yo, p1, k2, k2tog, ssk, k2, p1, yo, ssk, p1; repeat from * to end of round. *You now have* 13 stitches between the markers.

- **ROUND 6:** *K2, p1, k6, p1, k2, p1; repeat from * to end of round.

- **ROUND 7:** *Yo, ssk, p1, k1, k2tog, ssk, k1, p1, k2tog, yo, p1; repeat from * to end of round. *You now have* 11 stitches between the markers.

- **ROUND 8:** *K2, p1, k2tog, ssk, p1, k2, p1; repeat from * to end of round. *You now have* 9 stitches between the markers.

- **ROUND 9:** *K2, k2tog, ssk, k2, p1; repeat from * to end of round. *You now have* 7 stitches between the markers.

- **ROUND 10:** *K1, k2tog, ssk, k1, p1; repeat from * to end of round. *You now have* 5 stitches between the markers.

- **ROUND 11:** *K2tog, ssk, k1; repeat from * to end of round. *You now have* 3 stitches between the markers.

- **ROUND 12:** *S2kp; repeat from * to end of round. *You now have* 1 stitch between the markers.

Finishing

- Work k2tog around, removing markers. *You now have* 4 stitches.

- Slide 4 stitches onto one double-point needle and work 2 rounds of I-cord (see page 292). Cut the yarn leaving an 8"/20.5 cm tail. Thread tail onto yarn needle and draw through remaining stitches; pull up snugly and secure. Weave in ends. Block over dinner plate.

Twig Lace Cap

DESIGNED BY KERIN DIMELER-LAURENCE

The four sections of lace in this cap are decreased beautifully for the crown. The bright blue color is reminiscent of the romantic jewel tones of the Renaissance era.

21

Sizes and Finished Measurements

To fit 20"–22"/51–56 cm head, 17"/43 cm circumference and 8"/20.5 cm deep, unblocked

Yarn

Knit Picks Comfy Worsted, 75% pima cotton/25% acrylic, 109 yds (100 m)/1.75 oz (50 g), Color 25314 Celestial

Needles

US 9 (5.5 mm) circular needle 16"/40 cm long and set of US 9 (5.5 mm) double-point needles *or size you need to obtain correct gauge*
Circular needle 16"/40 cm one size smaller than gauge needle

Gauge

17 stitches and 22 rounds = 4"/10 cm in stockinette stitch on larger needle, unblocked; 18 stitches and 28 rounds = 4"/10 cm in Twig Lace pattern on larger needle, unblocked

Other Supplies

Stitch marker, cable needle, yarn needle

PATTERN ESSENTIALS

½ Left Cable Slip 1 stitch to cable needle and hold in front, k2 from left-hand needle, k1 from cable needle.

½ Right Cable Slip 2 stitches to cable needle and hold in back, k1 from left-hand needle, k2 from cable needle.

Left Decreasing Twist Slip 1 stitch to cable needle and hold in front; ssk from left-hand needle, k1 from cable needle — 3 stitches decreased to 2 stitches.

Right Decreasing Twist Slip 2 stitches to cable needle and hold in back; k1 from left-hand needle, k2tog from cable needle — 3 stitches decreased to 2 stitches.

Twig Lace

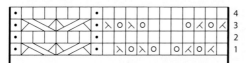

19-stitch repeat

Work pattern repeat 4 times.

□ knit	⩋	s2kp
• purl	▨	no stitch
⟍ k2tog	⟋	right decreasing twist
⟋ ssk	⟍	left decreasing twist
⟋ p2tog	⟍	1/2 right cable
○ yo	⟍	1/2 left cable

Twig Lace Crown

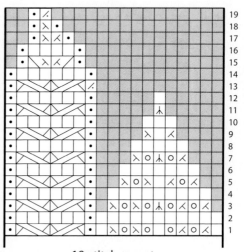

19-stitch repeat
decreased to 2-stitch repeat

Work pattern repeat 4 times.

Knitting the Band

- With smaller needle cast on 76 stitches. Place marker and and join into a round, being careful not to twist the stitches.
- **ROUNDS 1–5**: *K2, p2; repeat from * to end of round. Piece measures ¾"/ 2 cm.

Knitting the Lace

- Change to larger needle. Work Rounds 1–4 of Twig Lace chart eight times.

Decreasing for the Crown

- Work Rounds 1–19 of Twig Lace Crown chart, changing to double-point needles when necessary. *You now have 8 stitches.*

Finishing

- Cut yarn, leaving 6"/15 cm tail. Thread tail onto yarn needle, draw through remaining 8 stitches, pull up snugly, and fasten off. Weave in ends. Wash and block.

Alexandra Hat

DESIGNED BY JILLIAN MORENO

Jillian loves a close-fitting cap for showing lace, which can sometimes get lost in a slouchy hat. The diagonal lines combine with yarnovers to create a play of light across the surface of the fabric.

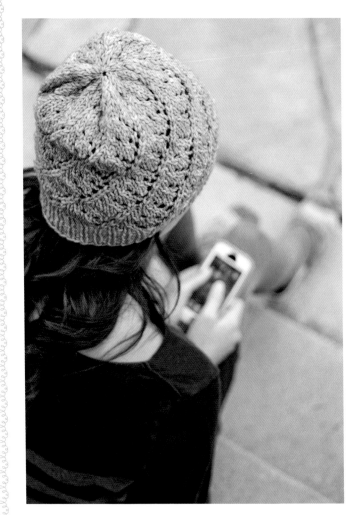

23

Sizes and Finished Measurements

To fit 19"–21"/48.5–53.5 cm head, 18"/45.5 cm circumference after blocking, unstretched

Yarn

Madelinetosh Tosh DK, 100% superwash merino wool, 225 yds (206 m)/3.5 oz (100 g), Caravan

Needles

US 5 (3.75 mm) circular needle 16"/40 cm long and set of US 5 (3.75 mm) double-point needles *or size you need to obtain correct gauge*

Gauge

18 stitches and 32 rounds = 4"/10 cm in Alexandra Lace pattern, blocked

Other Supplies

Stitch marker, yarn needle, head form or balloon for blocking

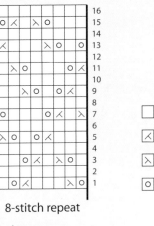

Alexandra Lace

8-stitch repeat

Work pattern repeat 10 times.

☐	knit
◿	k2tog
◺	ssk
○	yo

Knitting the Hat

- Cast on 80 stitches. Place marker and join into a round, being careful not to twist the stitches.

- **ROUND 1:** *K1, p1; repeat from * to end of round.

- Repeat Round 1 until piece measures 1½"/4 cm.

- Work Rounds 1–16 of Alexandra Lace chart three times (48 chart rounds total). Hat measures approximately 7½"/19 cm from cast-on edge. *Note:* The diagonal decrease lines of the pattern are not continuous and have deliberate "jogs" in Rounds 7 and 13.

Decreasing for the Crown

Note: Change to double-point needles when necessary.

- **NEXT 3 ROUNDS:** *K2tog; repeat from * to end of round. *You now have* 10 stitches.

Finishing

- Cut yarn, leaving a 6"/15 cm tail. Thread tail onto yarn needle and draw through remaining stitches; pull up snugly and fasten off.

- Weave in ends and block to open lace on a head form or an inflated balloon.

Hepatica Hats

DESIGNED BY MINDY VASIL

These beautiful lacy berets are perfect early spring accessories. The flower design on the crown adds a feminine and soft touch. The pattern offers the choice of two sizes.

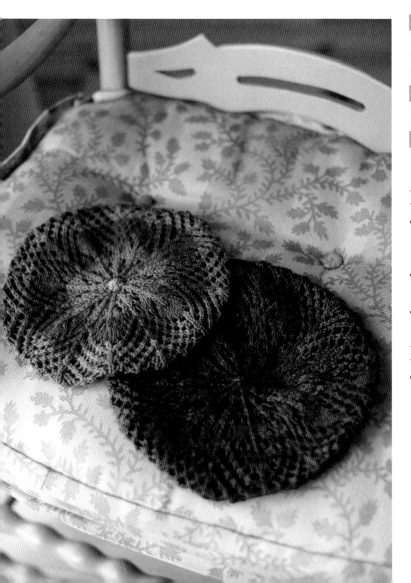

Sizes and Finished Measurements

Small (large), approximately 18.5 (21.5)"/ 47 (54.5) cm band circumference, unstretched

Yarn

Red Hat: Lorna's Laces Shepherd Sport, 100% superwash wool, 200 yds (183 m)/ 2.5 oz (70 g), Color 107 Red Rover
Blue Hat: Zitron Unisono, 100% superwash extrafine merino, 328 yds (300 m)/ 3.5 oz (100 g), Color 1220

Needles

US 7 (4.5 mm) circular needle 16"/40 cm long and set of US 7 (4.5 mm) double-point needles *or size you need to obtain correct gauge*

Gauge

18 stitches and 36 rounds = 4"/10 cm in k2, p2 ribbing

Other Supplies

Stitch marker, yarn needle

Knitting the Band

• Cast on 84 (96) stitches. Place marker and join into a round, being careful not to twist the stitches.

• **ROUND 1:** *K2, p2; repeat from * to end of round.

• Repeat Round 1 six more times.

Knitting the Hat Body

• **INCREASE ROUND (COUNTS AS ROUND 1 OF CHART):** *Yo, k1, (yo, k2tog) twice, yo, k1, (yo, ssk) twice, (yo, k1) twice; repeat from * six (seven) more times. *You now have* 112 (128) stitches.

Notes: Only odd-numbered rounds are charted, and Round 1 is not shown. Knit all even-numbered rounds from 2 through 32.

At the start of Rounds 5, 9, and 13, remove the end-of-round marker, k1, replace the marker, and then begin working the chart pattern; the k1 worked to shift the marker at the start of these rounds is included in the last 3-stitch decrease of the same round and maintains the pattern alignment.

- *For both sizes:* Work Rounds 2–32, working the pattern repeat seven (eight) times around.

Decreasing for the Crown

Note: At the start of odd-numbered Rounds 33–45, remove the end-of-round marker, k1, replace the marker, and then begin working the chart pattern; moving the marker in this manner maintains the pattern alignment.

- Continuing to knit all the even-numbered rounds, work Rounds 33–45. *You now have* 14 (16) stitches.

- Work final decreases as follows.

- **ROUND 46:** *K2tog; repeat from * to end of round. *You now have* 7 (8) stitches.

- **ROUNDS 47–49:** Knit.

- **ROUND 50:**

  - *For small size:* K1, *k2tog; repeat from * to end of round. *You now have* 4 stitches.

  - *For large size:* *K2tog; repeat from * to end of round. *You now have* 4 stitches.

Finishing

- Cut yarn, leaving a 6"/15 cm tail. Thread tail onto yarn needle and draw through remaining stitches; pull snugly and fasten off. Weave in ends. Block if desired.

Hepatica Lace

(Chart: 16-stitch repeat, odd-numbered rounds 3–45)

16-stitch repeat
decreased to 2-stitch repeat
Work pattern repeat 7 (8) times.

Only odd-numbered rounds are charted.
Knit all even-numbered rounds.

*See instructions.

	knit		yo
	k2tog		s2kp
	ssk		no stitch

Nicole's Angora Beanie

DESIGNED BY DIANA FOSTER

This lovely beanie features an easy-to-remember lace pattern, and it shows wonderfully knitted in white angora. The hat would be perfect for a winter bride — at least for getting to and from the church!

Finished Measurements

Approximately 20"/51 cm circumference and 7"/18 cm deep

Yarn

Schulana Angora-Fashion, 80% angora/ 20% nylon, 122 yds (112 m)/0.88 oz (25 g), Color 1 White

Needles

US 8 (5 mm) circular needle 16"/40 cm long and set of four US 8 (5 mm) double-point needles *or size you need to obtain correct gauge*

Gauge

16 stitches = 4"/10 cm in garter stitch; 17 stitches and 24 rounds = 4"/10 cm in Lace pattern

Other Supplies

Stitch marker, yarn needle

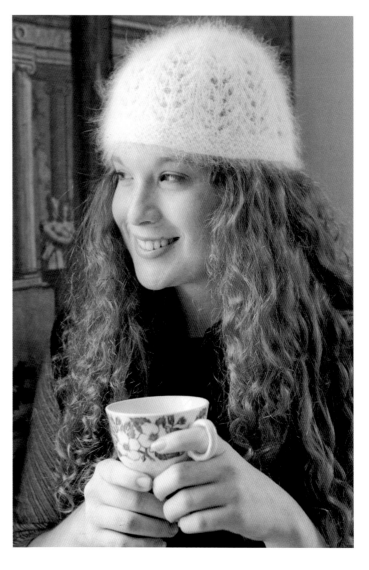

PATTERN ESSENTIALS

Lace (multiple of 7 stitches)

- **Round 1:** Knit.
- **Round 2:** *K1, k2tog, yo, k1, yo, ssk, k1; repeat from * to end of round.
- **Round 3:** Knit.
- **Round 4:** *K2tog, yo, k3, yo, ssk; repeat from * to end of round.
- Repeat Rounds 1–4 for pattern.

Knitting the Beanie

- With circular needle, cast on 84 stitches. Do not join into a round. Work back and forth in garter stitch (knit every row) for 1"/2.5 cm. Place marker and join into a round and work Rounds 1–4 of Lace pattern six times.

Decreasing for the Crown

Note: Change to double-point needles when necessary.

- **ROUND 1:** *K10, k2tog; repeat from * to end of round. *You now have 77 stitches.*

- **ROUNDS 2, 4, AND 6:** Knit.

- **ROUND 3:** *K9, k2tog; repeat from * to end of round. *You now have 70 stitches.*

- **ROUND 5:** *K8, k2tog; repeat from * to end of round. *You now have 63 stitches.*

- **ROUND 7:** *K7, k2tog; repeat from * to end of round. *You now have 56 stitches.*

- **ROUND 8:** *K6, k2tog; repeat from * to end of round. *You now have 49 stitches.*

- **ROUND 9:** *K5, k2tog; repeat from * to end of round. *You now have 42 stitches.*

- **ROUND 10:** *K4, k2tog; repeat from * to end of round. *You now have 35 stitches.*

- **ROUND 11:** *K3, k2tog; repeat from * to end of round. *You now have 28 stitches.*

- **ROUND 12:** *K2, k2tog; repeat from * to end of round. *You now have 21 stitches.*

- **ROUND 13:** *K1, k2tog; repeat from * to end of round. *You now have 14 stitches.*

- **ROUND 14:** *K2tog; repeat from * to end of round. *You now have 7 stitches.*

Finishing

- Cut yarn, leaving an 8"/20.5 cm tail. Thread tail onto yarn needle and draw through remaining stitches; pull up snugly and secure. Thread beginning tail onto yarn needle and sew garter ridge bumps together to close slit at start of beanie. Weave in ends and block.

Ellie's Orange Tam

Designed by Judith Durant

The best thing about this tam is the yarn. Check out Ellie's Reclaimed Cashmere (www.elliesreclaimedcashmere.com) for fabulous recycled luxury. This tam is worked in seven distinct sections, with decreases worked along the divisions.

Finished Measurements

Approximately 20"/51 cm circumference at ribbing

Yarn

Ellie's Reclaimed Cashmere, 100% recycled cashmere, 216 yds (198 m)/1.2 oz (34 g), Orange

Needles

US 3 (3.25 mm) circular 16"/40 cm long and set of US 3 (3.25 mm) double-point needles *or size you need to obtain correct gauge* and US 1½ (2.5 mm) circular 16"/40 cm long

Gauge

26 stitches and 38½ rounds = 4"/10 cm in Tam Lace pattern on larger needle, blocked

Other Supplies

Stitch marker, yarn needle, dinner plate for blocking

Knitting the Tam

- Using smaller circular needle, cast on 144 stitches. Place marker and join into a round, being careful not to twist the stitches.

- **ROUND 1:** *K1, p1; repeat from * to end of round.

- Repeat Round 1 until piece measures 1"/2.5 cm.

- Change to larger circular needle.

- **INCREASE ROUND:** *(K4, M1L) 17 times, (k2, M1L) twice; repeat from * once more. *You now have 182 stitches.*

- Repeat Rounds 1–4 of Tam Lace chart, working the 26-stitch repeat seven times in each round, until piece measures 3½"/9 cm from cast-on edge, ending with Round 4.

Decreasing for the Crown

Note: Before working odd-numbered Rounds 5–27, which have an s2kp decrease as the first decrease of the round, remove the end-of-round marker, slip the last stitch from the end of the previous even-numbered round to the left-hand needle, and replace the end-of-round marker.

- Work Rounds 5–28 of chart, changing to double-point needles when there are too few stitches for the circular needle. *You now have* 14 stitches.

- **NEXT ROUND:** *K2tog; repeat from * to end of round. *You now have* 7 stitches.

Finishing

- Cut yarn, leaving a 6"/15 cm tail. Thread tail onto yarn needle, draw through remaining stitches, pull up snugly, and fasten off. Weave in ends. Block over a 10"/25.5 cm dinner plate.

Tam Lace

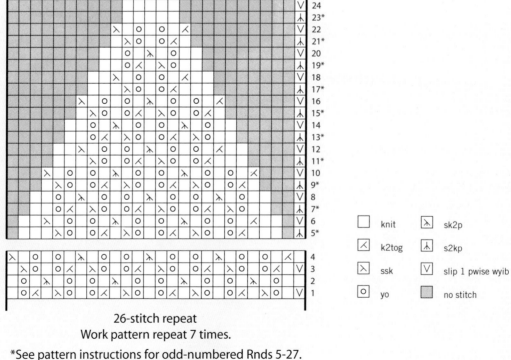

26-stitch repeat
Work pattern repeat 7 times.

*See pattern instructions for odd-numbered Rnds 5–27.

	knit		sk2p
	k2tog		s2kp
	ssk		slip 1 pwise wyib
	yo		no stitch

Flutter Toque

DESIGNED BY JENISE REID

This toque matches the Flutter Mitts on page 54. It is knit in the round on a circular needle and features evenly spaced staggered decreases instead of aligned decreases.

Finished Measurements

Approximately 18"/45.5 cm circumference, unstretched, and 8½"/21.5 cm deep

Yarn

Knit Picks Sugarbunny, 80% merino wool/20% angora, 136 yds (124 m)/1.75 oz (50 g), Topaz

Needles

US 4 (3.5 mm) circular needle 16"/40 cm long and set of four US 4 (3.5 mm) double-point needles *or size you need to obtain correct gauge*

Gauge

18 stitches and 26 rounds = 4"/10 cm in stockinette stitch

Other Supplies

Stitch marker, yarn needle

Knitting the Toque

- With circular needle, cast on 81 stitches; place marker and join into a round, being careful not to twist the stitches.

- **ROUND 1:** (K2tog, yo, p1) 27 times.

- **ROUND 2:** (K2, p1) 27 times.

- **ROUND 3:** (Yo, ssk, p1) 27 times.

- **ROUND 4:** Repeat Round 2.

- **ROUNDS 5–16:** Repeat Rounds 1–4 three more times; piece measures about 2¼"/5.5 cm.

- **ROUNDS 17–30:** Knit.

Decreasing for the Crown

Note: Change to double-point needles when necessary.

- **ROUND 31:** (K7, k2tog) nine times. *You now have* 72 stitches.

- **ROUNDS 32–40:** Knit.

- **ROUND 41:** (K4, k2tog) 12 times. *You now have* 60 stitches.

- **ROUNDS 42–46:** Knit.

- **ROUND 47:** (K1, k2tog) 20 times. *You now have* 40 stitches.

- **ROUNDS 48–51:** Knit.

- **ROUND 52:** (K2tog) 20 times. *You now have* 20 stitches.

- **ROUNDS 53 AND 54:** Knit.

- **ROUND 55:** (K2tog) 10 times. *You now have* 10 stitches.

- **ROUND 56:** Knit.

- **ROUND 57:** (K2tog) five times. *You now have* 5 stitches.

Finishing

- Cut yarn, leaving an 8"/20.5 cm tail. Thread tail onto yarn needle and draw through remaining stitches; pull up snugly and secure. Weave in ends and block.

Tilting Ladders Hat

DESIGNED BY SARAH JEAN HOOD

This lace is easy to knit because it's easy to read — you'll always know exactly where you are in the stitch pattern. The hat is knit top down, so the length can be adjusted for a custom fit. One skein is enough for two hats.

Finished Measurements

Approximately 22"/56 cm circumference

Yarn

Jade Sapphire Mongolian Cashmere 2-Ply, 100% cashmere, 400 yds (366 m)/ 1.9 oz (55 g), Color 61 Blue Spruce

Needles

US 3 (3.25 mm) circular needle 16"/40 cm long and set of five US 3 (3.25 mm) double-point needles, or one long circular needle for magic loop *or size you need to obtain correct gauge*

Gauge

26 stitches and 44 rounds = 4"/10 cm in Tilting Ladders Lace pattern

Other Supplies

Stitch marker, cable needle, yarn needle, one ½"/13 mm button, sewing needle and coordinating thread

Special Abbreviations

C4B cable 4 stitches back
C4F cable 4 stitches front

PATTERN ESSENTIALS

Cable 4 Stitches Back Slip next 2 stitches onto cable needle and hold in back, knit 2 stitches from left-hand needle, knit 2 stitches from cable needle.

Cable 4 Stitches Front Slip next 2 stitches onto cable needle and hold in front, knit 2 stitches from left-hand needle, knit 2 stitches from cable needle.

PATTERN NOTES

Instructions are for a 22"/56 cm circumference hat with 11 repeats of the 13-stitch Tilting Ladders Lace pattern. Increase to 24"/61 cm or decrease to 20"/51 cm by adding or subtracting one repeat, respectively. The crown begins with a circular cast on.

Knitting the Crown

• Using double-point needles and a circular cast-on method (see page 291) or magic loop method (see page 295), cast on 11 stitches. Place marker and join into a round, being careful not to twist the stitches. Knit 1 round. Work Rounds 1–34 of Crown Increase chart, working the chart 11 times in each round and changing to circular needle when necessary. *You now have 143 stitches.*

Knitting the Lace

• Work Rounds 1–24 of Tilting Ladders Lace chart twice, then work Rounds 1–12 once more. Knit one round.

Binding Off with I-Cord

• Following the instructions on page 292, work a 4-stitch I-cord bind off. When all hat stitches have been bound off, knit 3 I-cord stitches again, pick up and knit (see page 297) 1 stitch from the first stitch of hat round and work it together with the last I-cord

stitch as k2tog. Using two double-point needles, work 3 rounds of 4-stitch I-cord (see page 292) without attaching to the hat.

Making the Buttonhole Tab

• Work back and forth in rows on the 4 stitches of the I-cord as follows:

• ROW 1 (WS): Purl.

• ROW 2 (RS): Knit.

• ROW 3: Purl.

• ROW 4 (RS, BUTTONHOLE ROW): K2, yo, k2. *You now have 5 stitches.*

• ROWS 5–7: Repeat Rows 1–3.

• ROW 8: K1, s2kp, k1. *You now have 3 stitches.*

• ROW 9: Purl.

• ROW 10: S2kp. *You now have 1 stitch.*

• Cut yarn, leaving a 12"/30.5 cm tail. Thread tail onto a yarn needle, draw through the remaining stitch.

Finishing

• Weave in the tail at the end of the buttonhole tab by working it along the selvedge back to the I-cord join and tack it securely in place. Weave in ends. Block.

• Using a sewing needle and coordinating thread, sew the button to the I-cord underneath the buttonhole.

Tilting Ladders Lace

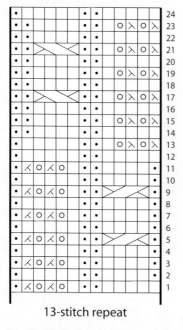

13-stitch repeat

Work pattern repeat 11 times.

Crown Increase

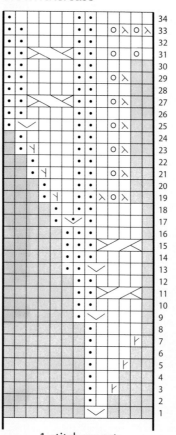

1-stitch repeat
increased to 13-stitch repeat

Work pattern repeat 11 times.

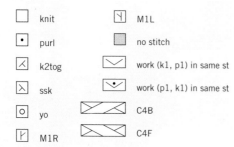

☐ knit	⅂ M1L
• purl	▨ no stitch
⟋ k2tog	⌣ work (k1, p1) in same st
⟍ ssk	⌣• work (p1, k1) in same st
○ yo	⟍⟋ C4B
⌐ M1R	⟍⟋ C4F

Sweet Pea Mitts

DESIGNED BY LISA SWANSON

These sweet mitts feature a Vine Lace pattern and an I-cord bind off. They are ambidextrous, making them easy to knit and to wear.

Finished Measurements

7½"/19 cm circumference and 7½"/19 cm long

Yarn

Brown Sheep Wildfoote, 75% superwash wool/25% nylon, 215 yds (197 m)/1.75 oz (50 g), Color SY-32 Little Lilac

Needles

Two US 1 (2.5 mm) circular needles 16"/40 cm long and set of four US 1 (2.5 mm) double-point needles *or size you need to obtain correct gauge*

Gauge

28 stitches and 42 rounds = 4"/10 cm in Vine Lace pattern

Other Supplies

Stitch markers, scrap yarn for holders, yarn needle

PATTERN ESSENTIALS

Vine Lace
(multiple of 9 stitches plus 4)

- **Round 1:** Knit.
- **Round 2:** K2, *k1, yo, k2, ssk, k2tog, k2, yo; repeat from * to last 2 stitches, k2.
- **Round 3:** Knit.
- **Round 4:** K2, *yo, k2, ssk, k2tog, k2, yo, k1, repeat from * to last 2 stitches, k2.
- Repeat Rounds 1–4 for pattern.

PATTERN NOTES

Instructions are written for knitting in the round on two circular needles. See page 291 for more information.

Knitting the Mitts (make 2)

- Cast on 58 stitches, join for working in the round, and divide stitches evenly onto two circular needles.

- Following written instructions or chart, work Rounds 1–4 of Vine Lace pattern 11 times, or to desired length from start of mitt to base of thumb.

Knitting the Thumb Gusset

- Slip the last 2 stitches from Needle 2 to the beginning of Needle 1; these stitches will be worked again at the start of the next round.

- Following written instructions or chart (see page 38), work Rounds 1–20 of Gusset pattern.

- **ROUND 1:** K1, place marker, M1L, k2, M1L, place marker, knit to end. *You now have* 4 stitches between thumb markers.

- **ROUND 2:** K1, slip marker, k4, slip marker, k1, *k1, yo, k2, ssk, k2tog, k2, yo; repeat from * to end of round.

- **ROUND 3:** K1, slip marker, M1L, knit to next marker, M1L, slip marker, knit to end — 2 stitches increased between thumb markers.

- **ROUND 4:** K1, slip marker, knit to marker, slip marker, k1, *yo, k2, ssk, k2tog, k2, yo, k1; repeat from * to end of round.

- **ROUND 5:** Repeat Round 3.

- **ROUNDS 6–15:** Repeat Rounds 2–5 two more times, then work Rounds 2 and 3 once more. *You now have* 18 stitches between thumb markers and 74 stitches total. **Note:** The increases are deliberately not mirrored.

- **ROUND 16:** K20 slipping markers, *yo, k2, ssk, k2tog, k2, yo, k1; repeat from * to end of round.

- **ROUND 17:** Knit.

- **ROUND 18:** K20 slipping markers, *k1, yo, k2, ssk, k2tog, k2, yo; repeat from * to end of round.

- **ROUND 19:** Knit.

- **ROUND 20:** Repeat Round 16.

- **NEXT ROUND (COUNTS AS ROUND 1 OF VINE LACE PATTERN):** K1, remove thumb markers and place 18 thumb stitches on scrap yarn holder, cast on 2 stitches across thumb gap, knit to end of round. *You now have* 58 stitches.

- Knit the first 2 stitches of Needle 1 onto the end of Needle 2 to restore the beginning of the round to its original position.

Continuing the Mitt

- Work Rounds 2–4 of Vine Lace pattern once, then repeat Rounds 1–4 three more times or to desired length, usually just below the knuckles.

- Bind off in 2-stitch I-cord (see page 292) until 2 I-cord stitches remain. Cut yarn, leaving a 6"/15 cm tail. Join last 2 I-cords stitches to base of first 2 I-cord stitches with yarn tail so I-cord appears continuous around the top edge.

Knitting the Thumb

- Divide the 18 held thumb stitches onto three double-point needles and join yarn to beginning of stitches with RS facing. K18, then pick up and knit (see page 297) 7 stitches from thumb gap. *You now have* 25 stitches. Knit 6 rounds or until thumb reaches the desired length. Bind off in 2-st I-cord as for top of mitt. Weave in ends.

Gusset

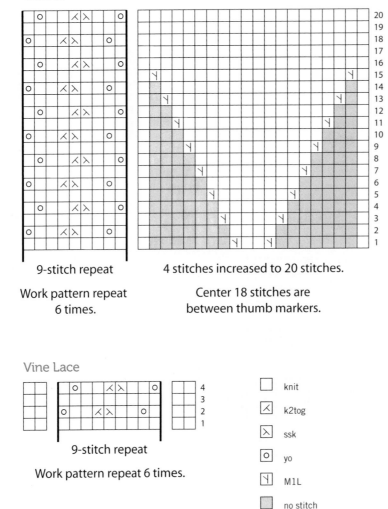

9-stitch repeat

Work pattern repeat
6 times.

4 stitches increased to 20 stitches.

Center 18 stitches are
between thumb markers.

Vine Lace

9-stitch repeat

Work pattern repeat 6 times.

	knit
⟑	k2tog
⟍	ssk
◦	yo
⅄	M1L
▨	no stitch

Lacy Hand Warmers

DESIGNED BY TAMARA DEL SONNO

These lovely little hand warmers have a touch of silk, which adds a little sheen to the wool. Knitted in a rib and lace pattern, they will stretch to fit many sizes.

Finished Measurements

Approximately 6½"/16.5 cm circumference at top of hand, unstretched, and 7½"/19 cm long

Yarn

Spud & Chloë Fine, 80% superwash wool/20% silk, 248 yds (227 m)/2.3 oz (65 g), Color 7800 Popcorn

Needles

US 2 (2.75 mm) double-point needles *or size you need to obtain correct gauge* and straight needles one size larger for cast on

Gauge

36 stitches and 40 rounds = 4"/10 cm in k2, p1 rib pattern, unstretched

Other Supplies

Stitch markers, scrap yarn for stitch holder, yarn needle

Special Abbreviations

LP (lift, purl) wyif, insert the right-hand needle under the strand between the needles from back to front, place the lifted strand on the left-hand needle, then purl the lifted strand and the stitch after it together

SLP (slip, lift, purl) wyif, slip the next purl stitch to the right-hand needle, insert the right-hand needle under the strand between the needles from back to front, place lifted strand on the left-hand needle, return the slipped stitch to the left-hand needle, and purl the stitch and the lifted strand after it together

sssk (slip, slip, slip, knit) slip 3 stitches knitwise, one at a time, to right-hand needle. Insert left-hand needle into front of the stitches and k3tog tbl — 2 stitches decreased.

WL (work lifted strand) insert right-hand needle under the strand between the needles from back to front, place lifted strand on the left-hand needle, then knit or purl it through its front loop as necessary to maintain the rib pattern — 1 stitch increased. ***Note:*** Do not twist the lifted strand; this increase deliberately creates a hole for decorative effect.

PATTERN ESSENTIALS

Side Lace

(worked over 4 stitches)

- **Round 1:** P1, yo, ssk, p1.
- **Round 2:** P1, k2, p1.
- **Round 3:** P1, k2tog, yo, p1.
- **Round 4:** Repeat Round 2.
- Repeat Rounds 1–4 for pattern.

Thumb Lace

(multiple of 3 stitches plus 1)

- **Round 1:** P1, *yo, ssk, p1; repeat from *.
- **Round 2:** P1, *k2, p1; repeat from *.
- **Round 3:** P1, *k2tog, yo, p1; repeat from *.
- **Round 4:** Repeat Round 2.
- Repeat Rounds 1–4 for pattern.

Knitting the Left Warmer

Knitting the Cuff

- Using larger needles and knitted-on method (see page 294), cast on 96 stitches loosely. Divide stitches evenly on smaller double-point needles. Place marker and join into a round, being careful not to twist the stitches.
- **ROUND 1:** Knit.
- **ROUND 2:** *Sssk, k3tog, yo; repeat from * to end of round. *You now have* 48 stitches.
- **ROUNDS 3–8:** *K2, pl; repeat from * to end of round. Piece measures about 1"/2.5 cm.

Knitting the Hand

- **ROUND 1:** K1, M1R, k1, place marker, work Round 1 of Thumb Lace over 13 stitches, place marker, k1, M1L, k1, (pl, k2) five times, place marker, work Round 1 of Side Lace over 4 stitches, place marker, (k2, pl) four times. *You now have* 50 stitches.
- **ROUND 2:** K3, slip marker, work 13 stitches Thumb Lace, slip marker, k3, (pl, k2) five times, slip marker, work 4 stitches Side Lace, slip marker, (k2, pl) four times.

- **ROUND 3:** K2, M1R, k1, slip marker, work 13 stitches Thumb Lace, slip marker, k1, M1L, k2, (pl, k2) five times, slip marker, work 4 stitches Side Lace, slip marker, (k2, pl) four times. *You now have* 52 stitches.
- **ROUND 4:** K4, slip marker, work 13 stitches Thumb Lace, slip marker, k4, (pl, k2) five times, slip marker, work 4 stitches Side Lace, slip marker, (k2, pl) four times.
- **ROUND 5:** Work as established to 2 stitches before marker, WL, k2, slip marker, work 13 stitches Thumb Lace, slip marker, k2, WL, work as established to next marker, slip marker, work 4 stitches Side Lace, slip marker, work as established to end — 2 stitches increased.
- **ROUND 6:** Working new stitches into established k2, pl rib pattern, work in pattern to 2 stitches before marker, k2, slip marker, work 13 stitches Thumb Lace, slip marker, k2, work in rib pattern to next marker, slip marker, work 4 stitches Side Lace, slip marker, work in rib pattern to end.
- **ROUNDS 7–23:** Repeat Rounds 5 and 6 eight more times, then work Round 5 once more, ending with Round 3 of both lace patterns. *You now have* 72 stitches: 14 rib stitches before Thumb Lace, 13 stitches Thumb Lace, 29 rib stitches between lace patterns, 4 stitches Side Lace, 12 rib stitches at end of round.
- **ROUND 24:** (K2, pl) four times, k2, slip marker, work 13 stitches Thumb Lace, slip marker, k2, (pl, k2) nine times, slip marker, work 4 stitches Side Lace, slip marker, (k2, pl) four

times, remove end-of-round marker, work first 12 stitches of round again as (k2, p1) four times, replace marker. *You now have* 2 knit stitches before Thumb Lace, 13 stitches Thumb Lace, 29 rib stitches for back of hand between lace patterns, 4 stitches Side Lace, 24 rib stitches for palm at end of round.

- **ROUND 25**: K2, slip marker, work 13 stitches Thumb Lace, slip marker, k2, LP, work in rib pattern to next marker, slip marker, work 4 stitches Side Lace, slip marker, work in rib pattern to last 3 stitches, SLP, k2. *Note:* The LP and SLP stitches imitate the decorative effect of the WL increases without adding any stitches.

- **ROUND 26**: K2, slip marker, work 13 stitches Thumb Lace, slip marker, k2, p1, work in rib pattern to next marker, slip marker, work 4 stitches Side Lace, slip marker, work in rib pattern to last 3 stitches, p1, k2.

- **ROUNDS 27–48**: Repeat Rounds 25 and 26 eleven more times, ending with Round 4 of both lace patterns.

Reserving the Thumb Stitches

- **ROUND 49 (ROUND 1 OF LACE PATTERNS)**: Removing thumb markers, k2, work 13 stitches Thumb Lace, k2, p1, place 18 stitches just worked on stitch holder, work in established patterns to end of round, remove marker, use the knitted-on method to cast on 3 stitches at end of round, work cast-on stitches as k2, p1, place marker for new beginning of round. *You now have* 57 stitches: 26 stitches before Side Lace pattern, 4 stitches Side Lace between markers, and 27 stitches after Side Lace pattern.

Continuing the Hand

- **ROUND 50 (ROUND 2 OF LACE PATTERNS)**: Work 26 stitches in established rib, slip marker, work 4 stitches Side Lace, slip marker, work 23 stitches in established rib, work last 4 stitches in Side Lace pattern.

- **ROUNDS 51–66**: Work 16 rounds even as established, ending with Round 2 of Side Lace patterns.

- Bind off using 2-stitch I-cord method (see page 292). Cut yarn, leaving a 6"/15 cm tail, and use the tail to join the last 2 I-cord stitches to the first 2 I-cord stitches so I-cord appears continuous around the bound-off edge.

Knitting the Thumb

- Return 18 held thumb stitches to needles and rejoin yarn to beginning of stitches with RS facing. K2, work Round 2 of Thumb Lace pattern over 13 stitches, k2, p1, pick up and knit (see page 297) 3 stitches from base of stitches cast on across thumb gap. *You now have* 21 stitches.

- **NEXT ROUND**: K2, work 13 stitches Thumb Lace, k2, work 4 stitches Side Lace.

- Work 7 more rounds as established, ending with Round 2 of both lace patterns. Bind off with 2-stitch I-cord method as for top of hand. Weave in ends.

Knitting the Right Warmer

- Cast on and work Rounds 1–8 of cuff as for left warmer. *You now have* 48 stitches; piece measures about 1"/2.5 cm.

Knitting the Hand

- **ROUND 1**: K1, M1R, k1, place marker, work Round 1 of Thumb Lace over 13 stitches, place marker, k1, M1L, k1, (p1, k2) four times, place marker, work Round 1 of Side Lace over 4 stitches, place marker, (k2, p1) five times. *You now have* 50 stitches.

- **ROUND 2**: K3, slip marker, work 13 stitches Thumb Lace, slip marker, k3, (p1, k2) four times, slip marker, work 4 stitches Side Lace, slip marker, (k2, p1) five times.

- **ROUND 3**: K2, M1R, k1, slip marker, work 13 stitches Thumb Lace, slip marker, k1, M1L, k2, (p1, k2) four times, slip marker, work 4 stitches Side Lace, slip marker, (k2, p1) five times. *You now have* 52 stitches.

- **ROUND 4**: K4, slip marker, work 13 stitches Thumb Lace, slip marker, k4, (p1, k2) four times, slip marker, work 4 stitches Side Lace, slip marker, (k2, p1) five times.

- **ROUND 5**: Work as established to 2 stitches before marker, WL, k2, slip marker, work 13 stitches Thumb Lace, slip marker, k2, WL, work as established to next marker, slip marker, work 4 stitches Side Lace, slip marker, work as established to end — 2 stitches increased.

- **ROUND 6**: Working new stitches into established k2, p1 rib pattern, work in pattern to 2 stitches before marker, k2, slip marker, work 13 stitches Thumb Lace, slip marker, k2, work in rib pattern to next marker, slip marker, work 4 stitches Side Lace, slip marker, work in rib pattern to end.

- **ROUNDS 7–23**: Repeat Rounds 5 and 6 eight more times, then work Round 5 once more, ending with Round 3 of both lace patterns. *You now have* 72 stitches: 14 rib stitches before Thumb Lace, 13 stitches Thumb Lace, 26 rib stitches between lace patterns, 4 stitches Side Lace, 15 rib stitches at end of round.

- **ROUND 24**: (K2, p1) four times, k2, slip marker, work 13 stitches Thumb Lace, slip marker, k2, (p1, k2) eight times, slip marker, work 4 stitches Side Lace, slip marker, (k2, p1) five times, remove end-of-round marker, work first 12 stitches of round again as (k2, p1) four times, replace marker. *You now have* 2 knit stitches before Thumb Lace, 13 stitches Thumb Lace, 26 rib stitches for palm between lace patterns, 4 stitches Side Lace, 27 rib stitches for back of hand at end of round.

- **ROUND 25**: K2, slip marker, work 13 stitches Thumb Lace, slip marker, k2, LP, work in rib pattern to next marker, slip marker, work 4 stitches Side Lace, slip marker, work in rib pattern to last 3 stitches, SLP, k2.

- **ROUND 26**: K2, slip marker, work 13 stitches Thumb Lace, slip marker, k2, p1, work in rib pattern to next marker, slip marker, work 4 stitches Side Lace, slip marker, work in rib pattern to last 3 stitches, p1, k2.

- **ROUNDS 27–48**: Repeat Rounds 25 and 26 eleven more times, ending with Round 4 of both lace patterns.

Reserving the Thumb Stitches

- **ROUND 49 (ROUND 1 OF LACE PATTERNS)**: Removing thumb markers, k2, work 13 stitches Thumb Lace, k2, p1, place 18 stitches just worked on stitch holder, work in established patterns to end of round, remove marker, use the knitted-on method to cast on 3 stitches at end of round, work cast-on stitches as k2, p1, place marker for new beginning of round. *You now have* 57 stitches: 23 stitches before Side Lace pattern, 4 stitches Side Lace between markers, and 30 stitches after Side Lace pattern.

Continuing the Hand

- **ROUND 50 (ROUND 2 OF LACE PATTERNS)**: Work 23 stitches in established rib, slip marker, work 4 stitches Side Lace, slip marker, work 26 stitches in established rib, work last 4 stitches in Side Lace pattern.

- **ROUNDS 51–66**: Work 16 rounds even as established, ending with Round 2 of Side Lace patterns.

- Bind off using 2-stitch I-cord method as for left warmer.

Knitting the Thumb

- Work as for left warmer.

Trellis Mitts

DESIGNED BY ANN McCLURE

These fancy fingerless mitts feature a Triple Leaf lace panel offset by twisted stitches and smocking at the cuff and top. Because they're worked from the top down, you'll also find a unique thumb construction. That's a lot of knitting adventure in one — well, okay, two — small projects.

Finished Measurements
Approximately 6"/15 cm circumference, unstretched, and 7"/18 cm long

Yarn
Ella Rae Lace Merino, 100% extra fine merino wool, 460 yds (420 m)/3.5 oz (100 g), Color 35 Emerald

Needles
Set of four US 2 (2.75 mm) double-point needles *or size you need to obtain correct gauge*

Gauge
28 stitches and 40 rounds = 4"/10 cm in Triple Leaf pattern

Other Supplies
Smooth scrap yarn for provisional cast on, crochet hook similar in size to knitting needles, stitch holders (or more scrap yarn), stitch markers, yarn needle

Special Abbreviations
LT (left twist)   with right-hand needle behind left-hand needle, knit the second stitch through the back loop and leave it on needle, knit the first stitch, and slip both stitches from left-hand needle
RT (right twist)   k2tog, leaving stitches on left-hand needle, knit the first stitch again, and slip both stitches from left-hand needle

PATTERN ESSENTIALS

Wrap 3 Wyib, slip 3 stitches purlwise to right-hand needle; bring yarn to front and slip 3 stitches back to left-hand needle; bring yarn to back and slip 3 stitches purlwise to right-hand needle.

Knitting the Right Mit

- Cast on 48 stitches and place 12 stitches on Needle 1, 24 stitches on Needle 2, and 12 stitches on Needle 3. ***Note:*** Needle 2 holds the back-of-hand stitches. Join into a round, being careful not to twist the stitches; the round begins in the center of the palm.

Knitting the Top Smocking

- **ROUND 1:** *P1, k1; repeat from * to end of round.
- **ROUND 2:** Repeat Round 1.

43

- **ROUND 3:** *P1, Wrap 3; repeat from * to end of round.

- **ROUNDS 4–6:** Repeat Round 1.

- **ROUND 7:** P1, k1, p1, *Wrap 3, p1; repeat from *, moving stitches between the needles as necessary to accommodate the wraps, to last 2 stitches, p1, then work Wrap 3 over the last stitch of this round and the first 2 stitches of the next round. *Note:* Do not change the starting point of the round; replace the end-of-round marker after the first stitch of the Wrap 3, and count the last 2 stitches of the Wrap 3 as the first 2 stitches of Round 8.

- **ROUNDS 8–10:** Repeat Round 1.

- **ROUND 11:** Repeat Round 3.

- **ROUNDS 12 AND 13:** Repeat Round 1.

Knitting the Triple Leaf Pattern

- Move 1 stitch from Needle 2 to Needle 3. On Needles 1 and 3, continue in rib as established (without any Wrap 3s). On the 23 stitches of Needle 2, following either the chart or the written version, work Rounds 1–12 of Triple Leaf pattern once, then work Rounds 1–10 once more.

- **ROUND 1:** P1, k2, p1, k15, p1, k2, p1.

- **ROUND 2:** P1, k2, p1, k1, yo, k2tog, k3tog, (yo, k1) three times, yo, k3tog tbl, ssk, yo, k1, p1, k2, p1.

- **ROUND 3:** P1, RT, p1, k15, p1, LT, p1.

- **ROUND 4:** P1, k2, p1, k1, yo, k3tog, yo, k7, yo, k3tog tbl, yo, k1, p1, k2, p1.

- **ROUND 5:** Repeat Round 1.

- **ROUND 6:** P1, RT, p1, k1, yo, k2tog, yo, k1, yo, k2, s2kp, k2, yo, k1, yo, ssk, yo, k1, p1, LT, p1. *You now have* 25 stitches.

- **ROUND 7:** P1, k2, p1, k17, p1, k2, p1.

- **ROUND 8:** P1, k2, p1, k1, yo, k2tog, yo, k3, yo, k1, s2kp, k1, yo, k3, yo, ssk, yo, k1, p1, k2, p1. *You now have* 27 stitches.

- **ROUND 9:** P1, RT, p1, k19, p1, LT, p1.

- **ROUND 10:** P1, k2, p1, k1, yo, (k2tog) twice, k3, yo, s2kp, yo, k3, (ssk) twice, yo, k1, p1, k2, p1. *You now have* 25 stitches.

- **ROUND 11:** P1, k2, p1, k17, p1, k2, p1.

- **ROUND 12:** P1, RT, p1, k1, yo, (k2tog) three times, (k1, yo) twice, k1, (ssk) three times, yo, k1, p1, LT, p1. *You now have* 23 stitches.

- Repeat Rounds 1–10 once more.

Knitting the Thumb Gusset

- With scrap yarn and crochet hook, chain 20 and set aside for thumb gusset.

- **ROUND 1:** On Needle 1, work 9 stitches in rib as established and place last 5 stitches worked on holder; work last 3 stitches on needle in rib. On Needles 2 and 3, continue in patterns as established.

- **ROUND 2:** On Needle 1, work 4 stitches in rib as established, place marker, k13 into crochet chain as for provisional cast on (see page 297), place marker, work last 3 stitches on needle in rib. On Needles 2 and 3, work in patterns as established to end of round. *You now have* 20 stitches total on Needle 1 and 13 stitches between thumb gusset markers.

- **ROUNDS 3 AND 4:** Keeping the thumb gusset stitches in stockinette stitch and other stitches in patterns as established, work 2 rounds even.

- **ROUND 5 (DECREASE ROUND):** Work 4 rib stitches, slip marker, k2tog tbl, knit to 2 stitches before next gusset marker, k2tog, slip marker, work in patterns as established to end of round — 2 gusset stitches decreased.

- Repeat Rounds 3–5 three more times. *You now have* 12 stitches total on Needle 1 and 5 stitches between thumb gusset markers.

- Resume working all stitches on Needle 1 in rib pattern, and continue in patterns as established until five repeats of 12-round Triple Leaf pattern have been completed from the beginning.

Knitting the Cuff Smocking

- Repeat Rounds 1–13 of top smocking.

- Bind off in rib.

Knitting the Thumb

- Carefully remove the crochet-chain scrap yarn, place 13 stitches from the base of the provisional cast on onto the needle, and join the yarn at end of these stitches. Pick up and knit (see page 297) 3 stitches before the stitches on the holder to close any gaps, k5 from holder, pick up and knit 3 stitches after stitches just worked to close any gaps. *You now have* 24 stitches.

- **ROUNDS 1–5:** Knit.

- **ROUND 6:** *K2tog, k6; repeat from * to end of round. *You now have* 21 stitches.

- **ROUNDS 7 AND 8:** Knit.

- **ROUND 9:** *K2tog, k5; repeat from * to end of round. *You now have* 18 stitches.

- **ROUND 10:** *K1, p1; repeat from * to end of round.

- Bind off in rib.

Knitting the Left Mitt

- Work as for right mitt to the thumb gusset.

Knitting the Thumb Gusset

- With scrap yarn and crochet hook, chain 20 and set aside for thumb gusset.

- **ROUND 1:** On Needles 1 and 2, work in patterns as established. On Needle 3, work 8 stitches in rib as established, place last 5 stitches worked on holder, work last 5 stitches in rib as established.

- **ROUND 2:** On Needles 1 and 2, work in patterns. On Needle 3, work 3 stitches in rib as established, place marker, k13

into crochet chain as for provisional cast on, place marker, work last 5 stitches on needle in rib. *You now have* 21 stitches total on Needle 3 and 13 stitches between thumb gusset markers.

- **ROUNDS 3 AND 4:** Keeping the thumb gusset stitches in stockinette stitch and other stitches in patterns as established, work 2 rounds even.

- **ROUND 5 (DECREASE ROUND):** On Needles 1 and 2, work in pattern. On Needle 3, work 3 rib stitches, slip marker, k2tog tbl, knit to 2 stitches before next thumb marker, k2tog, slip marker, work 5 rib stitches — 2 gusset stitches decreased.

- Repeat Rounds 3–5 three more times. *You now have* 13 stitches total on Needle 3 and 5 stitches between thumb gusset markers.

- Resume working all stitches on Needle 3 in rib pattern, and continue in patterns as established until five repeats of 12-round Triple Leaf pattern have been completed from the beginning.

- Work cuff smocking and thumb as for right mitt.

Finishing

- Weave in ends. Block lightly, if desired.

Triple Leaf

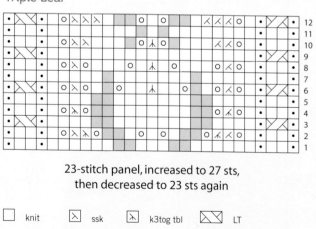

23-stitch panel, increased to 27 sts, then decreased to 23 sts again

☐ knit	⊠ ssk	⟋ k3tog tbl
• purl	○ yo	⋏ s2kp
⟍ k2tog	⟋ k3tog	▨ no stitch

LT
RT

Vine Lace Fingerless Gloves

DESIGNED BY OHMAY DESIGNS

Knit these gloves in the round without a thumb gusset — you'll leave an opening for the thumb where you'll pick up and knit thumb stitches. An optional cord between the second and third fingers keeps the mitts in place.

Finished Measurements

Approximately 7"/18 cm circumference and 7½"/19 cm long

Yarn

Grignasco Cuzco 2, 60% extra fine merino wool/40% superfine alpaca, 109 yds (100 m)/1.75 oz (50 g), Color 6610 Natural

Needles

Set of five US 6 (4 mm) double-point needles *or size you need to obtain correct gauge*

Gauge

20½ stitches and 26 rounds = 4"/10 cm in Vine Lace pattern

Other Supplies

Stitch marker, stitch holder, crochet hook similar in size to knitting needles (optional), yarn needle

PATTERN ESSENTIALS

Vine Lace
(multiple of 9 stitches)

- **Rounds 1 and 3:** Knit.
- **Round 2:** *Yo, k2, ssk, k2tog, k2, yo, k1; repeat from * to end of round.
- **Round 4:** *K1, yo, k2, ssk, k2tog, k2, yo; repeat from * to end of round.

Knitting the Left Glove

- Cast on 36 stitches and divide onto four double-point needles. Place marker and join into a round, being careful not to twist the stitches; round begins on thumb side of hand, at start of back-of-hand stitches. Work Vine Lace pattern for 5½"/14 cm, ending with Round 3 of pattern. *Note:* Take care that you do not accidentally drop any yarnovers that occur at the ends of the needles.

Creating the Thumb Opening

- **NEXT ROUND (COUNTS AS ROUND 4 OF PATTERN):** K1, (yo, k2, ssk, k2tog, k2, yo, k1) twice, yo, k2, ssk; k6 and place on holder; k3, k2tog, k2, yo. *You now have* 30 stitches on needles and 6 stitches on hold.

- **NEXT ROUND (COUNTS AS ROUND 1 OF PATTERN):** Knit to thumb opening, cast on 6 stitches across gap, knit to end of round. *You now have* 36 stitches.

- **NEXT ROUND (COUNTS AS ROUND 2 OF PATTERN):** (Yo, k2, ssk, k2tog, k2, yo, k1) twice, yo, k2, ssk, k9, k2tog, k2, yo, k1.

Finishing the Hand

- Beginning with Round 3, resume working Vine Lace pattern as established on all stitches. Continue in pattern until piece measures 1½"/4 cm from thumb opening, ending with Round 2 or 4 of pattern.

- Bind off with 3-stitch attached I-cord (see page 292).

- *Optional:* Crochet a chain of 4 or 5 stitches connecting the back of hand with the palm between the second and third fingers.

Knitting the Thumb

- Place the 6 stitches from the holder onto a needle. With WS facing, attach yarn to beginning of these stitches and purl 1 WS row. Turn work so RS is facing.

- **ROUND 1:** K6, pick up and knit (see page 297) 10 stitches evenly from base of stitches cast on across the thumb opening. Place marker and join to work in the round. *You now have* 16 stitches.

- **ROUNDS 2–8:** Knit.

- Bind off all stitches.

Knitting the Right Glove

- Work as for left glove to thumb opening, ending with Round 3 of pattern; round begins on the thumb side of the hand, at the start of the palm stitches.

Creating the Thumb Opening

- **NEXT ROUND (COUNTS AS ROUND 4 OF PATTERN):** K1, yo, k2, ssk, k3, k6 and place on holder; k2tog, k2, yo, (k1, yo, k2, ssk, k2tog, k2, yo) twice. *You now have* 30 stitches on needle and 6 stitches on hold.

- **NEXT ROUND (COUNTS AS ROUND 1 OF PATTERN):** Knit to thumb opening, cast on 6 stitches across gap, knit to end of round. *You now have* 36 stitches.

- **NEXT ROUND (COUNTS AS ROUND 2 OF PATTERN):** Yo, k2, ssk, k9, k2tog, k2, yo, k1, (yo, k2, ssk, k2tog, k2, yo, k1) twice.

Finishing the Hand and Thumb

- Beginning with Round 3 of pattern, finish hand as for left glove. Work thumb as for left glove.

Finishing

- Weave in ends. Wash and block.

Travel-Worthy Mitts

DESIGNED BY SARAH JEAN HOOD

Luxury and function go hand in hand with these lovely cashmere mitts. Travel worthy for their lightness and warmth, they provide both wrist and knuckle coverage. One skein is enough for two pairs of mitts.

Finished Measurements
Approximately 6¾"/17 cm circumference and 8½"/21.5 cm long

Yarn
Jade Sapphire Mongolian Cashmere 2-Ply, 100% cashmere, 400 yds (366 m)/ 1.9 oz (55 g), Color 61 Blue Spruce

Needles
Set of US 3 (3.25 mm) double-point needles or long circular for magic loop *or size you need to obtain correct gauge* Needles one size larger for cast on

Gauge
28 stitches and 44 rounds = 4"/10 cm in cuff pattern, slightly stretched

Other Supplies
Stitch markers, small stitch holder, yarn needle

Knitting the Left Mitt

- With larger double-point needles, cast on 48 stitches using knitted-on cast on (see page 294). **Note:** A loose cast on allows the edge to naturally zigzag. Join into a round, being careful not to twist the stitches; round begins at the pinky side of the hand, at the start of the palm stitches.

Knitting the Cuff

Note: The s2kp (centered double decrease) at the beginning of Round 4 uses the last stitch of Round 3 and the first 2 stitches of Round 4. The end-of-round marker is repositioned at the end of Round 3 so all the stitches of the s2kp will be on the same side of the marker. To reposition the marker, knit to the last stitch in Round 3, temporarily slip the last stitch to the right-hand needle, remove the marker, return the slipped stitch to the left-hand needle, and replace the marker.

- **ROUND 1:** Knit. Change to smaller double-point needles.
- **ROUND 2:** *S2kp, (k1, yo) twice, k1; repeat from * to end of round.
- **ROUND 3:** Knit to the last stitch, reposition marker at end of round (see Note above).
- **ROUND 4:** *S2kp, (k1, yo) twice, k1; repeat from * to end of round.
- **ROUNDS 5–10:** Repeat Rounds 3 and 4 three more times.
- **ROUND 11:** Knit to the last stitch, reposition marker at end of round.

Knitting the Wrist

- **ROUND 12:** *S2kp, (k1, yo) twice, k1; repeat from * to end of round.
- **ROUNDS 13–15:** Knit.
- **ROUND 16:** *K1, yo, k1, s2kp, k1, yo; repeat from * to end of round.
- **ROUNDS 17–19:** Knit, repositioning the marker at end of Round 19 only.
- **ROUNDS 20–44:** Repeat Rounds 12–19 three more times, then work Round 12 once more.

Knitting the Thumb Gusset

- **ROUND 45:** K17, place marker, work Round 45 of Thumb chart over 7 stitches, place marker, k24.
- **ROUNDS 46 AND 47:** Knit to thumb marker, slip marker, work next round of Thumb chart, slip marker, knit to end.

- **ROUND 48:** (P2, k1 tbl) five times, p2, slip marker, work next round of Thumb chart, slip marker, work Round 1 of Back-of-Hand chart over 24 stitches.
- **ROUNDS 49–57:** Working first 17 stitches in established p2, k1 tbl rib pattern for the palm, continue chart patterns for thumb and back of hand, ending with Round 57 of Thumb chart and Round 2 of Back-of-Hand chart. *You now have 19 stitches between the thumb markers and 60 stitches total.*
- **ROUND 58:** Work established rib pattern over 17 palm stitches, remove thumb marker, k1 tbl (first thumb stitch), slip next 17 stitches to small stitch holder, cast on 5 stitches using backward loop method (see page 290), k1 tbl (last thumb stitch), remove thumb marker, work Round 3 of Back-of-Hand chart over 24 stitches. *You now have 48 stitches.*
- **ROUND 59:** (P2, k1 tbl) eight times for palm, work Round 4 of Back-of-Hand chart over 24 stitches.
- **ROUNDS 60–90:** Continue in established patterns, ending with Round 3 of Back-of-Hand chart.
- **ROUNDS 91–95:** (P2, k1 tbl) 16 times.
- Bind off all stitches knitwise.

Knitting the Thumb

- Transfer the 17 held stitches to smaller needles. Join yarn to beginning of stitches with RS facing, (p2, k1 tbl) five times, p2, pick up and knit (see page 297) 1 stitch before the stitches cast on across thumb gap, 5 stitches from base of cast on, and 1 stitch after cast-on stitches. *You now have 24 stitches.*

- **ROUNDS 1–12:** *P2, k1 tbl; repeat from * to end of round.

- Bind off all stitches knitwise. Weave in ends.

Knitting the Right Mitt

- Work cuff and wrist as for left mitt. Round begins at the pinky side of the hand, at the start of the back-of-hand stitches.

Knitting the Thumb Gusset

- **ROUND 45:** K24, place marker, work Round 45 of Thumb chart over 7 stitches, place marker, k17.

- **ROUNDS 46 AND 47:** Knit to thumb marker, slip marker, work next round of Thumb chart, slip marker, knit to end.

- **ROUND 48:** Work Round 1 of Back-of-Hand chart over 24 stitches, slip marker, work next round of Thumb chart, slip marker, (p2, k1 tbl) five times, p2.

- **ROUNDS 49–57:** Working last 17 stitches in established p2, k1 tbl rib pattern for palm, continue chart patterns for thumb and back of hand, ending with Round 57 of Thumb chart and Round 2 of Back-of-Hand chart. *You now have* 19 stitches between the thumb markers and 60 stitches total.

- **ROUND 58:** Work Round 3 of Back-of-Hand chart over 24 stitches, remove thumb marker, k1 tbl (first thumb stitch), slip next 17 stitches to small stitch holder, cast on 5 stitches using backward loop method, k1 tbl (last

thumb stitch), remove thumb marker, work established rib pattern over 17 palm stitches. *You now have* 48 stitches.

- **ROUND 59:** Work Round 4 of Back-of-Hand chart over 24 stitches, (k1 tbl, p2) eight times for the palm.

- **ROUNDS 60–90:** Continue in established patterns, ending with Round 3 of Back-of-Hand chart.

- **ROUNDS 91–95:** (K1 tbl, p2) 16 times.

- Bind off all stitches knitwise.

Knitting the Thumb

- Work as for left thumb.

Back-of-Hand

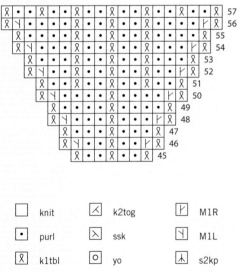

Thumb

□ knit	⊼ k2tog	⊬ M1R
• purl	⊠ ssk	⅄ M1L
ℛ k1tbl	○ yo	⋏ s2kp

Pine Needle Mittens

DESIGNED BY JENISE REID

With stockinette stitch on the palm and a lace pattern on the back of the hand, these mittens are both lovely and practical. They feature an "afterthought" thumb so you can place it exactly where you want it. Since you have to snip the knitting, this method is not for wimps! Pair the mittens with the Pine Needle Toque on page 16.

Finished Measurements

7½"/19 cm circumference and 11"/28 cm long

Yarn

Knit Picks Palette, 100% Peruvian Highland wool, 231 yds (211 m)/1.75 oz (50 g), Color Bittersweet Heather

Needles

Set of five US 3 (3.25) double-point needles *or size you need to obtain correct gauge*

Gauge

23 stitches and 32 rounds = 4"/10 cm in stockinette stitch

Other Supplies

Yarn needle

Knitting the Mittens (make 2)

- Cast on 44 stitches and divide evenly onto four double-point needles. Join into a round, being careful not to twist the stitches. Work Rounds 1–19 of chart.

- **NEXT ROUND:** Work Round 20 of chart, decreasing as shown. *You now have 33 stitches. Cuff measures about 3"/ 7.5 cm from deepest point on back of hand.*

- Work Rounds 21–25 of chart once.

- **NEXT ROUND:** Work Round 26 of chart, increasing as shown. *You now have 44 stitches.*

- Work Rounds 29–36 five times for mittens pictured. ***Note:*** To adjust length, repeat Rounds 29–36 more or fewer times as desired; every 8-round repeat added or removed lengthens or shortens the mitten hand by about 1"/2.5 cm.

- Work Rounds 37–42 of chart once; piece measures about 9½"/24 cm from deepest point on back of hand, or 1½"/4 cm less than desired length.

- Work Rounds 43–55 of chart. *You now have 11 stitches.*

- Cut yarn, leaving an 8"/20.5 cm tail. Thread tail onto yarn needle and draw through remaining stitches; pull up snugly and secure. Weave in end.

Adding the Thumbs

- Try mittens on and mark where your thumbs begin on the side of each mitten. Check that they match, adjusting one mitten or the other if necessary.

Make sure you mark one mitten for the right hand and the other for the left hand.

- Pick up and knit (see page 297) 9 palm stitches in the row above the marked thumb position, then use a separate needle to pick up and knit 9 palm stitches in the row below the marker; these stitches should begin next to the lace pattern on the back of the hand and extend into the stockinette palm. You should have 1 row between the picked-up stitches.

- Hold your breath, lift the center stitch of the row between the picked-up stitches with the tip of the scissors, and snip it. Unravel the yarn from the snipped center outward until all of the picked-up stitches have been freed. Tie the working yarn to one of the ends you just unraveled and knit the first 9 thumb stitches. Tie the other unraveled end to the working yarn and knit the remaining 9 thumb stitches. *You now have 18 stitches.*

- Knit all stitches until the thumb measures 2½"/6.5 cm or ¼"/6 mm less than desired length.

- **NEXT ROUND:** *K3tog; repeat from * to end of round. *You now have 6 stitches.*

- Knit 1 round. Cut yarn, leaving an 8"/20.5 cm tail. Thread tail onto yarn needle and draw through remaining stitches; pull up snugly and secure.

- Weave in ends. Block.

Pine Needle Mittens

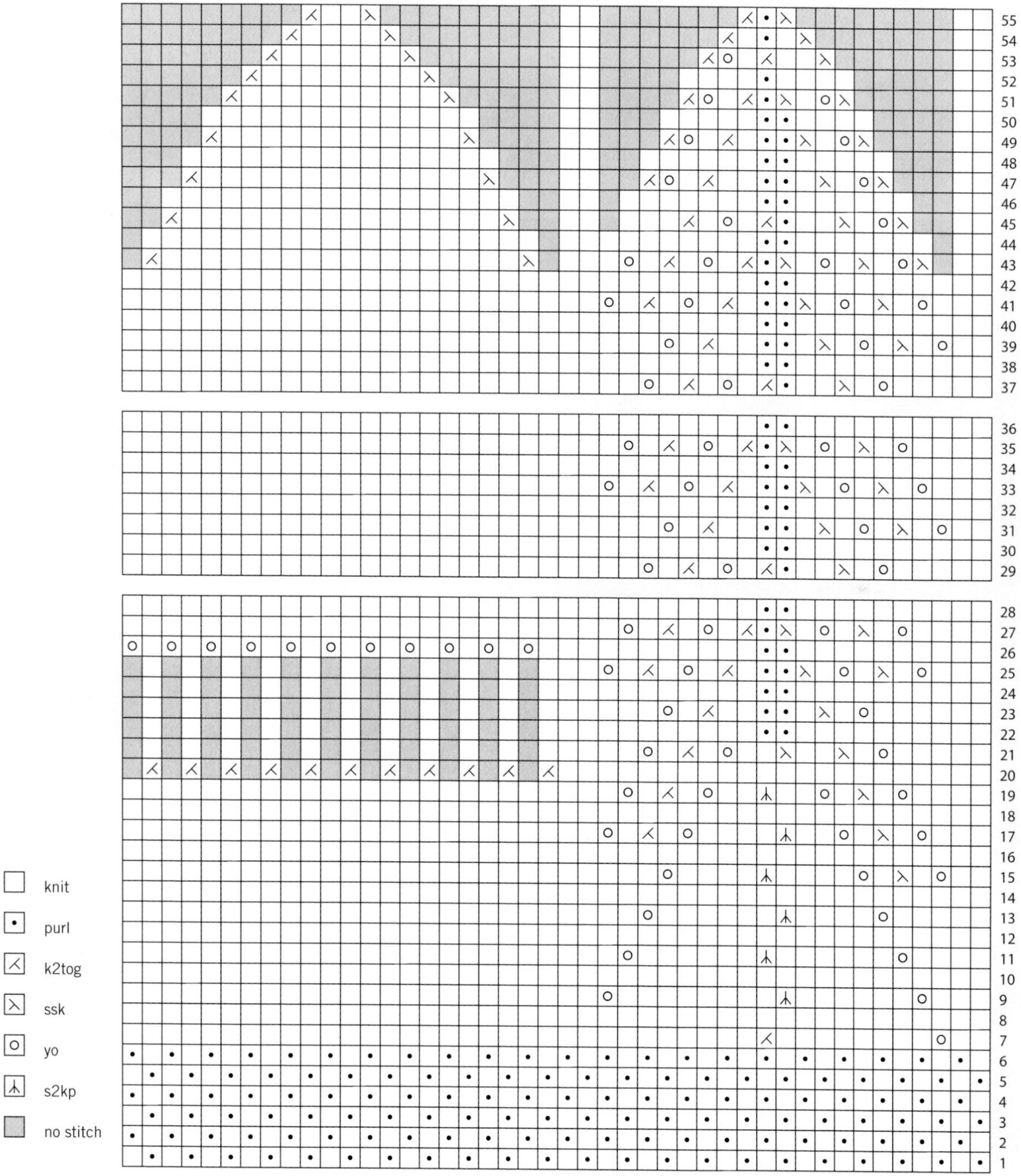

Legend:

Symbol	Meaning
☐	knit
•	purl
⋋	k2tog
⋌	ssk
○	yo
⋏	s2kp
▨	no stitch

Flutter Mitts

DESIGNED BY JENISE REID

These mittens are named for the way the lace ribbing flutters back and forth. They are knit in the round, and the lace continues from the ribbing to outline the sides of each mitten. Pair these with the Flutter Toque shown on page 31.

Finished Measurements

8"/20.5 cm hand circumference and 9½"/24 cm long

Yarn

Knit Picks Sugarbunny, 80% merino wool/ 20% angora, 136 yds (124 m)/1.75 oz (50 g), Topaz

Needles

Set of five US 4 (3.5 mm) double-point needles *or size you need to obtain correct gauge*

Gauge

18 stitches and 26 rounds = 4"/10 cm in stockinette stitch

Other Supplies

Scrap yarn for thumb opening, yarn needle

Knitting the Cuff

- Cast on 36 stitches and divide evenly onto four double-point needles. Join into a round, being careful not to twist the stitches.

- ROUND 1: *K2tog, yo, p1; repeat from * to end of round.

- ROUND 2: *K2, p1; repeat from * to end of round.

- ROUND 3: *Yo, ssk, p1; repeat from * to end of round.

- ROUND 4: Repeat Round 2.

- **ROUNDS 5–14:** Repeat Rounds 1–4 twice, then work Rounds 1 and 2 once more.
- **ROUND 15:** *Yo, ssk, (p1, ssk) five times, p1; repeat from * once more; cuff measures about 2"/5 cm. *You now have* 26 stitches.

Knitting the Hand

- **ROUNDS 16 AND 18:** (K2, p1, k9, p1) twice.
- **ROUND 17:** (K2tog, yo, p1, k9, p1) twice.
- **ROUND 19:** *Yo, ssk, p1, (M1R, k2) four times, M1R, k1, p1; repeat from * once more. *You now have* 36 stitches.
- **ROUND 20:** (K2, p1, k14, p1) twice.
- **ROUND 21:** (K2tog, yo, p1, k14, p1) twice.
- **ROUND 22:** (K2, p1, k14, p1) twice.
- **ROUND 23:** (Yo, ssk, p1, k14, p1) twice.
- **ROUND 24:** Repeat Round 22.
- **ROUNDS 25–38:** Repeat Rounds 21–24 three more times, then work Rounds 21 and 22 once more; piece measures about 5½"/14 cm. *Note:* To adjust the position of the thumb opening, repeat Rounds 21–24 more or fewer times before working Rounds 21 and 22; every 4 rounds added or removed lengthen or shorten the piece by about ½"/13 mm.

Reserving the Thumb Stitches

- Work Round 39 for the right or left hand as follows to mark thumb placement.

For the right hand: Yo, ssk, p1, use scrap yarn to knit the next 6 stitches, return the stitches just worked to the left-hand needle and knit them again using the main yarn, k8, p1, yo, ssk, p1, k14, p1.

For the left hand: Yo, ssk, p1, k8, use scrap yarn to knit the next 6 stitches, return the stitches just worked to the left-hand needle and knit them again using the main yarn, p1, yo, ssk, p1, k14, p1.

Knitting the Upper Hand

- **ROUND 40:** (K2, p1, k14, p1) twice.
- **ROUND 41:** (K2tog, yo, p1, k14, p1) twice.
- **ROUND 42:** Repeat Round 40.
- **ROUND 43:** (Yo, ssk, p1, k14, p1) twice.
- **ROUNDS 44–57:** Repeat Rounds 40–43 three more times, then work Rounds 40 and 41 once more; piece measures about 8½"/21.5 cm. *Note:* To adjust the length, repeat Rounds 40–43 more or fewer times before working Rounds 40 and 41; every 4 rounds added or removed lengthen or shorten the hand by about ½"/13 mm.

Shaping the Mitten Top

- **ROUND 58:** (K2, p1, k2tog, k10, ssk, p1) twice. *You now have* 32 stitches.
- **ROUND 59:** (Yo, ssk, p1, k2tog, k8, ssk, p1) twice. *You now have* 28 stitches.
- **ROUND 60:** (K2, p1, k2tog, k6, ssk, p1) twice. *You now have* 24 stitches.
- **ROUND 61:** (K2tog, yo, p1, k2tog, k4, ssk, p1) twice. *You now have* 20 stitches.
- **ROUND 62:** (K2, p1, k2tog, k2, ssk, p1) twice. *You now have* 16 stitches.
- **ROUND 63:** (Yo, ssk, p1, k2tog, ssk, p1) twice. *You now have* 12 stitches.
- **ROUND 64:** *K2, (p2tog) twice; repeat from * once more. *You now have* 8 stitches.

Cut yarn, leaving an 8"/20.5 cm tail. Thread tail onto yarn needle and draw through remaining stitches; pull up snugly and secure on WS.

continued on next page

Knitting the Thumb

- Carefully remove scrap yarn from the thumb opening and place 6 stitches from the base of the opening on one needle and 7 stitches from the top of the opening on another needle. *You now have* 13 stitches.

- Redistribute stitches as evenly as possible on three or four needles, and join yarn at side of opening with RS facing. Work in stockinette stitch until thumb measures 2"/5 cm or ¼"/6 mm less than desired length.

- **NEXT ROUND:** (K1, k2tog) four times, k1. *You now have* 9 stitches.

- **NEXT ROUND:** (K2tog) four times, k1. *You now have* 5 stitches.

- Cut yarn, leaving an 8" (20.5 cm) tail. Thread tail onto yarn needle and draw through remaining stitches; pull up snugly and secure on WS.

Finishing

- Weave in ends and block.

Damask Lace Gloves

DESIGNED BY YUMIKO SAKURAI

These delicate and feminine gloves are knitted in lace-weight yarn with simple lace stitches on the cuffs. The finger lengths can be adjusted to fit several sizes. The gloves are ambidextrous — both knitted exactly alike.

Finished Measurements

Approximately 7½"/19 cm hand circumference

Yarn

Malabrigo Lace, 100% baby merino wool, 470 yds (430 m)/ 1.75 oz (50 g), Color 130 Damask

Needles

Sets of five US 3 (3.25 mm) and US 1 (2.25 mm) double-point needles *or size you need to obtain correct gauge*

Gauge

38 stitches and 52 rounds = 4"/10 cm in stockinette stitch with smaller needles

Other Supplies

Stitch markers, scrap yarn for holders, yarn needle

Damask Lace

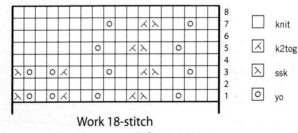

Work 18-stitch
pattern repeat 4 times.

PATTERN ESSENTIALS

Damask Lace

(multiple of 18 stitches)

- **Round 1:** *K3, yo, k2, ssk, k2tog, k2, yo, k2, k2tog, yo, k1, yo, ssk; repeat from * to end of round.
- **Rounds 2, 4, 6, and 8:** Knit.
- **Round 3:** *K2, yo, k2, ssk, k2tog, k2, yo, k3, k2tog, yo, k1, yo, ssk; repeat from * to end of round.
- **Round 5:** *K3, yo, k2, ssk, k2tog, k2, yo, k7; repeat from * to end of round.
- **Round 7:** *K2, yo, k2, ssk, k2tog, k2, yo, k8; repeat from * to end of round.
- Repeat Rounds 1–8 for pattern.

Knitting the Cuff

- Using larger needles, cast on 72 stitches loosely. Distribute stitches evenly onto 4 double-point neeldes, place marker and join into a round, being careful not to twist the stitches; round begins at little finger side of hand. Purl 1 round.

- Working from text or chart, work Rounds 1–8 of Damask Lace three times (24 rounds completed).

- Change to smaller needles and work Rounds 1–8 of Damask Lace once.

- Continuing with smaller needles, work in stockinette stitch for 4 rounds.

Note: Use smaller needles for rest of hand, fingers, and thumb.

Knitting the Thumb Gusset

- **ROUND 1:** K35, place marker, M1R, k2, M1L, place marker, k35. *You now have 4 stitches between the gusset markers.*

- **ROUNDS 2 AND 3:** Knit.

- **ROUND 4:** K35, slip marker, M1R, knit to next marker, M1L, slip marker, k35 — 2 stitches increased between the gusset markers.

- Repeat Rounds 2–4 eight more times. *You now have 22 stitches between the gusset markers.*

- Knit 2 rounds.

Reserving the Thumb Stitches

- K35, remove marker, place next 22 stitches on scrap yarn to hold, remove marker, cast on 3 stitches, k35. *You now have 73 stitches on the needles for the hand and 22 stitches on scrap yarn for the thumb.*

Knitting the Upper Hand

- Work all stitches in stockinette stitch for 1"/2.5 cm above where thumb stitches were put on hold, or until hand reaches base of little finger.

Knitting the Little Finger

- **NEXT ROUND:** K8, place next 57 stitches on scrap yarn to hold, cast on 2 stitches, k8. *You now have 18 stitches for the little finger.*

- Distribute stitches onto 3 double-point needles, place marker, and work little finger in stockinette stitch until it measures 2¼"/5.5 cm or ¼"/6 mm less than desired length.

- **NEXT ROUND:** (K2tog, k1) six times. *You now have 12 stitches.*

- **NEXT ROUND:** Knit.

- **NEXT ROUND:** K2tog six times. *You now have 6 stitches.*

- Cut yarn, leaving a 6"/15 cm tail. Thread tail onto yarn needle and draw through remaining stitches; pull up snugly and secure. Weave in the end.

Continuing the Hand

- Attach new yarn to the beginning of the held stitches with RS facing, k57 stitches from scrap yarn, pick up and knit (see page 297) 2 stitches from base of little finger. *You now have 59 stitches.* Distribute evenly onto 4 double-point needles, place marker, and work in stockinette stitch for ¼"/6 mm or desired length to base of ring finger.

Knitting the Ring Finger

- **NEXT ROUND:** K10, place next 39 stitches on scrap yarn, cast on 2 stitches, and knit remaining 10 stitches. *You now have 22 stitches on needles for the ring finger.*

- Distribute evenly onto 3 double-point needles, place marker and work even in stockinette stitch until finger measures 3"/7.5 cm or ¼"/6 mm less than desired length.

- **NEXT ROUND:** K2tog 11 times. *You now have 11 stitches.*

- **NEXT ROUND:** Knit.

- **NEXT ROUND:** K2tog five times, k1. *You now have 6 stitches.*

- Cut yarn, leaving a 6"/15 cm tail. Thread tail onto yarn needle and draw through remaining stitches; pull up snugly and secure. Weave in the end.

Knitting the Middle Finger

- Attach new yarn to beginning of held stitches with RS facing, k39 stitches from scrap yarn, pick up and knit 2 stitches from the base of the ring finger. *You now have 41 stitches for the hand.*

- Place marker and work in stockinette stitch for 2 rounds or desired length to base of middle finger.

- **NEXT ROUND:** K10, place next 21 stitches on scrap yarn, cast on 3 stitches, and knit remaining 10 stitches. *You now have* 23 stitches on needles for the middle finger.

- Distribute evenly onto 3 double-point needles, place marker and work even in stockinette stitch until finger measures 3¼"/8.5 cm or ¼"/6 mm less than desired length.

- **NEXT ROUND:** K2tog 11 times, k1. *You now have* 12 stitches.

- **NEXT ROUND:** Knit.

- **NEXT ROUND:** K2tog six times. *You now have* 6 stitches.

- Cut yarn, leaving a 6"/15 cm tail. Thread tail onto yarn needle and draw through remaining stitches; pull up snugly and secure. Weave in the end.

Knitting the Index Finger

- Attach new yarn to beginning of held stitches with RS facing, k21 stitches from scrap yarn, pick up and knit 3 stitches from base of middle finger. *You now have* 24 stitches on needles for the index finger.

- Distribute evenly onto 3 double-point needles, place marker and work even in stockinette stitch until finger measures 3"/7.5 cm or ¼"/6 mm less than desired length.

- **NEXT ROUND:** K2tog 12 times. *You now have* 12 stitches.

- **NEXT ROUND:** Knit.

- **NEXT ROUND:** K2tog six times. *You now have* 6 stitches.

- Cut yarn, leaving a 6"/15 cm tail. Thread tail onto yarn needle and draw through remaining stitches; pull up snugly and secure. Weave in the end.

Knitting the Thumb

- Attach new yarn to beginning of held thumb stitches with RS facing, knit 22 stitches from scrap yarn, pick up and knit 3 stitches from the base of the stitches cast on across the thumb gap. *You now have* 25 stitches on needles for the thumb.

- Distribute evenly onto 3 double-point needles, place marker and work even in stockinette stitch until thumb measures 2½"/6.5 cm or ¼"/6 mm less than desired length.

- **NEXT ROUND:** K2tog 12 times, k1. *You now have* 13 stitches.

- **NEXT ROUND:** Knit.

- **NEXT ROUND:** K2tog six times, k1. *You now have* 7 stitches.

- Cut yarn, leaving a 6"/15 cm tail. Thread tail onto yarn needle and draw through remaining stitches; pull up snugly and secure. Weave in the end.

Finishing

- Close any openings at base of fingers using yarn tails. Weave in all ends, block.

- Make a second glove like the first.

Spicy Lace Cuffs

DESIGNED BY REBECCA MERCIER

Add a feminine touch to any outfit with these lace cuffs. Wear them ruffle up over the end of a plain sleeve, or wear them ruffle down to peek out from under a larger sleeve. The pattern is written for two circular needles, but you can use double-point needles if you prefer.

Finished Measurements

Approximately 5"/12.5 cm circumference at wrist, unstretched, and 5"/12.5 cm long

Yarn

SWTC Tofutsies, 50% superwash wool/ 25% Soysilk/22.5% cotton/2.5% chitin, 465 yds (425 m)/3.5 oz (100 g), Color 938 TOEtally TOEmented

Needles

Two US 3 (3.25 mm) circular needles 16"/ 40 cm long *or size you need to obtain correct gauge*

Gauge

28 stitches and 36 rounds = 4"/10 cm in stockinette stitch; 33½ stitches and 45 rounds = 4"/10 cm in pattern from Rounds 22 and 23 of chart, unstretched

Other Supplies

Yarn needle

Knitting the Cuffs (make 2)

- Cast on 114 stitches and divide evenly onto two circular needles. Join into a round, being careful not to twist the stitches.

Knitting the Picot Edge

- **ROUNDS 1–5:** Knit.

- **ROUND 6 (PICOT FOLD LINE):** *K2tog, yo; repeat from * to end of round.

- **ROUNDS 7–11:** Knit.

Knitting the Ruffle

- Work Rounds 1–21 of chart once, working the chart pattern six times in each round, and decreasing as shown. *You have* 42 stitches after completing Round 19.

Knitting the Wrist

- Work Rounds 22 and 23 fifteen times.

- Bind off loosely.

Finishing

- Fold edge of ruffle to WS along Picot Fold Line, and sew hem invisibly in place; this creates the lovely picot edge along the belled end of each cuff. Weave in ends. Block.

Ruffle and Wrist

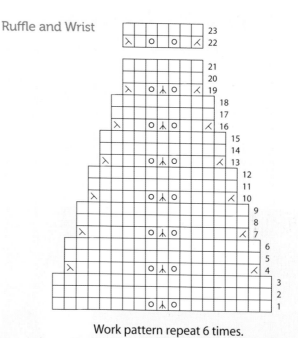

Work pattern repeat 6 times.

☐ knit	⊡ yo
⟋ k2tog	slip 2tog kwise, k1, pass 2 slipped sts over k st
⟍ ssk	

Downy Buffalo Socks

DESIGNED BY MELISSA MORGAN-OAKES

Ever see a buffalo near a space heater? Probably not! You won't need one either when you wrap your cold tootsies in these delicious socks knit from yarn with just a hint of bison down. The open pattern helps to keep off the chill by trapping air between the open spaces.

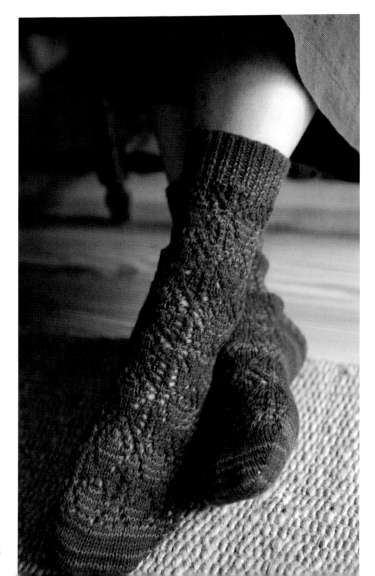

Size and Finished Measurements

Woman's medium, 8"/20.5 cm circumference, foot length as desired (socks shown measure 8"/20.5 cm long)

Yarn

Buffalo Wool Company Tracks, 90% superwash wool/10% bison down, 400 yds (366 m)/3.5 oz (100 g), Cayman

Needles

Set of four US 1 (2.25 mm) double-point needles *or size you need to obtain correct gauge*

Gauge

30 stitches and 42 rounds = 4"/10 cm in Buffalo Lace pattern

Other Supplies

Yarn needle

Knitting the Leg

- Cast on 60 stitches and divide evenly onto three double-point needles (20 stitches on each needle). Join into a round, being careful not to twist the stitches.

- **ROUND 1:** *K1, p1; repeat from * to end of round.

- Repeat Round 1 for 1½"/4 cm.

- Work Rows 1–16 of Buffalo Lace chart three times (48 chart rounds total); piece measures about 6"/15 cm from cast-on edge.

Knitting the Heel Flap

- Knit the first 10 stitches from Needle 2 onto the end of Needle 1. *You now have 30 stitches on one needle for the heel flap. Leave the remaining 30 stitches to rest on two needles while working the heel flap.*

- Work back and forth in rows on the 30 stitches of Needle 1 as follows.

- **ROW 1 (WS):** Slip 1 purlwise wyif, purl to end of row.

- **ROW 2 (RS):** *Slip 1 purlwise wyib, k1; repeat from * to end of row.

- Repeat Rows 1 and 2 fourteen more times, ending with a RS row (30 rows total).

Turning the Heel

- Continue working in rows on heel flap stitches only as follows.

- **ROW 1 (WS):** P17, p2tog, p1, turn.

- **ROW 2 (RS):** Slip 1 purlwise wyib, k5, k2tog tbl, k1, turn.

- **ROW 3:** Slip 1 purlwise wyif, purl to 1 stitch before gap, p2tog to close gap, p1, turn.

- **ROW 4:** Slip 1 purlwise wyib, knit to 1 stitch before gap, k2tog tbl to close gap, k1, turn.

- Repeat Rows 3 and 4 until all stitches of the heel flap have been worked, but do not turn at the end of the final Row 4. *You now have 18 heel stitches.*

- Slip the 30 unworked instep stitches of Needles 2 and 3 onto one needle, reserving the empty needle for picking up gusset stitches.

Buffalo Lace

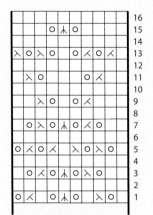

knit	
k2tog	
ssk	
yo	
s2kp	

10-stitch repeat

Work pattern repeat
6 times for leg,
3 times for instep.

Knitting the Heel Gusset

- Using the needle holding 18 heel stitches (now Needle 1), pick up and knit (see page 297) 15 stitches down side of heel flap; on Needle 2, work Row 1 of chart pattern as established on 30 instep stitches; on Needle 3, pick up and knit 15 stitches up other side of heel flap, then knit the first 9 stitches from Needle 1 again. *You now have 78 stitches total: 24 stitches each on Needles 1 and 3 (heel gusset and sole), and 30 stitches on Needle 2 (instep).* Work gusset decreases as follows.

- **ROUND 1:** On Needle 1, knit to the last 3 stitches, k2tog, k1; on Needle 2, work in charted pattern as established; on Needle 3, k1, ssk, knit to end — 2 stitches decreased.

- **ROUND 2:** On Needle 1, knit; on Needle 2, work in charted pattern as established; on Needle 3, knit.

- Repeat Rounds 1 and 2 eight more times. *You now have 60 stitches: 15 stitches each on Needles 1 and 3, and 30 stitches on Needle 2.*

Knitting the Foot

- Continuing the charted pattern on instep stitches of Needle 2, work stitches on Needles 1 and 3 in stockinette until sock measures 2"/5 cm less than desired finished length from heel to toe.

Shaping the Toe

- **ROUND 1:** On Needle 1, knit to the last 3 stitches, k2tog, k1; on Needle 2, k1, ssk, knit to the last 3 stitches, k2tog, k1; on Needle 3, k1, ssk, knit to end — 4 stitches decreased.

- **ROUND 2:** Knit.

- Repeat Rounds 1 and 2 six more times. *You now have 32 stitches:* 8 stitches each on Needles 1 and 3, and 16 stitches on Needle 2. Repeat Round 1 only (i.e., decrease every round) four times. *You now have 16 stitches total.*

Finishing

- Knit the 8 stitches of Needle 1 onto the end of Needle 3 so you have 8 instep stitches on one needle and 8 sole stitches on another needle. Break yarn, leaving a 10"/25.5 cm tail, and graft the stitches together with Kitchener stitch (see page 293). Weave in ends. Block.

Tribute Socks

DESIGNED BY BRENDA PATIPA

Tribute socks use an adaptation of the Frost Flowers Lace pattern found in Barbara Walker's Treasury of Knitting Patterns *(Schoolhouse Press, 1998). This stitch pattern dates back to the early nineteenth century.*

Size and Finished Measurements
Woman's medium, 8"/20.5 cm foot circumference, length as desired (socks shown measure 9"/23 cm long)

Yarn
Lisa Souza Knitwear and Dyeworks Super Sport Merino, 100% superwash merino, 375 yds (343 m)/4 oz (113 g), Ginger Peach

Needles
One US 1 (2.25 mm) circular needle 32"/80 cm long or two shorter circular needles *or size you need to obtain correct gauge*

Gauge
36 stitches and 44 rounds = 4"/10 cm in stockinette stitch

Other Supplies
Stitch markers, yarn needle

PATTERN NOTES

This pattern is easier to work with the magic loop method (see page 295) or on two circular needles (see page 291), rather than double points. With circulars, there is less shifting of stitches between needles to work the lace.

When working the leg, pay attention to the note about slipping stitches at the start of certain chart rounds. Rearrange your stitches as necessary for ease of working.

Knitting the Cuff

- Loosely cast on 68 stitches, leaving a 12"/30.5 cm tail for sewing the cuff facing later. Place a marker and join into a round, being careful not to twist the stitches.

- Work even in stockinette stitch for 1"/2.5 cm.

- PICOT ROUND: *K2tog, yo; repeat from * to end of round.

- Work even in stockinette stitch for 1"/2.5 cm.

Knitting the Lace

- Work Rounds 1–24 of Frost Flowers chart A (see page 67), working the repeat twice in each round.

  Notes: At the beginning of Rounds 15, 16, 19, 20, 23, and 24, remove the marker, slip the first stitch of the round purlwise wyib, then replace the marker on the right-hand needle. This shifts the start of the round 1 stitch to the left to compensate for the 2 decreases at the end of these chart rounds and keeps the pattern aligned.

- Work Rounds 1–24 of Frost Flowers chart A again (48 chart rounds total). Piece measures about 5½"/14 cm from the Picot Round.

Knitting the Heel Flap

- Turn the work so the WS is facing, and slip the last 2 stitches worked in Round 24 of Frost Flowers chart A from the left-hand needle to the right-hand needle. The heel flap is worked back and forth in rows on the next 34 stitches, beginning with the third stitch from the end of the original

round. The 34 instep stitches not being worked can rest on the cable portion of the needle while working the heel.

- ROW 1 (WS): K3, p31.

- ROW 2 (RS): P3, *k1, slip 1 purlwise wyib; repeat from * to last 3 stitches, k3.

- Repeat Rows 1 and 2 sixteen more times (34 rows total), ending with a RS row.

Turning the Heel

- **ROW 1 (WS):** Slip 1, p18, p2tog, p1, turn.
- **ROW 2 (RS):** Slip 1, k5, ssk, k1, turn.
- **ROW 3:** Slip 1, p6, p2tog, p1, turn.
- **ROW 4:** Slip 1, k7, ssk, k1, turn.
- **ROW 5:** Slip 1, p8, p2tog, p1, turn.
- **ROW 6:** Slip 1, k9, ssk, k1, turn.
- **ROW 7:** Slip 1, p10, p2tog, p1, turn.
- **ROW 8:** Slip 1, k11, ssk, k1, turn.
- **ROW 9:** Slip 1, p12, p2tog, p1, turn.
- **ROW 10:** Slip 1, k13, ssk, k1, turn.
- **ROW 11:** Slip 1, p14, p2tog, p1, turn.
- **ROW 12:** Slip 1, k15, ssk, k1, turn.
- **ROW 13:** Slip 1, p16, p2tog, p1, turn.
- **ROW 14:** Slip 1, k17, ssk, k1. *You now have* 20 stitches.

Knitting the Gusset

- **SETUP ROUND:** With RS of heel flap facing, pick up and knit (see page 297) 18 stitches along side of heel flap for the right gusset; place marker for new start of round; work Row 1 of Frost Flowers chart B across 34 instep stitches, place marker; pick up and knit 18 stitches along side of heel flap for the left gusset; knit the 20 heel flap stitches and the 18 right gusset stitches again. *You now have* 90 stitches. Round now begins with the instep stitches.

Decreasing the Gusset

- **ROUND 1:** Work in pattern to the end of the instep stitches; k1, ssk; knit to last 3 stitches of the round, k2tog, k1 — 2 stitches decreased.

- **ROUND 2:** Working sole stitches in stockinette, work instep stitches even in patterns as established.

- Repeat Rounds 1 and 2 ten more times. *You now have* 68 stitches: 34 instep stitches and 34 sole stitches.

Knitting the Foot

- Work even as established on 68 stitches until 60 rounds of Frost Flowers chart B have been completed, ending with Round 12 of the chart. If necessary, work all stitches even in stockinette until the foot length reaches the base of the toes when measured from the back of the heel, or about 2"/5 cm less than desired total length.

Shaping the Toe

- **ROUND 1:** K1, ssk, knit to 3 stitches before second marker at end of instep, k2tog, k1, slip marker, k1, ssk, knit to last 3 stitches of round, k2tog, k1 — 4 stitches decreased.

- **ROUND 2:** Knit.

- Repeat Rounds 1 and 2 seven more times. *You now have* 36 stitches. Repeat Round 1 only four more times. *You now have* 20 stitches.

- Arrange stitches so 10 instep stitches are on one needle and 10 sole stitches are on another. Graft toe stitches together with Kitchener stitch (see page 293).

Finishing

- Turn sock inside out. Fold cuff facing to WS along Picot Round, then use cast-on tail to sew the facing to the inside, matching the elasticity of the knitting. Weave in ends. Block lightly.

Frost Flowers B

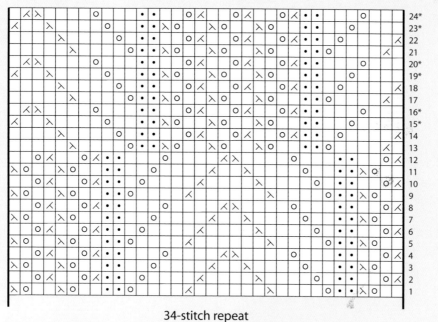

34 instep stitches

Frost Flowers A

34-stitch repeat

Work pattern repeat 2 times.
*See instructions for Rnds 15, 16, 19, 20, 23, and 24.

☐	knit
•	purl
o	yo
⟋	k2tog
⟍	ssk

Galvez Socks

DESIGNED BY DEBBIE HAYMARK

While this Seafoam Stitch pattern isn't technically speaking lace, it does produce a nice open fabric and one great-looking sock! The colorway is reminiscent of the waves in the Gulf of Mexico, and the sock is named for the historic Galvez Hotel in Galveston, Texas, which sits on its shore.

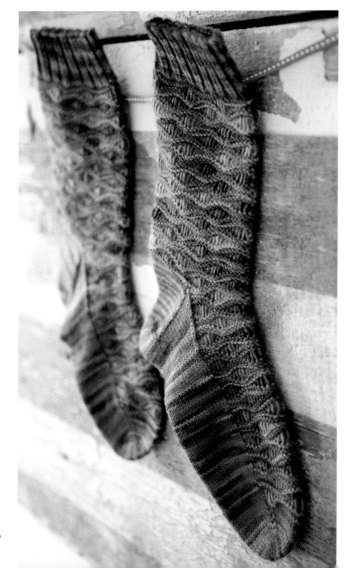

Size and Finished Measurements

Woman's medium, approximately 7½"/19 cm foot circumference, length as desired (socks shown measure 7½"/19 cm long)

Yarn

Lorna's Laces Shepherd Sock, 80% superwash merino wool/20% nylon, 430 yds (393 m)/ 3.5 oz (100 g), Lakeview

Needles

US 1 (2.5 mm) circular needle 9"–12"/23–30 cm long and set of four US 1 (2.25 mm) double-point needles *or size you need to obtain correct gauge*

Gauge

36 stitches and 49 rounds = 4"/10 cm in Seafoam Stitch pattern; 40 stitches and 54 rounds = 4"/10 cm in stockinette stitch

Other Supplies

Three stitch markers (one in a unique color), yarn needle

PATTERN NOTES

Because of the number of yarnovers in the Seafoam Stitch pattern, it's easier to work the sock on a short circular needle rather than double points, but you could also use the magic loop method (see page 295) or two circular needles. You won't need the double-point needles until you reach the toe of the sock.

PATTERN ESSENTIALS

Twisted Rib

- **Round 1:** *K1 tbl twice, p2; repeat from * to end of round.
- Repeat Round 1 for pattern.

Seafoam Stitch (multiple of 10 stitches)

- **Round 1:** Knit.
- **Round 2:** Purl.
- **Round 3:** *K5, yo, k1, yo twice, k1, yo three times, k1, yo twice, k1, yo, k1; repeat from * to end of round. *You now have* 19 stitches in each pattern repeat.
- **Round 4:** Purl, dropping all yos off the needle. *You now have* 10 stitches in each pattern repeat.
- **Round 5:** Knit.
- **Round 6:** Purl.
- **Round 7:** *K1, yo, k1, yo twice, k1, yo three times, k1, yo twice, k1, yo, k5; repeat from * to end of round. *You now have* 19 stitches in each pattern repeat.
- **Round 8:** Purl, dropping all yos off the needle. *You now have* 10 stitches in each pattern repeat.
- Repeat Rounds 1–8 for pattern.

Knitting the Cuff

- Cast on 64 stitches. Place the unique-colored marker for the beginning of round and join, being careful not to twist the stitches. Work Twisted Rib for 1½"/4 cm. Knit 1 round, decreasing 4 stitches evenly spaced. *You now have* 60 stitches.

Knitting the Leg

- Work Rounds 1–8 of Seafoam Stitch pattern seven times. Piece measures approximately 6"/15 cm from cast-on edge.

Knitting the Heel Flap

- Heel flap is worked back and forth in rows on the first 30 stitches of the round using the circular needle. The 30 instep stitches not being worked simply rest on the cable portion of the needle, out of the way. Knit the first 30 stitches, turn.

- **ROW 1 (WS):** Slip 1 purlwise, p29, turn.
- **ROW 2 (RS):** Slip 1 knitwise, k29, turn.
- Repeat Rows 1 and 2 fourteen more times. *You now have* completed 30 heel flap rows.

Turning the Heel

- Continue with the 30 heel flap stitches only.
- **ROW 1 (WS):** Slip 1 purlwise, p21, p2tog, turn.
- **ROW 2 (RS):** Slip 1 knitwise, k14, ssk, turn.
- **ROW 3:** Slip 1 purlwise, p14, p2tog, turn.
- Repeat Rows 2 and 3 five more times, then work Row 2 once more. *You now have* 16 stitches.

Knitting the Gusset

- **ROUND 1:** With RS of heel facing, pick up and knit (see page 297) 15 slipped edge stitches *through the back loop only* along the first side of the heel flap, place marker; work Round 1 of Seafoam Stitch pattern on 30 instep stitches, place marker; pick up and knit 15 slipped edge stitches *through the back loop only* along the second side of the heel flap; knit the first 8 heel stitches again; place marker for beginning of round at the center back of the heel. *You now have* 76 stitches: 23 heel and gusset stitches on each side and 30 instep stitches in the center.
- **ROUND 2:** K8, k1 tbl 15 times, slip marker, work Round 2 of Seafoam Stitch pattern on instep stitches, slip marker, k1 tbl 15 times, k8.

- **ROUND 3**: Knit to 2 stitches before first marker, k2tog, slip marker; work Seafoam Stitch pattern as established on instep stitches; slip marker, ssk, knit to end of round — 2 stitches decreased.

- **ROUND 4**: Knit to marker, slip marker, work Seafoam Stitch pattern as established on the instep stitches, slip marker, knit to the end of the round.

- Repeat Rounds 3 and 4 seven more times. *You now have 60 stitches: 15 heel and gusset stitches on each side and 30 instep stitches in the center.*

Knitting the Foot

- Continue in patterns as established, working the instep stitches in Seafoam Stitch pattern and sole stitches in stockinette stitch, until seven pattern repeats from the start of the gusset are complete. Foot measures approximately 6"/15 cm from center back heel. ***Note:*** To adjust foot length, work more or fewer pattern repeats here, ending with Round 8 of the pattern; every repeat added or removed lengthens or shortens the foot by about ¾"/2 cm.

Shaping the Toe

- Transfer stitches to three double-point needles as follows: Knit the first 15 stitches onto Needle 1, knit the 30 instep stitches onto Needle 2, and knit the remaining 15 stitches onto Needle 3.

- **ROUND 1**: On Needle 1, knit to last 2 stitches, k2tog; on Needle 2, ssk, knit to last 2 stitches, k2tog; on Needle 3, ssk, knit to end — 4 stitches decreased.

- **ROUND 2**: Knit.

- Repeat Rounds 1 and 2 six more times. *You now have 32 stitches total: 8 stitches each on Needles 1 and 3, and 16 stitches on Needle 2.*

- Knit 8 stitches from Needle 1 onto the end of Needle 3. *You now have 16 stitches each on two needles.*

- Graft stitches together with Kitchener stitch (see page 293). Weave in ends. Block.

Buckhorn Socks

DESIGNED BY HÉLÈNE RUSH

These lovely lace socks, named for the colorway of the yarn, are knit from the top down. Instructions are given for two sizes, and the stretchiness of the lace allows each size to fit a range of foot widths.

Finished Measurements

Approximately 7½ (8)"/19 (20.5) cm circumference, foot length as desired (socks shown have an 8"/20.5 cm circumference and 9¼"/23.5 cm foot length)

Yarn

Knit One, Crochet Too Crock-O-Dye, 65% superwash wool/20% nylon/15% silk, 416 yds (380 m)/3.5 oz (100 g), Color 855 Buckhorn

Needles

Set of US 1 (2.25 mm) double-point needles *or size you need to obtain correct gauge*

Gauge

34 stitches and 46 rounds = 4"/10 cm in stockinette stitch

Other Supplies

Yarn needle

PATTERN NOTES

When only one set of instructions is given, it applies to both sizes. Otherwise, instructions for the larger size appear in parentheses.

Knitting the Cuff

- Cast on 60 stitches. Join to knit in the round, being careful not to twist the stitches.

- **ROUND 1:** *K2, p2; repeat from * to end of round.

- Repeat Round 1 until piece measures 1"/2.5 cm.

- **NEXT ROUND:** Knit around, increasing 4 (8) stitches evenly spaced. *You now have 64 (68) stitches.*

PATTERN ESSENTIALS

Leg (multiple of 16 [17] stitches)

- **Round 1:** *K2tog, yo, k1, yo, k3, sk2p, k3, yo, k1, yo, ssk, p1 (2); repeat from * to end of round.
- **Rounds 2, 4, and 6:** *K15, p1 (2); repeat from * to end of round.
- **Round 3:** *K2tog, (yo, k2) twice, sk2p, (k2, yo) twice, ssk, p1 (2); repeat from * to end of round.
- **Round 5:** *K2tog, yo, k3, yo, k1, sk2p, k1, yo, k3, yo, ssk, p1 (2); repeat from * to end of round.
- **Round 7:** *K2tog, yo, k4, yo, sk2p, yo, k4, yo, ssk, p1 (2); repeat from * to end of round.
- **Round 8:** Repeat Round 2.
- Repeat Rounds 1–8 for pattern.

Instep
(worked over 33 [35] stitches)

- **Round 1:** K2tog, k3, yo, k1, yo, ssk, p1 (2), k2tog, yo, k1, yo, k3, sk2p, k3, yo, k1, yo, ssk, p1 (2), k2tog, yo, k1, yo, k3, ssk.
- **Rounds 2, 4, and 6:** K8, p1 (2), k15, p1 (2), k8.
- **Round 3:** K2tog, (k2, yo) twice, ssk, p1 (2), k2tog, (yo, k2) twice, sk2p, (k2, yo) twice, ssk, p1 (2), k2tog, (yo, k2) twice, ssk.
- **Round 5:** K2tog, k1, yo, k3, yo, ssk, p1 (2), k2tog, yo, k3, yo, k1, sk2p, k1, yo, k3, yo, ssk, p1 (2), k2tog, yo, k3, yo, k1, ssk.
- **Round 7:** K2tog, yo, k4, yo, ssk, p1 (2), k2tog, yo, k4, yo, sk2p, yo, k4, yo, ssk, p1 (2), k2tog, yo, k4, yo, ssk.
- **Round 8:** Repeat Round 2.
- Repeat Rounds 1–8 for pattern.

Instep

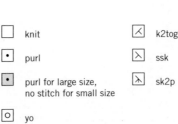

Worked over 33 (35) stitches

Leg

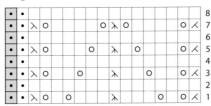

16 (17) stitch repeat
Work pattern repeat 4 times.

	knit		$\boxtimes$	k2tog
	purl		$\boxtimes$	ssk
	purl for large size, no stitch for small size		$\boxtimes$	sk2p
	yo			

Knitting the Leg

- Following Leg chart or written instructions, work Rounds 1–8 seven times, then work Rounds 1–7 once more (63 pattern rounds total). Piece measures about 6½"/16.5 cm from cast on.

Knitting the Heel Flap

- The heel is worked back and forth on 31 (33) stitches, the first 23 (24) and last 8 (9) stitches of the original round. The remaining 33 (35) stitches are held for the instep.

- **ROW 1 (RS):** K23 (24); turn.

- **ROW 2 (WS):** Slip 1 purlwise wyif, (p1, slip 1 purlwise wyif) 14 (15) times, p2; turn.

- **ROW 3:** Slip 1 purlwise wyib, k30 (32); turn.

- Repeat Rows 2 and 3 fifteen more times, then work WS Row 2 once more (34 heel rows total).

Turning the Heel

- **ROW 1 (RS):** Slip 1 purlwise wyib, k17 (19), k2tog, k1; turn.

- **ROW 2 (WS):** Slip 1 purlwise wyif, p6 (8), p2tog, p1; turn.

- **ROW 3:** Slip 1 purlwise wyib, knit to slipped stitch at beginning of previous row, work k2tog with slipped stitch and stitch after it, k1; turn.

- **ROW 4:** Slip 1 purlwise wyif, purl to slipped stitch at beginning of previous row, work p2tog with slipped stitch and stitch after it, p1; turn.

- Repeat Rows 3 and 4 until all stitches have been worked, ending with a WS row. *You now have* 19 (21) stitches.

Knitting the Gussets

- Knit the 19 (21) heel stitches, pick up and knit (see page 297) 17 stitches on the side of the heel flap, pick up 1 stitch in the yo at the corner, work Round 1 of Instep pattern over 33 (35) held stitches, pick up and knit 1 stitch in yo at the corner, pick up and knit 17 stitches on the side of the heel flap. *You now have* 88 (92) stitches.

- **NEXT ROUND:** Knit to the last 2 stitches before instep stitches, k2tog; continue in established pattern on instep stitches; ssk first 2 stitches after instep stitches, knit to end of round — 2 stitches decreased.

- **NEXT ROUND:** Knit to instep stitches, continue in established pattern on instep stitches, knit to end of round.

- Repeat the last 2 rounds 11 more times. *You now have* 64 (68) stitches: 31 (33) stockinette stitches for sole and 33 (35) stitches for instep.

Knitting the Foot

- Work in established patterns until foot is 1½"/4 cm less than desired finished foot length, ending with Round 8 of Instep pattern (socks shown have 10 repeats of Instep pattern).

- **NEXT ROUND:** Knit to end of instep stitches, decreasing 2 stitches evenly on instep. *You now have* 62 (66) stitches total: 31 (33) stitches for both sole and instep. Round begins at start of sole stitches.

Shaping the Toe

Note: The remainder of the sock is worked in stockinette stitch.

- **ROUND 1:** *K1, ssk, knit to last 3 sole stitches, k2tog, k1; repeat from * on instep stitches — 4 stitches decreased.

- **ROUND 2:** Knit.

- Repeat Rounds 1 and 2 seven more times. *You now have* 30 (34) stitches total: 15 (17) stitches each for sole and instep. Graft the sole and instep stitches together with Kitchener stitch (see page 293). Weave in ends.

Vesta Socks

DESIGNED BY REBECCA MERCIER

Knit from the toe up, these lacy socks feature a figure-8 cast on and a short-row heel. There's plenty of knitting adventure to be had with a different pattern on the front and the back and the use of both lace and cable techniques. The pattern is written for two circular needles, but you may choose any method you prefer.

Sizes and Finished Measurements

Woman's US shoe sizes 8–9, approximately 7"/18 cm foot circumference and 9½"/24 cm foot length

Yarn

SWTC Tofutsies, 50% superwash wool/25% Soysilk/22.5% cotton/2.5% chitin, 465 yds (425 m)/3.5 oz (100 g), Color 940 TOE Up

Needles

Two US 2 (2.75 mm) circular needles *or size you need to obtain correct gauge* and two US 1 (2.25 mm) circular needles or sets of US 2 (2.75 mm) and US 1 (2.25 mm) double-point needles, depending on preferred knitting method

Gauge

36½ stitches and 44 rounds = 4"/10 cm in Vesta Lace pattern on larger needles

Other Supplies

Cable needle, yarn needle

Special Abbreviations

C8B cable 8 back
LT left twist
RT right twist
WT wrap and turn

PATTERN ESSENTIALS

C8B (cable 8 back) Slip 4 stitches onto cable needle and hold in back of work, k4, then k4 from cable needle.

LT (left twist) With the right-hand needle behind the left-hand needle, knit the second stitch through the back loop and leave it on the needle, knit the first stitch, and slip both stitches from the left-hand needle.

RT (right twist) K2tog, leaving stitches on left-hand needle, knit the first stitch again, and slip both stitches from the left-hand needle.

WT (wrap and turn) On RS rows, bring yarn to front and slip next stitch purlwise, bring yarn to back, slip stitch back to left-hand needle, turn work. On WS rows, bring yarn to back and slip next stitch purlwise, bring yarn to front, slip stitch back to left-hand needle, turn work. The first stitch on the right-hand needle now has the working yarn wrapped around its base.

Knitting the Foot

- With larger needle, use the figure-8 method (see page 292) to cast on 24 stitches. The first 12 stitches are the sole, and the last 12 stitches are the instep.

- ROUND 1: On Needle 1 (sole), k1, kfb, knit to last 2 stitches, kfb, k1; on Needle 2 (instep), k1, kfb, knit to last 2 stitches, kfb, k1 — 4 stitches increased total: 2 stitches each on sole and instep.

- ROUND 2: Knit.

- Repeat Rounds 1 and 2 nine more times. *You now have 64 stitches: 32 stitches each for sole and instep.*

- Keeping the first 32 stitches of the round in Stockinette stitch for the sole, work the remaining 32 instep stitches in pattern from the Vesta Lace chart (see page 78) by working Setup Rounds 1–4 once, then repeat Rounds 1–12 of chart until foot measures 7½"/19 cm or 2"/5 cm less than desired finished length. Make note of the last chart round worked so you can resume the pattern on the front of the leg with the correct round after the heel has been completed.

Knitting the Heel

Note: Heel is worked back and forth on 32 sole stitches only. Leave instep stitches idle until heel is completed.

Decreasing the Heel Stitches

- ROW 1 (RS): K30, WT. **Note:** *The next-to-last stitch was wrapped; the last stitch on the needle is not wrapped.*

- ROW 2 (WS): P28, WT. **Note:** *The next-to-last stitch was wrapped; the last stitch on the needle is not wrapped.*

- ROW 3: Knit to last stitch before wrapped stitch, WT.

- ROW 4: Purl to last stitch before wrapped stitch, WT.

- Repeat Rows 3 and 4 seven more times. *You now have 9 wrapped stitches at each side and 12 unwrapped stitches in the center.*

Increasing the Heel Stitches

- ROW 1: Knit to the first wrapped stitch, pick up the wrap with the stitch, and knit them together, WT. **Note:** *This stitch now has 2 wraps.*

- ROW 2: Purl to the first wrapped stitch, pick up the wrap with the stitch and purl them together, WT. **Note:** *This stitch now has 2 wraps, as will all wrapped stitches from here on except the 2 end stitches, which were not wrapped at the start of the heel.*

- ROW 3: Knit to the wrapped stitch, pick up both wraps with the stitch, and knit all 3 together, WT.

- ROW 4: Purl to the wrapped stitch, pick up both wraps with the stitch and purl all 3 together, WT.

- Repeat Rows 3 and 4 until you have worked all of the double-wrapped stitches. The 2 end stitches each have 1 wrap. Knit to the last stitch, pick up the wrap with the stitch, and knit them together. *Do not turn.*

- With RS still facing, work next chart row on the instep stitches. Pick up the wrap on the first heel stitch with the stitch and knit them together; knit to end of heel stitches. The round now begins at the start of the instep stitches.

Knitting the Leg

Notes: It's easier to keep track of the two lace patterns if they are both on the same numbered round. If the next round of the instep is not Round 1 of the Vesta Lace chart, work the back-of-leg stitches in Stockinette stitch until Round 12 of the Vesta Lace pattern has been completed, and then begin working both charts on Round 1.

- Continue in established patterns, repeating Rounds 1–12 of both charts, until leg measures approximately 7"/18 cm from where you resumed working in the round at the top of the heel, or 2¼"/5.5 cm less than desired finished length, ending with Round 12 of both charts.

- Work Rounds 13–18 of Vesta Lace chart on instep stitches and Rounds 1–6 of Back of Leg on remaining stitches once. Leg measures about 7¼"/18.5 cm from the top of the heel.

Knitting the Cuff

- Change to smaller needles.

- **ROUND 1:** *K1, p1; repeat from * to end of round.

- Repeat Round 1 nineteen more times or until cuff measures 2"/5 cm.

- Bind off as follows: K1, p1; slip these 2 stitches back to the left-hand needle, p2tog; *k1, slip these 2 stitches back to the left-hand needle, k2tog; p1, slip these 2 stitches back to the left-hand needle, p2tog; repeat from * until 1 stitch remains. Fasten off the last stitch.

- Weave in ends. Block.

Back of Leg

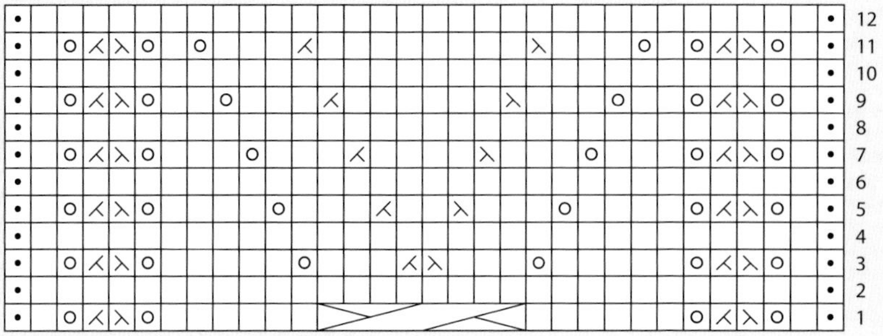
12
11
10
9
8
7
6
5
4
3
2
1

Vesta Lace

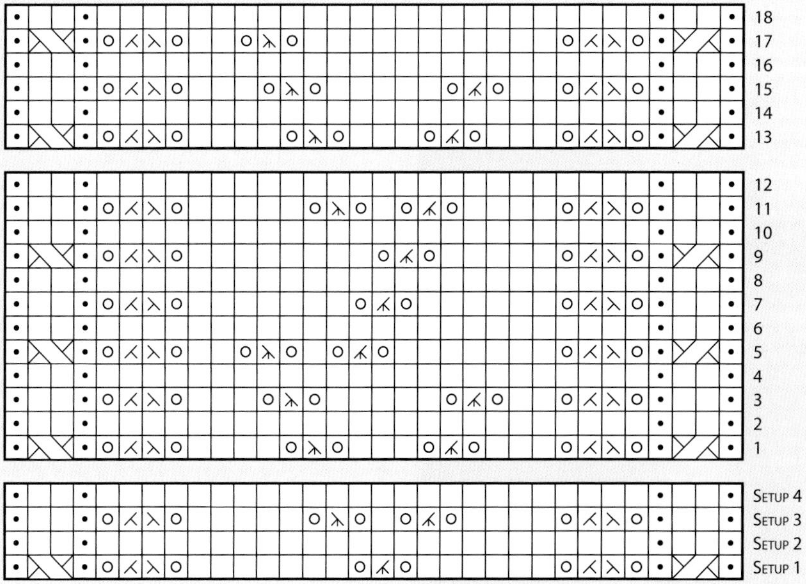
18
17
16
15
14
13
12
11
10
9
8
7
6
5
4
3
2
1
Setup 4
Setup 3
Setup 2
Setup 1

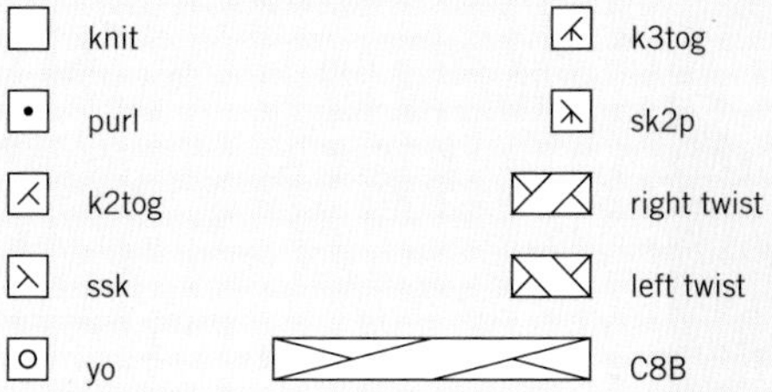
knit
purl
k2tog
ssk
yo
k3tog
sk2p
right twist
left twist
C8B

Flemish Lace Socks

Designed by Naomi Herzfeld

This sock uses a pattern stitch adapted from Barbara Walker's Second Treasury of Knitting Patterns *(Schoolhouse Press, 1998). The heel is a modified version of a technique from Wendy Johnson's* Socks from the Toe Up *(Potter Craft, 2009). Daisy Blinn — talented, caring, and persistent test knitter — produced the sample socks, and Cambria Washington shared her gift for sock heel math.*

Size and Finished Measurements

Woman's medium, 7¾"/19.5 cm foot circumference, 8"/20.5 cm leg circumference, foot length and leg height as desired (socks shown measure 8"/20.5 cm in both length and height)

Yarn

Fyberspates Scrumptious 4-Ply, 55% superwash merino/45% silk, 399 yds (365 m)/3.5 oz (100 g), Color 304 Water

Needles

Two US 2½ (3 mm) circular needles *or size you need to obtain correct gauge*

Gauge

30 stitches and 44 rounds = 4"/10 cm in stockinette stitch; 28 stitches and 44 rounds = 4"/10 cm in Flemish Block Lace pattern

Other Supplies

Stitch markers, yarn needle

PATTERN ESSENTIALS

Flemish Block Lace
(multiple of 14 stitches worked in the round)

- **Round 1 and all odd-numbered rounds:** Knit.
- **Round 2:** *K2tog, yo, k1, yo, ssk, k3, k2tog, yo, k4; repeat from * to end of round.
- **Round 4:** *Yo, k3, yo, ssk, k1, k2tog, yo, k4, k2tog; repeat from * to end of round.
- **Round 6:** *K5, yo, sk2p, yo, k4, k2tog, yo; repeat from * to end of round.
- **Round 8:** *Yo, ssk, k4, yo, ssk, k3, k2tog, yo, k1; repeat from * to end of round.
- **Round 10:** *K1, yo, ssk, k4, yo, ssk, k1, k2tog, yo, k2; repeat from * to end of round.
- **Round 12:** *K2, yo, ssk, k4, yo, k3tog, yo, k3; repeat from * to end of round.
- Repeat Rounds 1–12 for pattern.

PATTERN NOTES

Flemish Block Lace uses a multiple of exactly 14 stitches, so the best way to change the circumference is to adjust the yarn gauge rather than the number of stitches. Try 7½ stitches per inch in the pattern stitch for a small woman, or 6½ per inch for a larger woman or a man. The ankle and leg can also be shaped by changing needle size. For the heel, instead of picking up and knitting the edges of a flap, a series of increases and decreases shape the elegant, comfortable, and fun-to-knit heel. The socks are knitted toe-up with the two circular needles method (see page 291).

Knitting the Toe

- Using Judy's Magic Cast On (see page 292), cast on 8 stitches onto each needle. *You now have 16 stitches.* Place a marker for the beginning of the round.

- Knit 1 round, then start the toe increases.

- **ROUND 1:** *Kfb, knit to last 2 stitches on needle, kfb, k1; repeat from * on second needle — 4 stitches increased.

- **ROUND 2:** Knit.

- Repeat Rounds 1 and 2 nine more times. *You now have 56 stitches total: 28 stitches on each needle.*

Knitting the Foot and Heel

- Place a marker in the middle of the stitches on the second needle so there are 14 stitches on each side of it. The unmarked first needle holds the sole stitches, the marked second needle holds the instep stitches, and the marker separates the two 14-stitch lace repeats on the instep.

- Knitting the sole stitches every round and working Flemish Block Lace pattern on the instep stitches every round, repeat Rounds 1–12 of Flemish Block Lace pattern on instep stitches until sock is 2½"/6.5 cm shorter than desired finished foot length.

Notes: The diagonal decrease lines of the pattern are not continuous and have a deliberate "jog" in Round 4.

Make a note of the last pattern round completed so you can begin the heel shaping of the second sock with the same round.

Increasing for the Heel

- **ROUND 1:** Kfb, knit to last 2 sole stitches, kfb, k1; work Flemish Block Lace on instep stitches as established — 2 stitches increased on the sole needle.

- **ROUND 2:** Work even in patterns as established.

- Repeat Rounds l and 2 eleven more times. *You now have* 52 sole stitches and 28 instep stitches. Note the last pattern round completed so you can resume working the pattern for the leg with the correct round.

Turning the Heel

- Work back and forth on the sole stitches only, as follows.

- **ROW 1 (RS):** K30, turn.

- **ROW 2 (WS):** Slip l purlwise wyif, p6, p2tog, pl, turn.

- **ROW 3:** Slip l purlwise wyib, k7, ssk, kl, turn.

- **ROW 4:** Slip l purlwise wyif, purl to 1 stitch before gap, p2tog (1 stitch on each side of gap), pl, turn.

- **ROW 5:** Slip l purlwise wyib, knit to 1 stitch before gap, ssk (1 stitch on each side of gap), kl, turn.

- Repeat Rows 4 and 5 until all the stitches have been worked, but do not turn at the end of the last row. *You now have* 28 sole stitches. Place a marker in the center of the sole stitches, with 14 stitches on each side.

Knitting the Leg

- Resume working in the round as follows: Work 28 instep stitches in established pattern, then work the same pattern round on the 28 sole stitches for the back of the leg. *You now have* 56 leg stitches.

Notes: If there are holes between the needles where you began working in the round again, don't worry; they will be camouflaged by the eyelets in the lace pattern. If you can't ignore them, darn the holes after the sock is finished, or — if you're certain it won't throw off the lace pattern — you can try to tighten the holes by working an M1 increase at each end of one needle, and then knit each increased stitch together with the stitch next to it in the following round.

You can accommodate size changes in the ankle and calf by switching to a slightly smaller needle for the ankle, and a larger one for the calf. Try the sock on as you go to check the fit.

- Continue in Flemish Block Lace pattern as established until the leg is about 2"/5 cm shorter than desired finished length or you have slightly more than half the yarn left.

Knitting the Cuff

- Work 2"/5 cm in kl, pl rib, then bind off loosely. *Note:* If you want to make sure your socks won't slip down, carry some thin elastic thread along with your sock yarn in the cuff ribbing.

- Weave in ends. Block.

Flemish Block Lace

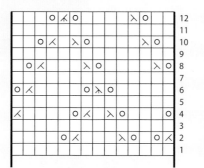

14-stitch repeat

Work pattern repeat twice
for 28 instep stitches
and 4 times for 56 leg stitches.

Small Falls Socks

Designed by Christiane Burkhard

These playful lace socks are reminiscent of cascading waterfalls in Maine. They are worked top down and with an easy-to-memorize pattern repeat that is fast and fun to knit.

Size and Finished Measurements

Woman's medium, 7½"/19 cm foot circumference, length as desired (socks shown measure 8½"/21.6 cm in length)

Yarn

Cascade Heritage Solid, 75% superwash merino wool/25% nylon, 437 yds (400 m)/3.5 oz (100 g), Color 5626 Turquoise

Needles

US 1 (2.25 mm) circular needle 32"/80 cm long or set of US 1 (2.25 mm) double-point needles *or size you need to obtain correct gauge*

Gauge

34 stitches and 43 rounds = 4"/10 cm in pattern; 32 stitches and 43 rounds = 4"/10 cm in stockinette stitch

Other Supplies

Stitch markers, stitch holder (optional), yarn needle

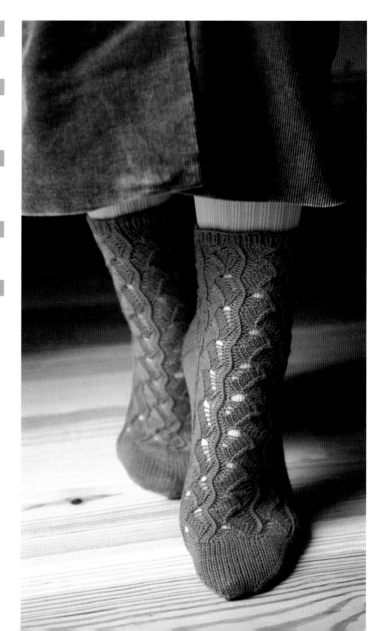

Knitting the Cuff

- Cast on 60 stitches. Place marker and join into a round, being careful not to twist the stitches.

- **ROUND 1:** *P1, k1; repeat from * to end of round.

- Repeat Round 1 until cuff measures ½"/13 mm.

Knitting the Leg

- Work Rounds 1–12 of Leg chart (see page 84) four times, working the repeat six times in each round. Piece measures about 5"/12.5 cm.

Knitting the Heel Flap

- Slip 1 stitch purlwise; place the next 31 stitches for the instep on a stitch holder or allow them to rest on the needle while working the heel flap.

  Note: The remaining 29 stitches are worked back and forth for the heel flap. Slip all stitches purlwise.

- Turn work so that WS is facing.

- **ROW 1 (WS):** Slip 1 wyif, purl to last stitch, k1.

- **ROW 2 (RS):** (Slip 1 wyib) twice, *k1, slip 1 wyib; repeat from * to last stitch, k1.

- Repeat Rows 1 and 2 until heel flap measures 2¼"/5.5 cm or desired length, ending with WS Row 1.

Turning the Heel

- **ROW 1 (RS):** Slip 1 wyib, k15, ssk, k1, turn.

- **ROW 2 (WS):** Slip 1 wyif, p4, p2tog, p1, turn.

- **ROW 3:** Slip 1 wyif, knit to 1 stitch before gap created on previous row, ssk (1 stitch from each side of the gap), k1, turn.

- **ROW 4:** Slip 1 wyif, purl to 1 stitch before gap created on previous row, p2tog, p1, turn.

- Repeat Rows 3 and 4 until all stitches have been worked. *You now have* 17 heel stitches.

Shaping the Gussets

- Turn work so RS is facing. *Note:* If you are using double-point needles you can arrange the instep and sole stitches on separate needles instead of using markers to indicate the different sections.

- **SETUP ROUND:** Slip 1 wyib, k7, place marker (for beginning of the round), k9, pick up and knit (see page 297) 1 stitch in each slipped stitch along the edge of the heel flap, pick up and knit 1 stitch in the corner between the heel flap and the instep, place marker (for right side of the foot), work Round 1 of Instep chart (see page 84) on 31 held instep stitches, place marker (for left side of the foot), pick up and knit 1 stitch in the corner between top of foot and heel flap, pick up and knit 1 stitch in each slipped stitch along the edge of heel flap, knit the first 8 heel flap stitches again. Round now begins in center of heel.

- **ROUND 1:** Knit to 2 stitches before first marker, k2tog, slip marker, work instep stitches in pattern to second marker, slip marker, ssk, knit to end of round — 2 stitches decreased.

- **ROUND 2:** Knit to first marker, slip marker, work in established instep pattern to second marker, slip marker, knit to end of round.

- Repeat Rounds 1 and 2 until 62 stitches remain: 31 instep stitches and 31 sole stitches.

Knitting the Foot

- Work even in established patterns, knitting all sole stitches and working instep stitches in chart pattern until foot measures 2"/5 cm less than desired finished length from the back of the heel, ending with Row 6 or Row 12 of chart. If necessary, end the chart early and continue in stockinette stitch until foot reaches desired length before starting the toe.

Shaping the Toe

- Remove end-of-round marker and knit to first marker. Round now begins at start of instep stitches.
- **ROUND 1:** Knit.
- **ROUND 2:** *K1, ssk, knit to 3 stitches before marker, k2tog, k1, slip marker; repeat from * once more — 4 stitches decreased.
- Repeat Rounds 1 and 2 ten more times. *You now have 18 stitches.*

Finishing

- Divide stitches evenly onto two needles, 9 stitches each for sole and instep. Cut yarn, leaving a 10"/25.5 cm tail. Graft stitches together with Kitchener stitch (see page 293). Weave in ends. Block.

Instep

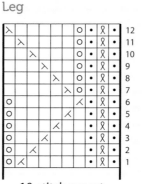

10-stitch repeat plus 1

Work pattern repeat 3 times.

Leg

10-stitch repeat

Work pattern repeat 6 times.

	knit
•	purl
ℛ	ktbl
⟋	k2tog
⟍	ssk
○	yo

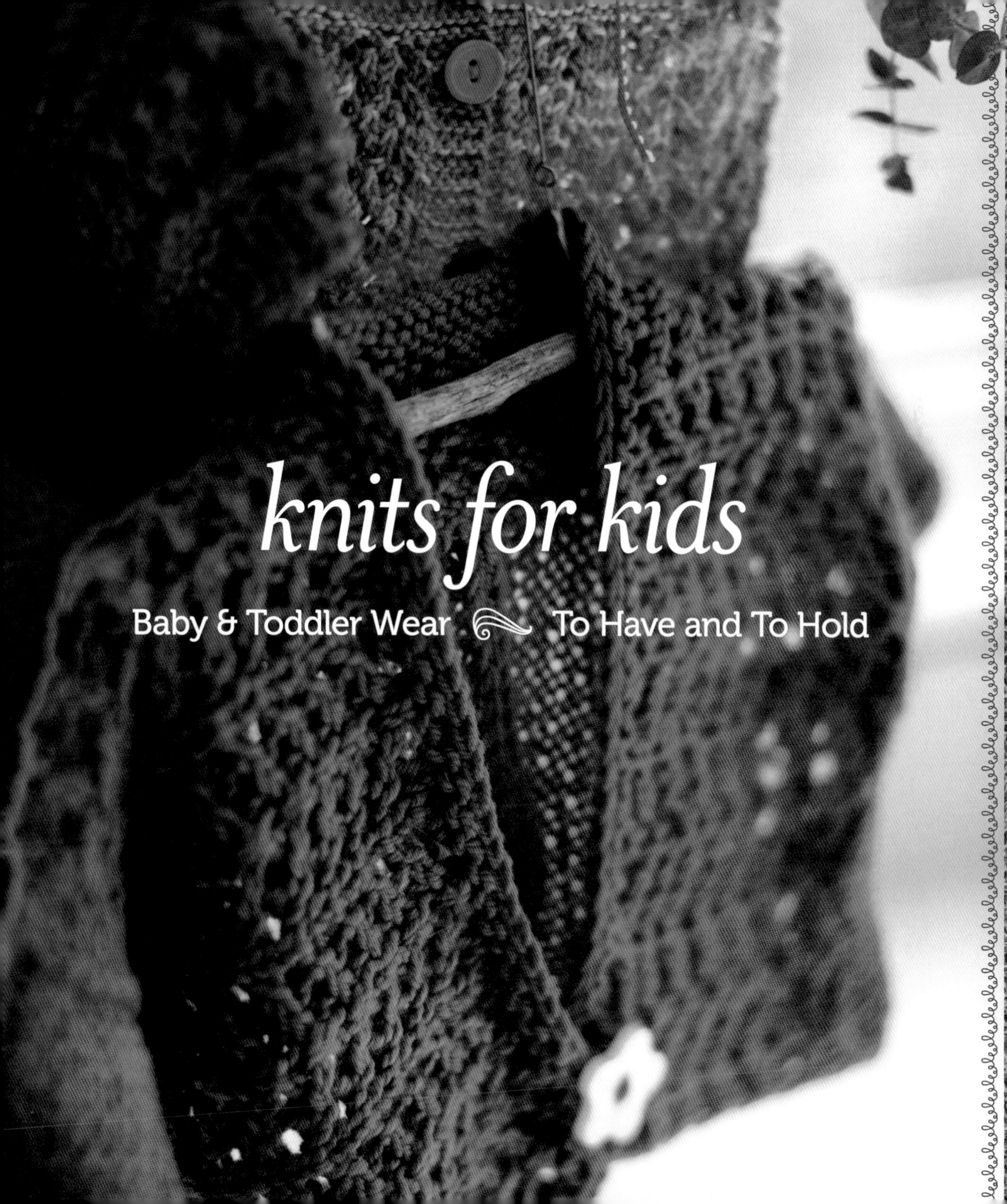

knits for kids

Baby & Toddler Wear ⟡ To Have and To Hold

Coral Reef Hat

DESIGNED BY TONIA BARRY

Beginning at the bottom and ending with the picot top knot, this whimsical little hat is sure to trigger smiles wherever it goes.

PATTERN ESSENTIALS

Picot Bind Off *Using cable method (see page 290), cast on 2 stitches, bind off 4 stitches; slip remaining stitch on right-hand needle to left-hand needle; repeat from * to bind off all stitches; cut yarn and pull through the last stitch.

Knitting the Hat

- With smaller needle, cast on 68 stitches. Place marker and join into a round, being careful not to twist the stitches.

- RIB ROUND: *P2, k2; repeat from * to end of round.

- Repeat the Rib Round until piece measures 1"/2.5 cm.

- INCREASE ROUND: *P2, k2, M1L; repeat from * to end of round. *You now have* 85 stitches.

- Work Rounds 1–8 of Coral Reef Lace chart until hat measures approximately 7"/18 cm from cast on, ending with Round 2.

- NEXT ROUND: *P2tog, k1, yo, k2tog; repeat from * to end of round. *You now have* 68 stitches. Place a locking stitch marker in this round.

- Change to larger needle and work Rounds 4–8 of Crown chart once, then repeat Rounds 1–8 of Crown chart until hat measures approximately 9"/23 cm from cast on.

- Bind off using Picot Bind Off.

- Weave in ends.

Finishing

- Cut twelve 24"/61 cm lengths of yarn. Thread all 12 lengths onto a yarn needle and weave them through the eyelets in the round marked by the locking stitch marker. Pull ends tightly and tie in an overhand knot, leaving two equal lengths of 12 strands each. Divide the 24 strands evenly into three groups of 8 strands and braid. Knot the end and trim to about 1½"/4 cm to form a tassel.

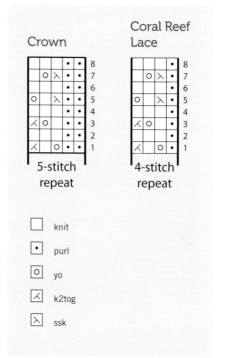

Crown

5-stitch repeat

Coral Reef Lace

4-stitch repeat

☐ knit

• purl

○ yo

╱ k2tog

╲ ssk

Sea Mist Baby Hat

DESIGNED BY TERRY COLLARD

Sea Mist Baby Hat features a picot edge and a simple lace pattern. Offered in three sizes, you can knit one for any baby you know or may come to know!

Finished Measurements

11¾ (14, 16¼)"/30 (35.5, 41.5) cm circumference and 5 (5½, 6½)"/12.5 (14, 16.5) cm deep

Yarn

Harrisville Designs Silk & Wool, 50% silk/50% wool, 175 yds (160 m)/1.75 oz (50 g), Color 206 Sea Mist

Needles

Set of four or five US 6 (4 mm) double-point needles *or size you need to obtain correct gauge*

Gauge

22 stitches and 36 rounds = 4"/10 cm in stockinette stitch; 17½ stitches and 35 rounds = 4"/10 cm in Sea Mist Lace pattern

Other Supplies

Stitch marker, yarn needle

PATTERN ESSENTIALS

Sea Mist Lace

(multiple of 10 stitches plus 1)

- **Round 1:** K1, *(yo, skp) twice, k1, (k2tog, yo) twice, k1; repeat from * to end of round.
- **Round 2:** Knit.
- **Round 3:** K2, *yo, skp, yo, sk2p, yo, k2tog, yo, k3; repeat from * to last 9 stitches, yo, skp, yo, sk2p, yo, k2tog, yo, k2.
- **Round 4:** Knit.
- Repeat Rounds 1–4 for pattern.

Knitting the Hat

- Cast on 50 (60, 70) stitches. Place marker and join into a round, being careful not to twist the stitches.

- ROUNDS 1–4: Knit.

- ROUND 5 (PICOT ROUND): *K2tog, yo; repeat from * to end of round.

- ROUNDS 6–9: Knit.

- ROUND 10: Knit around, increasing 1 stitch. *You now have* 51 (61, 71) stitches.

Knitting the Lace Pattern

- Work Rounds 1–4 of Sea Mist Lace pattern until piece measures 3½ (4, 5)"/9 (10, 12.5) cm from the Picot Round, ending with Round 4 of pattern, and decreasing 1 stitch in the last round. *You now have* 50 (60, 70) stitches.

Decreasing for the Crown

- ROUND 1: *K8, k2tog; repeat from * to end of round. *You now have* 45 (54, 63) stitches.

- ROUND 2 AND ALL EVEN-NUMBERED ROUNDS THROUGH ROUND 12: Knit.

- ROUND 3: *K7, k2tog; repeat from * to end of round. *You now have* 40 (48, 56) stitches.

- ROUND 5: *K6, k2tog; repeat from * to end of round. *You now have* 35 (42, 49) stitches.

- ROUND 7: *K5, k2tog; repeat from * to end of round. *You now have* 30 (36, 42) stitches.

- ROUND 9: *K4, k2tog; repeat from * to end of round. *You now have* 25 (30, 35) stitches.

- ROUND 11: *K3, k2tog; repeat from * to end of round. *You now have* 20 (24, 28) stitches.

- ROUND 13: *K2, k2tog; repeat from * to end of round. *You now have* 15 (18, 21) stitches.

- ROUND 14: (K2tog) seven (nine, ten) times, k1 (0, 1). *You now have* 8 (9, 11) stitches.

- ROUND 15: (K2tog) four (four, five) times, k0 (1, 1). *You now have* 4 (5, 6) stitches.

Finishing

- Cut yarn, leaving a 6"/15 cm tail. Thread tail onto yarn needle and draw through remaining stitches; pull up snugly and secure. Fold lower edge to WS along Picot Round and sew loosely to the inside. Weave in ends. Block.

Bunny Check Baby Hat

DESIGNED BY JILL WRIGHT

This baby cap is worked from the bottom up, in the round with no seaming. The pattern shifts from a garter stitch border to a simple lace pattern of double eyelets sitting on top of a double purl ridge, the result of which looks like the face of a bunny. Use your imagination!

Sizes and Finished Measurements

To fit 0–6 (6–18) months, 14½ (16)"/37 (41) cm circumference

Yarn

Classic Elite Yarns Fresco, 60% wool/30% baby alpaca/10% angora, 164 yds (150 m)/1.75 oz (50 g), Color 5321 Celadon

Needles

US 5 (3.75 mm) 16"/40 cm circular needle and set of four US 5 (3.75 mm) double-point needles *or size you need to obtain correct gauge*

Gauge

22 stitches and 36 rounds = 4"/10 cm in Bunny Check Stitch pattern

Other Supplies

Stitch marker, yarn needle

PATTERN ESSENTIALS

Bunny Check Stitch

(multiple of 8 stitches)

- **Rounds 1 and 2:** Knit.
- **Rounds 3 and 4:** *K1, p3, k4; repeat from * to end of round.
- **Round 5:** *K1, yo, s2kp, yo, k4; repeat from * to end of round.
- **Rounds 6–8:** Knit.
- **Rounds 9 and 10:** *K5, p3; repeat from * to end of round.
- **Round 11:** *K5, yo, s2kp, yo; repeat from * to end of round.
- **Round 12:** Knit.
- **Repeat Rounds 1–12 for pattern.**

90

Knitting the Hat

- Using the circular needle, cast on 80 (88) stitches. Place marker and join into a round, being careful not to twist the stitches.

- ROUND 1: Knit.

- ROUND 2: Purl.

- Repeat Rounds 1 and 2 once more.

- Following chart or written instructions, work Rounds 1–12 of Bunny Check Stitch pattern until hat measures 4 (4½)"/ 10 (11.5 cm) from cast-on edge, ending with Round 6 or 12 of pattern.

Knitting the Crown

Note: Change to double-point needles when necessary.

- ROUND 1 (DECREASE ROUND): *K8 (9), k2tog; repeat from * seven more times. *You now have* 72 (80) stitches.

- ROUND 2: Knit.

- ROUND 3 (DECREASE ROUND): *K7 (8), k2tog; repeat from * seven more times. *You now have* 64 (72) stitches.

- ROUND 4: Knit.

- Continue in this manner, decreasing 8 stitches every other round, until 8 (16) stitches remain.

- NEXT ROUND: *K2tog; repeat from * to end of round. *You now have* 4 (8) stitches.

- *For 6–18 months size only:* Repeat last round once more. *You now have* 4 stitches.

Finishing

- Cut yarn, leaving an 8"/20.5 cm tail; thread tail on yarn needle and draw through remaining stitches; pull up snugly and fasten off. Weave in ends, block to size.

Bunny Check Stitch

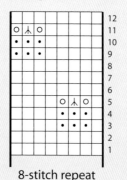

8-stitch repeat

	knit
•	purl
O	yo
⋏	s2kp

Little Leg Warmers

DESIGNED BY GWEN STEEGE

The lace pattern stitch for these bright and cozy leg warmers is Lace Chain, adapted from Barbara Walker's Craft of Lace Knitting *(Scribner's, 1971). We don't know a little girl who could resist these!*

Size and Finished Measurements

To fit a 4- to 6-year-old, 6"/23 cm circumference and 11"/28 cm long, unstretched (stretches to 9"/23 cm circumference)

Yarn

Jwrayco Hand Painted Yarns & Fibers, 50% superwash merino/ 25% bamboo/25% nylon, 460 yds (420 m)/3.5 oz (100 g), Flowers on the Beach

Needles

Set of four US 3 (3.25 mm) double-point needles *or size you need to obtain correct gauge*

Gauge

28 stitches and 40 rounds = 4"/10 cm in Lace Chain pattern, unstretched

Other Supplies

Yarn needle

Casting On with Picots

- Use the cable cast-on method (see page 290) to cast on 3 stitches. *Bind off 2 stitches; return stitch on right-hand needle to left-hand needle; use the cable cast-on method to cast on 4 stitches; repeat from * 16 more times, bind off 2 stitches; return stitch on right-hand needle to left-hand needle; use the cable cast on to cast on 1 more stitch. *You now have 36 stitches.*

- Place 12 stitches on each of three double-point needles; join into a round, being careful not to twist the stitches.

PATTERN ESSENTIALS

Lace Chain (multiple of 14 stitches)

- **Rounds 1, 3, and 5:** *P4, k10; repeat from * to end of round.

- **Round 2:** *P4, k2, k2tog, yo; k2tog but before slipping stitches from left-hand needle insert right-hand needle between the 2 knit-together stitches and knit the first stitch again, then slip the 2 stitches off the needle together; yo, ssk, k2; repeat from * to end of round.

- **Round 4:** *P4, k1, k2tog, yo, k4, yo, ssk, k1; repeat from * to end of round.

- **Round 6:** *P4, k2tog, yo, k1, k2tog, yo twice, ssk, k1, yo, ssk; repeat from * to end of round.

- **Round 7:** *P4, k4, work (k1, p1) in double yo of previous round, k4; repeat from * to end of round.

- **Round 8:** *P4, k2, yo, ssk, k2, k2tog, yo, k2; repeat from * to end of round.

- **Round 9:** Repeat Round 1.

- **Round 10:** *P4, k3, yo, ssk, k2tog, yo, k3; repeat from * to end of round.

- Repeat Rounds 1–10 for pattern.

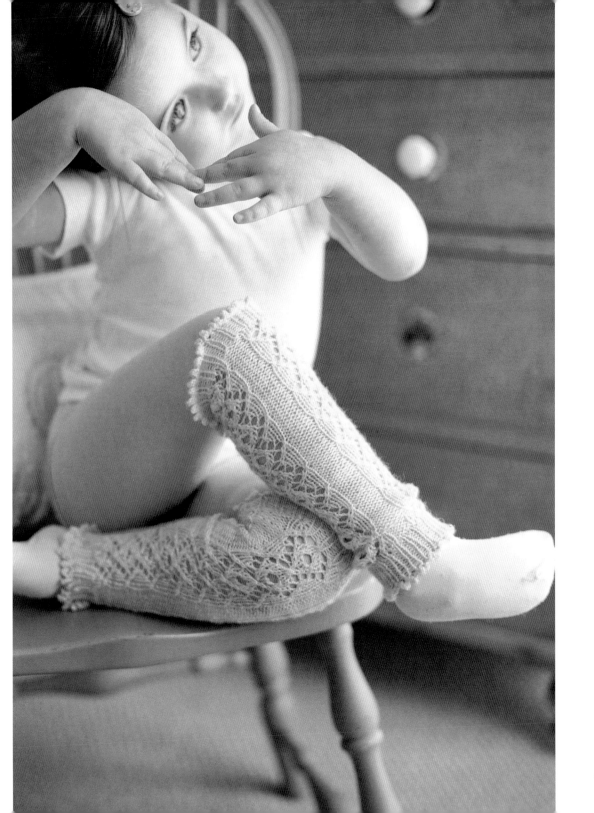

Knitting the Leg

- ROUNDS 1–10: *K1, p1; repeat from * to end of round.

- INCREASE ROUND: *K6, M1L; repeat from * to end of round. You now have 42 stitches: 14 on each needle.

- Following written instructions or chart, work Rounds 1–10 of Lace Chain pattern nine times or until piece measures 1"/2.5 cm less than desired length.

Knitting the Top Rib

- ROUNDS 1–10: *K1, p1; repeat from * to end of round.

Binding Off with Picots

- Knit the first 2 stitches and bind off 1 stitch using a regular bind off; *return stitch on right-hand needle to left-hand needle and use the knitted-on method (see page 294) to cast on 2 stitches; bind off 3 stitches (the 2 stitches just cast on and the stitch returned to the left-hand needle); repeat from * until 1 stitch remains. Cut yarn and pull it through the last stitch. Weave in the ends.

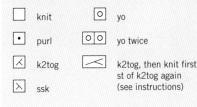

Lace Chain

14-stitch repeat

Work pattern repeat 3 times.

☐ knit	⊙ yo
• purl	⊙⊙ yo twice
⋌ k2tog	⤬ k2tog, then knit first st of k2tog again (see instructions)
⋋ ssk	

Kaya Baby Sweater

DESIGNED BY BRENDA PATIPA

Lace diamonds are strategically placed in this baby sweater, which is knit in one piece to the armholes, then divided for front and back. It's made to wear open at the front.

Size and Finished Measurements

To fit 12–18 months, 22½"/57 cm chest circumference, 9"/23 cm body length, and 6½"/16.5 cm sleeve length

Yarn

A Verb for Keeping Warm Creating, 100% superwash merino wool, 385 yds (352 m)/3.5 oz (100 g), Tilda

Needles

US 2 (2.75 mm) circular needle 16"/40 cm long *or size you need to obtain correct gauge*

Gauge

27 stitches and 40 rows = 4"/10 cm in pattern

Other Supplies

Stitch holders, yarn needle

Knitting the Body

Note: Sweater is knitted back and forth on a circular needle to accommodate the number of stitches in the body.

- Cast on 153 stitches. Work Rows 1–46 of Kaya Body chart (see page 96) once, then work Rows 27–34 once more (54 chart rows total). Piece measures 5½"/14 cm from cast on.

Kaya Body

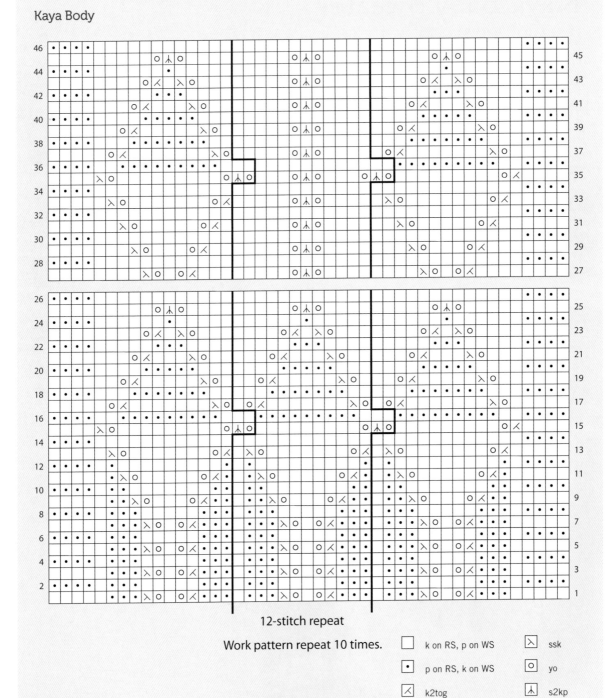

12-stitch repeat

Work pattern repeat 10 times.

	k on RS, p on WS		⟋	ssk
	p on RS, k on WS		○	yo
	k2tog			s2kp

Dividing for Fronts and Back

- **NEXT ROW (ROW 35 OF BODY CHART, RS):** Work 38 stitches in pattern for right front and place stitches on holder, bind off next 5 stitches, work in pattern until there are 67 back stitches after bind-off gap; place these stitches on a separate holder, bind off next 5 stitches, work in pattern to end of row. *You now have 38 left front stitches on the needle.*

Knitting the Left Front

SHAPING THE ARMHOLE

- Continuing in pattern as established, work 1 WS row. Decrease 1 stitch at beginning of next 5 RS rows by working first 3 stitches as k1, ssk; and end with the final RS Decrease Row (Row 45 of Body chart). *You now have 33 stitches.*

SHAPING THE NECK

Note: Continue the (yo, s2kp, yo) column as established while working remaining stitches in stockinette.

- **NEXT ROW (WS):** Bind off 14 stitches at neck edge, work in pattern to end. *You now have 19 stitches.*

- Decrease 1 stitch at end of next 5 RS rows by working last 3 stitches as k2tog, k1. *You now have 14 stitches.*

- Work even until armhole measures 3½"/9 cm, ending with a WS row.

SHAPING THE SHOULDER

- Bind off 7 stitches at beginning of next RS row, purl 1 WS row, then bind off remaining 7 stitches.

Knitting the Right Front

- Return the 38 held right front stitches to the needle and rejoin yarn with WS facing.

SHAPING THE ARMHOLE

- Continuing in pattern as established, work 1 WS row. Decrease 1 stitch at the end of the next 5 RS rows by working to last 3 stitches, k2tog, k1; then work 1 WS row (Row 46 of Body chart) after the final RS decrease row. *You now have 33 stitches.*

SHAPING THE NECK

Note: As for the left front, continue the (yo, s2kp, yo) column as established while working remaining stitches in stockinette.

- **NEXT ROW (RS):** Bind off 14 stitches at neck edge, work in pattern to end. *You now have 19 stitches.*

- Decrease 1 stitch at beginning of next 5 RS rows by working the first 3 stitches as k1, ssk. *You now have 14 stitches.*

- Work even until armhole measures 3½"/9 cm, ending with a RS row.

SHAPING THE SHOULDER

- Bind off 7 stitches at beginning of next WS row, knit 1 RS row, then bind off remaining 7 stitches.

Knitting the Back

- Return the 67 held back stitches to needle and rejoin yarn with WS facing.

SHAPING THE ARMHOLE

Note: As for the fronts, continue the (yo, s2kp, yo) columns as established while working remaining stitches in stockinette.

- **ROW 1 (WS):** Purl.

- **ROW 2 (RS):** K1, ssk, work in pattern to last 3 stitches, k2tog, k1.

- Repeat Rows 1 and 2 four more times. *You now have 57 stitches.*

- Work even until back armhole measures 2½"/6.5 cm, ending with a WS row.

SHAPING THE LEFT BACK NECK

- **NEXT ROW (RS):** Work 17 stitches in pattern and place stitches on a holder for right neck and shoulder, bind off next 23 stitches, and work in pattern to end. *You now have* 17 left neck and shoulder stitches on the needle.

- ROW 1 (WS): Purl.

- ROW 2: K1, ssk, work in pattern to end of row.

- Repeat Rows 1 and 2 two more times. *You now have* 14 stitches.

- Work even until back armhole measures 3½"/9 cm, ending with a RS row.

SHAPING THE LEFT SHOULDER

- Bind off 7 stitches at beginning of next WS row, knit 1 RS row, then bind off remaining 7 stitches.

SHAPING THE RIGHT BACK NECK

- Return the 17 held right neck and shoulder stitches to the needle and rejoin yarn with WS facing.

- ROW 1 (WS): Purl.

- ROW 2: Work in pattern to last 3 stitches, k2tog, k1.

- Repeat Rows 1 and 2 two more times. *You now have* 14 stitches. Work even until back armhole measures 3½"/9 cm, ending with a WS row.

SHAPING THE RIGHT SHOULDER

- Bind off 7 stitches at beginning of next RS row, purl 1 WS row, then bind off remaining 7 stitches.

Knitting the Sleeves (make 2)

- Cast on 37 stitches. Work Rows 1–6 of Kaya Sleeve chart.

- **NEXT ROW (RS):** K1, M1R, work to last st, M1L, k1 — 2 stitches increased.

- Continuing the center stitches in pattern and working the new stitches in stockinette, increase 1 stitch at each side in this manner every 6 rows five more times. *You now have* 49 stitches.

Note: After completing Row 46 of Sleeve chart, repeat Rows 27–46 to the end.

- Work even in pattern until 64 chart rows total have been completed, ending with Row 44 of Sleeve chart; sleeve measures about 6½"/16.5 cm.

Shaping the Sleeve Cap

- Continuing in pattern, bind off 3 stitches at the beginning of the next 2 rows. *You now have* 43 stitches.

- ROW 1 (RS): K1, ssk, work in pattern to last 3 stitches, k2tog, k1.

- ROW 2 (WS): Purl.

- Repeat Rows 1 and 2 four more times. *You now have* 33 stitches.

- Bind off 3 stitches at beginning of next 8 rows. *You now have* 9 stitches.

- Work 2 rows even to end with Row 46 of Sleeve chart. Bind off remaining stitches.

Finishing

- Block pieces to size. Sew shoulder and sleeve seams. Sew in sleeves.

Making the Neckband

- Starting at the left front neck edge, pick up and knit (see page 297) 33 stitches along left neck to shoulder seam, 39 stitches along back neck, and 33 stitches along right front neck edge. *You now have* 105 stitches. Knit 6 rows. Bind off all stitches. Weave in ends.

Kaya Sleeve

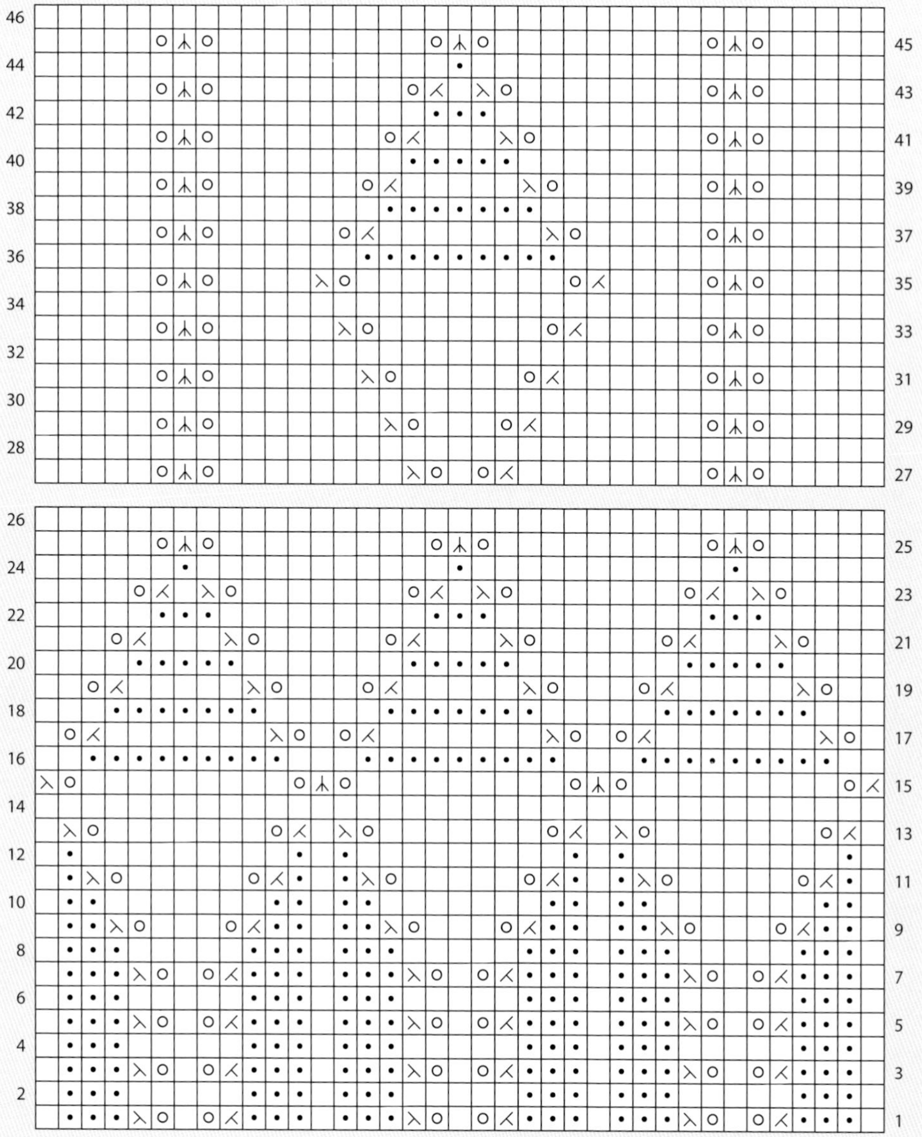

□	k on RS, p on WS	
⟩	ssk	
•	p on RS, k on WS	
○	yo	
⟨	k2tog	
人	s2kp	

Lace Baby Top

DESIGNED BY LORNA MISER

Is it possible for something to be sophisticated yet adorable at the same time? We think so, and here's proof! The top is worked back and forth in one piece to the armholes and then divided for fronts and back.

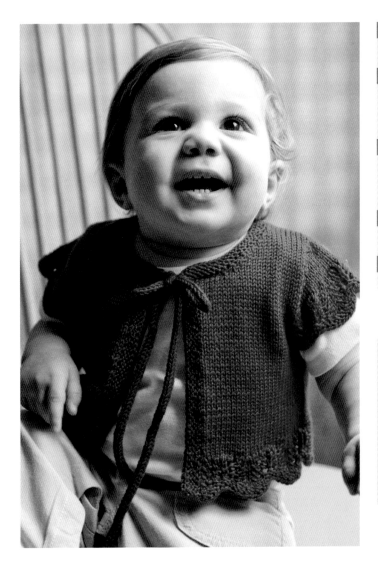

Size and Finished Measurements

To fit 6 months, 20"/51 cm chest circumference

Yarn

Cascade Heritage Sock, 75% super-wash merino wool/25% nylon, 437 yds (400 m)/ 3.5 oz (100 g), Color 5655 Como Blue

Needles

US 4 (3.5 mm) straight needles and two US 4 (3.5 mm) double-point needles for I-cord *or size you need to obtain correct gauge*

Gauge

26 stitches and 39 rows = 4"/10 cm in stockinette stitch

Other Supplies

Stitch holders, yarn needle

PATTERN ESSENTIALS

Scalloped Lace Edging
(multiple of 12 stitches plus 1)

- **Row 1 (RS):** K1, *k2tog twice, (yo, k1) three times, yo, ssk twice, k1; repeat from * to end of row.
- **Row 2 (WS):** Purl.
- Repeat Rows 1 and 2 for pattern.

Knitting the Bottom Section

- Cast on 157 stitches. Knit 4 rows. Work 8 rows Scalloped Lace Edging, ending with a WS row.
- **NEXT ROW (RS):** *K2tog, k4; repeat to last 7 stitches, k2tog, k3, k2tog. *You now have* 130 stitches.
- **NEXT ROW:** Purl 1 row.
- **NEXT ROWS:** Work in stockinette stitch until body measures 4¼"/11 cm from cast on at deepest point of scalloped edging, ending with a WS row.

Dividing for Front and Back

- **NEXT ROW (RS):** K28 and place on a holder for the right front, bind off 9 stitches, knit until there are 56 stitches after the bind-off gap and place them on a holder for the back, bind off 9 stitches, knit to the end for the left front. *You now have* 28 stitches for the left front on the needle.

Knitting the Left Front

- Working on 28 left front stitches, continue in stockinette stitch and decrease 1 stitch at the armhole edge (beginning of RS rows) every RS row five times by working the first 3 stitches as k1, ssk. *You now have* 23 stitches.

{ Casting on Lots of Stitches }

If you're instructed to cast on hundreds of stitches, place a marker after every 20th or 30th stitch so you don't have to count each stitch if you get interrupted and lose track.

- Work even until body measures 6¼"/16 cm from cast on, ending with a RS row. Bind off 6 stitches at neck edge at beginning of next WS row, then decrease 1 stitch at neck edge (end of RS rows) every RS row seven times by working the last 3 stitches as k2tog, k1. *You now have* 10 stitches.
- Work even on remaining 10 stitches until body measures 8¼"/21 cm from cast on. Bind off all stitches.

Knitting the Right Front

- Place 28 right front stitches on the needle and rejoin yarn with WS facing. Continue in stockinette stitch, and decrease 1 stitch at armhole edge (end of RS rows) every RS row five times by working the last 3 stitches as k2tog, k1. *You now have* 23 stitches.
- Work even until body measures 6¼"/16 cm from cast on, ending with a WS row. Bind off 6 stitches at neck edge at beginning of next RS row, then decrease 1 stitch at neck edge (beginning of RS rows) every RS row seven times by working the first 3 stitches as k1, ssk. *You now have* 10 stitches.
- Work even on remaining 10 stitches until the body measures 8¼"/21 cm from cast on. Bind off all stitches.

Knitting the Back

- Place 56 back stitches on the needle and rejoin yarn with WS facing. Working in stockinette stitch, decrease 1 stitch at each edge every RS row five times. *You now have* 46 stitches.

- Work even on 46 stitches until back measures 8¼"/21 cm from cast on. Bind off all stitches. Sew back to fronts at shoulder seams.

Knitting the Sleeve Caps (make 2)

- Cast on 49 stitches. Work 8 rows of Scalloped Lace Edging, ending with a WS row.
- **NEXT ROW (RS):** K5, *k1, k2tog; repeat from * to last 5 stitches, k5. *You now have* 36 stitches.
- Purl 1 row.
- Bind off 5 stitches at the beginning of the next 2 rows. *You now have* 26 stitches.
- Bind off 2 stitches at the beginning of the next 6 rows. *You now have* 14 stitches.
- Bind off remaining stitches.
- Block pieces. Center each cap on a shoulder seam and sew in place along shaped stockinette edge of the cap. Sew sides of lace edging to armhole edges, ending on either side of the stitches bound off at the base of the armhole opening (i.e., do not sew caps to underarm bind-off edges).

Finishing

- Pick up and knit (see page 297) 40 stitches along the right front edge from cast on to neck. Knit 5 rows. Bind off.
- Pick up and knit 40 stitches along the left front edge from neck to cast on. Knit 5 rows. Bind off.
- Pick up and knit 23 stitches along the right front neck edge, 28 stitches along the back neck edge, and 23 stitches along the left front neck edge. *You now have* 74 stitches.
- Knit 5 rows. Bind off.
- Using double-point needles, cast on 4 stitches and work I-cord (see page 292) for 12"/30.5 cm. Cut yarn and thread yarn through the stitches. Fasten off. Make a second I-cord in the same manner. Sew an I-cord tie to each side of the neck opening. Weave in ends.

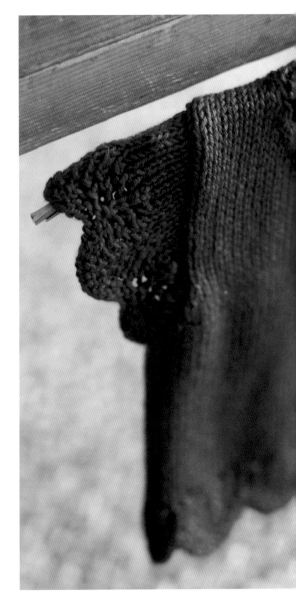

Baby Twist Pullover

DESIGNED BY LIZ NIELDS

The Baby Twist Pullover uses a simple four-row cable-and-lace pattern. It's made in two pieces, with stitches for the sleeves cast on at each side of the front and back pieces. The top of the sweater is joined with a three-needle bind off, and simple neck shaping and borders are worked as the pieces are knit.

Size and Finished Measurements

To fit 6–9 months, 19"/48.5 cm chest circumference, 9"/23 cm body length, and 7"/18 cm sleeve length

Yarn

Cascade Heritage Sock, 75% superwash merino wool/25% nylon, 437 yds (400 m)/ 3.5 oz (100 g), Color 5602 Steel

Needles

US 2 (2.75 mm) straight needles *or size you need to obtain correct gauge*

Gauge

28 stitches and 44 rows = 4"/10 cm in Baby Twist pattern

Other Supplies

Stitch holders, yarn needle

Special Abbreviations

TW3 skip the first 2 stitches on left-hand needle, insert right-hand needle into third stitch on left-hand needle and knit it, leaving the stitch on the needle; knit the first stitch then the second stitch and slip all 3 stitches from the needle together

Knitting the Back

- Cut two 1-yd/1 m lengths of yarn for casting on the sleeves, one 2-yd/2 m length of yarn for working the second back shoulder, and one 6-yd/5.5 m length of yarn for working the second front shoulder; set aside.

- Cast on 71 stitches. Knit 3 rows, beginning and ending with a WS row.

- Work Rows 1–4 of Baby Twist pattern 12 times, then work Rows 1–3 once more. Do not turn after last RS row. Piece measures about 4¾"/12 cm.

Casting On for the Sleeves

- With working yarn and a 1-yd/1 m length of yarn, use the long-tail method (see page 294) to cast on 50 stitches at the end of the last RS row completed. Turn. *You now have 121 stitches.*

- **NEXT ROW (WS):** K3, *(yo, p2tog) twice, p3; repeat from * to last 6 stitches, (yo, p2tog) twice, p2. Do not turn.

- Using the long-tail method as before with the other 1-yd/ 1 m length of yarn, cast 50 stitches on at the end of the last WS row completed. *You now have 171 stitches.* Continue as follows.

- **ROW 1 (RS):** K3, *(yo, p2tog) twice, k3; repeat from * to end of row.

- **ROW 2 (WS):** K3, *(yo, p2tog) twice, p3; repeat from * to last 7 stitches, (yo, p2tog) twice, k3.

- **ROW 3:** K3, *(yo, p2tog) twice, TW3; repeat from * to last 7 stitches (yo, p2tog) twice, k3.

- **ROW 4:** Repeat Row 2.

- Repeat Rows 1–4 eight more times — 22 full 4-row pattern repeats have been worked, counting from the bottom edge of sweater. Piece measures about 8"/20.5 cm.

Shaping the Back Neck

- **NEXT ROW (RS):** Work 63 stitches in established pattern, k45, work 63 stitches in pattern.

- Work 3 more rows in this manner, knitting the center 45 stitches every row, and working stitches on each side as established, ending with Row 4 of Baby Twist pattern.

- **NEXT ROW (RS):** Work 63 stitches in pattern, k3, join the 2-yd/2 m length of yarn, bind off 39 stitches, k3, work in pattern to end of row. *You now have 66 stitches on each side.*

- Working each side separately and knitting 3 stitches at each neck edge every row, continue in pattern as established for 3 more rows, ending with Row 4 of pattern — 24 full pattern repeats have been worked. Piece measures about 9"/23 cm. Place stitches on separate holders.

Knitting the Front

- Work as for back until 19 full pattern repeats have been completed from the beginning, ending with Row 4 of pattern. Piece measures about 7"/18 cm. *You now have 171 stitches.*

Shaping the Front Neck

- **NEXT ROW (RS):** Work 63 stitches in established pattern, k45, work 63 stitches in pattern.

- Work 3 more rows in this manner, knitting the center 45 stitches every row, and working stitches on each side as established, ending with Row 4 of Baby Twist pattern.

- **NEXT ROW (RS):** Work 63 stitches in pattern, k3, join the 6-yd/5.5 m length of yarn, bind off 39 stitches, k3, work in pattern to end of row. *You now have* 66 stitches on each side.

- Working each side separately and knitting 3 stitches at each neck edge every row, continue in pattern as established for 15 more rows, ending with Row 4 of Baby Twist pattern — 24 full pattern repeats have been worked. Piece measures about 9"/23 cm. Place stitches for each side on separate holders.

Joining Front and Back

- With RS together, use the three-needle bind off (see page 299) to join live stitches of the front and back shoulders. Sew side seams, weave in ends, and block to measurements.

Three-Button Baby Sweater

Designed by Carol J. Sorsdahl

You can work two different sizes of this sweater with the same instructions simply by changing needle size. Knit from the top down, the sweater features two lace patterns along with stockinette stitch, garter stitch, and knit 1, purl 1 ribbing.

105

Sizes and Finished Measurements

Small, to fit 6–12 months: 20"/51 cm chest circumference
Large, to fit 12–24 months: 22"/56 cm chest circumference

Yarn

Fly Designs Cashmara, 80% superwash merino wool/10% cashmere/10% nylon, 290 yds (265 m)/4 oz (113 g), Hyacinth (small), Lavender (large)

Needles

Small: US 3 (3.25 mm) circular needle 24"/60 cm long and set of four US 3 (3.25 mm) double-point needles; US 5 (3.75 mm) circular needle 24"/60 cm long and set of four US 5 (3.75 mm) double-point needles *or size you need to obtain correct gauge*
Large: US 5 (3.75 mm) circular needle 24"/60 cm long and set of four US 5 (3.75 mm) double-point needles; US 7 (4.5 mm) circular needle 24"/60 cm long and set of four US 7 (4.5 mm) double-point needles *or size you need to obtain correct gauge*

Gauge

Small: 24 stitches and 28 rows = 4"/10 cm in body lace pattern on larger needle
Large: 21 stitches and 26 rows = 4"/10 cm in body lace pattern on larger needle

Other Supplies

Four locking stitch markers, 18 regular stitch markers, scrap yarn for holders, yarn needle, three ½"–⅝" (13–16 mm) buttons, sewing needle and coordinating thread

Knitting the Neckband

- With smaller circular needle, cast on 83 stitches using the backward loop method (see page 290).

- ROW 1 (RS): K1, *p1, k1; repeat from * to end of row.

- ROW 2 (WS): K1, *k1, p1; repeat from * to last 2 stitches, k2.

- Repeat Rows 1 and 2 two more times.

Knitting the Yoke

- Change to larger circular needle.

- ROW 1 (RS): Purl.

- ROW 2 (WS): Purl.

- ROW 3: Knit.

- ROWS 4 AND 5: Repeat Rows 2 and 3.

- ROW 6 (INCREASE ROW): (K4, M1L) three times, (k5, M1L, k4, M1L) six times, (k4, M1L) three times, k5. *You now have 101 stitches.*

- ROW 7: Knit.

- ROWS 8–11: Repeat Rows 2 and 3 twice.

- ROW 12 (INCREASE ROW): (K5, M1L) four times, (k6, M1L, k5, M1L) five times, (k5, M1L) four times, k6. *You now have 119 stitches.*

- ROW 13: Knit.

- ROWS 14 AND 15: Repeat Rows 2 and 3.

- ROW 16 (INCREASE ROW): (K6, M1L) five times, (k7, M1L, k6, M1L) four times, (k6, M1L) five times, k7. *You now have 137 stitches.*

Knitting the Raglan Shaping

- Divide the yoke into sections by placing locking markers between stitches 20 and 21, 48 and 49, 89 and 90, and 117 and 118. *You now have 137 stitches total: 20 stitches for the left front, 28 stitches for the first sleeve, 41 stitches for the back, 28 stitches for the second sleeve, and 20 stitches for the right front.*

- ROW 1 (RS): *Knit to 2 stitches before marker, kfb, k1, slip marker, kfb; repeat from * three more times, knit to end of row. *You now have 145 stitches.*

- ROW 2 (WS): Purl.

- ROW 3: Repeat Row 1. *You now have 153 stitches: 22 stitches for each front, 32 stitches for each sleeve, and 45 back stitches.*

- **ROW 4:**

  - (*right front*) P2, *yo, p2tog; repeat from * to 2 stitches before marker, p2, slip marker — 9 eyelets worked;

  - (*right sleeve*) P2, *yo, p2tog; repeat from * to 2 stitches before marker, p2, slip marker — 14 eyelets worked;

  - (*back*) P3, *yo, p2tog; repeat from * to 2 stitches before marker, p2, slip marker — 20 eyelets worked;

  - (*left sleeve*) work as for right sleeve;

  - (*left front*) work as for right front.

- **ROWS 5–7:** Repeat Rows 1–3. *You now have* 169 stitches: 24 stitches for each front, 36 stitches for each sleeve, and 49 back stitches.

- **ROW 8:**

  - (*right front*) P2, *yo, p2tog; repeat from * to 2 stitches before marker, p2, slip marker — 10 eyelets worked;

  - (*right sleeve*) P2, *yo, p2tog; repeat from * to 2 stitches before marker, p2, slip marker — 16 eyelets worked;

  - (*back*) P3, *yo, p2tog; repeat from * to 2 stitches before marker, p2, slip marker — 22 eyelets worked;

  - (*left sleeve*) work as for right sleeve;

  - (*left front*) work as for right front.

- **ROWS 9–11:** Repeat Rows 1–3. *You now have* 185 stitches total: 26 stitches for each front, 40 stitches for each sleeve, and 53 back stitches.

- **ROW 12:** Knit.

Dividing the Sleeves from the Body

- **NEXT ROW (RS):** Knit to first marker, place the next 40 sleeve stitches on scrap yarn holder, cast on 6 stitches and join to the back; knit across back to next marker, place next 40 sleeve stitches on scrap yarn holder, cast on 6 stitches and join to the right front; knit to end. *You now have* 117 stitches.

- **NEXT ROW (WS):** Knit.

Knitting the Body

Note: Place markers between pattern repeats, if desired.

- **ROW 1 (RS):** K2, *yo, k1, sk2p, k1, yo, k1; repeat from * to last st, k1.

- **ROW 2 (WS):** Purl.

- **ROWS 3–34:** Repeat Rows 1 and 2 sixteen times.

- **ROW 35:** Repeat Row 1.

- ROWS 36–40: Change to smaller circular needle and knit, removing markers in the first row.
- Bind off using sewn bind-off method (see page 298).

Knitting the Sleeves (make 2)

- With larger double-point needles and beginning at center of underarm stitches, pick up and knit (see page 297) 3 underarm stitches, knit the 40 held sleeve stitches, then pick up and knit 3 underarm stitches, place marker. *You now have* 46 stitches.
- ROUND 1 (DECREASE ROUND): Working in the round, (p2tog, p1) four times, (p2tog, p2, p2tog, p1) three times, (p2tog, p1) four times, p1. *You now have* 32 stitches.
- Change to smaller double-point needles.
- ROUND 2: *K1, p1; repeat from * to end of round.
- ROUNDS 3–6: Repeat Round 2 four times.
- Bind off loosely in pattern.

{ Stitch Markers Are Your Friends }

Even if you usually work complicated patterns without stitch markers, consider using lots of them when knitting lace. Because mistakes are so difficult to find and then even more difficult to fix without ripping back, if you use a stitch marker between each repeat you can more easily count the number of stitches between the markers with each repeat to make sure you're staying on track.

Knitting the Left Front Button Band

- With RS of left front facing and smaller circular needle, and beginning at neck edge, pick up and knit 20 stitches evenly along yoke and 25 stitches along front edge. *You now have* 45 stitches.
- ROWS 1–10: Knit.
- Bind off loosely knitwise.

Knitting the Right Front Buttonhole Band

- With RS of right front facing and smaller circular needle, and beginning at lower edge, pick up and knit 25 stitches along front edge and 20 stitches evenly along yoke. *You now have* 45 stitches.
- ROWS 1–5: Knit.
- ROW 6 (RS, BUTTONHOLE ROW): K25, (yo, k2tog, k6) twice, yo, k2tog, k2.
- ROWS 7–10: Knit.
- Bind off loosely knitwise.

Finishing

- Weave in ends. Sew buttons to the button band, opposite the buttonholes.

Hana

DESIGNED BY CHERYL OBERLE

Hana is a traditional Japanese girl's name that means "flower." Hana is knitted side to side in two halves that are joined at the center back. The sleeves are knitted from the shoulder down. The front band and collar are knitted in one piece as a continuation of the lace pattern on the fronts.

Size and Finished Measurements

To fit 12–18 months, 22"/56 chest circumference, 9"/23 cm body length, and 3"/7.5 cm sleeve length

Note: Measurements are for blocked garment; the lace pattern expands once blocked.

Yarn

Cascade 220 Superwash, 100% superwash wool, 220 yds (201 m)/ 3.5 oz. (100 g), Color 834 Strawberry Pink

Needles

US 9 (5.5 mm) circular needle 24"/60 cm long *or size you need to obtain correct gauge*

Gauge

13 stitches and 18 rows = 4"/10 cm in stockinette stitch; 13 stitches and 20 rows = 4"/10 cm in Hana Lace pattern, blocked

Other Supplies

Stitch holders, locking stitch markers, yarn needle, US H/8 (5 mm) crochet hook, sewing needle and coordinating thread (optional), one 1"/2.5 cm button

PATTERN ESSENTIALS

Hana Lace (multiple of 6 stitches plus 1)

- **Rows 1 and 3 (WS):** Purl.
- **Row 2 (RS):** K1, *yo, ssk, k1, k2tog, yo, k1; repeat from * to end of row.
- **Row 4:** K2, *yo, s2kp, yo, k3; repeat from * to last 5 stitches, yo, s2kp, yo, k2.
- Repeat Rows 1–4 for pattern.

PATTERN NOTES

Each half begins at the side and is worked in toward the center.

The front and back panels are identical up to where the front and back divide.

Knitting the Right Front/Back

- Cast on 61 stitches. Beginning with a WS row, purl 3 rows, then knit 1 RS row.

Knitting the Lace

- Work Rows 1–4 of the Hana Lace pattern five times (20 pattern rows total), ending with a RS row.

Dividing the Right Front and Back

- **ROW 1 (WS):** Purl. Cut yarn.
- **ROW 2 (RS):** Place the first 34 stitches on a holder. Join yarn to remaining stitches with RS facing and knit to end. *You now have* 27 back stitches.
- Continue on back stitches as follows.
- **ROW 3:** K3, purl to end of row.
- **ROW 4:** Knit.
- Repeat Rows 3 and 4 four more times. Purl 2 rows and bind off loosely knitwise.

Knitting the Left Front/Back

- Work as for right front/back up to Dividing the Right Front and Back.

Dividing the Left Front and Back

- ROW 1 (WS): Purl.

- ROW 2 (RS): K27, place remaining 34 stitches on a holder for the front. *You now have 27 back stitches.*

- Continue on back stitches as follows.

- ROW 3: Purl to last 3 stitches, k3.

- ROW 4: Knit.

- ROW 5: Repeat Row 3.

- Repeat Rows 4 and 5 three more times, then work Row 4 once more. Purl 2 more rows. Bind off loosely knitwise.

Knitting the Sleeves (make 2)

Note: The sleeves are picked up and knit down from the shoulder to the cuff.

- On the side seam edges of each back and front, place a locking stitch marker 18 stitches up from the bottom edge; this marks the underarm. With RS facing, pick up and knit (see page 297) 26 stitches between the markers from underarm to underarm with the shoulder line in the center of the picked-up stitches.

- Beginning and ending with a WS row, work in stockinette stitch until sleeve measures 2½"/6.5 cm. Purl 2 rows. Bind off knitwise.

Finishing

Note: When sewing seams on Hana make sure that the finished seam is very flexible and will stretch to accommodate the lace, which will relax and open up when blocked.

- Join the side seams and the center back seam by sewing just inside the cast-on edge so that the purl ridges meet on the RS. Sew sleeve seams.

Knitting the Front Band/Collar

- With RS facing and beginning at the bottom of the right front, place the 34 held right front stitches on the needle. Join yarn at lower edge of right front. Beginning with RS Row 2 of the pattern, work these 34 stitches in pattern as established; pick up and knit 8 stitches across the right back neck to the center seam, pick up 1 stitch in the seam, pick up 8 stitches across the left back neck to the held left front stitches. Beginning at the bottom of the left front, place the 34 held left front stitches onto the free end of the needle and then work Row 2 of lace pattern as established (from the shoulder down to the bottom). *You now have 85 stitches.*

- Work Rows 3 and 4 of the pattern as established on these 85 stitches.

- Repeat Rows 1–4 of the pattern two more times. Purl 3 rows. Bind off very loosely knitwise.

Making the Button and Button Loop

- With the crochet hook, attach the yarn with a slip stitch just inside the right front edge, about 1"/2.5 cm up from the bottom. Chain 9, or work a crochet chain long enough to fit around the chosen button, and attach it again with a slip stitch to the inside edge about 2"/5 cm up from the bottom. With yarn or matching sewing thread, sew button to the left front to correspond to the button loop.

- Block to measurements. Weave in ends.

Haru

DESIGNED BY CHERYL OBERLE

Haru is a traditional Japanese boy's name that means "sunshine." Haru is knitted side to side in two halves that are joined at the center back. The sleeves are knitted from the shoulder down and the garter stitch front band and collar are worked in a single piece that is knitted onto the sewn-together garment.

Size and Finished Measurements

To fit 12–18 months, 22"/56 cm chest circumference, 9"/23 cm body length, and 3"/7.5 cm sleeve length
Note: Measurements are for blocked garment; the lace pattern expands once blocked.

Yarn

Cascade 220 Superwash, 100% superwash wool, 220 yds (201 m)/3.5 oz. (100 g), Color 841 Moss

Needles

US 9 (5.5 mm) circular needle 24"/60 cm long *or size you need to obtain correct gauge*

Gauge

13 stitches and 18 rows = 4"/10 cm in stockinette stitch; 14½ stitches and 24 rows = 4"/10 cm in Haru Lace pattern, blocked

Other Supplies

Stitch holders, locking stitch markers, yarn needle, US H/8 (5 mm) crochet hook, sewing needle and coordinating thread (optional), one 1"/2.5 cm button

Knitting the Right Front/Back

- Cast on 65 stitches. Beginning with a WS row, purl 3 rows, then knit 1 RS row.

Knitting the Lace

Note: Only even-numbered RS rows are charted; work all odd-numbered WS rows as k3, purl to last 3 stitches, k3.

- ROWS 1–20: Keeping the first 3 and last 3 stitches of the rows in garter stitch (knit every row) and working the center 59 stitches in chart pattern, work Rows 1–4 of Haru Lace chart (see page 114) five times (20 chart rows total).

- ROW 21 (WS): K3, purl to last 3 stitches, k3.

- ROW 22: Knit.

- Repeat Rows 21 and 22 once more, ending with a RS row.

Dividing the Right Front and Back

- ROW 1 (WS): Knit. Cut yarn.

- ROW 2 (RS): Place the first 35 stitches on a stitch holder. With RS facing, join yarn to the remaining stitches and knit to end. *You now have* 30 back stitches.

- Continue on back stitches as follows.

PATTERN NOTES

Each half begins at the side and is worked in toward the center.

The front and back panels are identical up to where the front and back divide.

- ROWS 3 AND 4: Knit.

- ROW 5 (WS, EYELET ROW): K1, *yo, k2tog; repeat from * to last stitch, k1.

- ROWS 6–8: Knit.

- ROW 9: Repeat Row 5.

- ROWS 10–16: Knit.

- Bind off loosely.

Knitting the Left Front/Back

- Work as for right front/back to Dividing the Right Front and Back.

Dividing the Left Front and Back

- ROW 1 (WS): Knit.

- ROW 2 (RS): K30, place the remaining 35 stitches on a stitch holder for the front. *You now have* 30 back stitches.

- Continue on back stitches as follows.

- ROWS 3 AND 4: Knit.

- ROW 5 (WS, EYELET ROW): K1, *k2tog, yo; repeat from * to last st, k1.

- ROWS 6–8: Knit.

- ROW 9: Repeat Row 5.

- ROWS 10–16: Knit.

- Bind off loosely.

Knitting the Sleeves (make 2)

Note: Sleeves are picked up and knit down from the shoulder.

- On the side seam edges of each back and front place a locking stitch marker 19 stitches up from the bottom edge; this marks the underarm. With RS facing, pick up and knit (see page 297) 27 stitches between the markers from underarm to underarm, with the shoulder line in the center of the picked-up stitches.

- Beginning and ending with a WS row, work in stockinette stitch until sleeve measures 2½"/6.5 cm. Purl 2 rows. Bind off knitwise.

Finishing

Note: When sewing seams, make sure that the finished seam is very flexible and will stretch to accommodate the lace, which will relax and open up when blocked.

- Join the side seams by sewing just inside the cast-on edge so that the purl ridges meet on the RS. Sew the sleeve seams.

- Join the center back seam by placing WS together and sewing so that the seam ridge shows on the RS of the garment.

Knitting the Front Band/Collar

- With RS facing and beginning at the bottom of the right front, place the 35 held right front stitches on the needle. Join yarn at the lower edge of the right front and knit these 35 stitches; pick up and knit 8 stitches across right back neck to the center seam, pick up 1 stitch in the seam, pick up and knit 8 stitches across left back neck to the held left front stitches. Beginning at the bottom of the left front, place the 35 held left front stitches onto the free end of the needle and then knit them (from the shoulder down to the bottom). *You now have* 87 stitches.

- Knit 13 rows, ending with a RS row. Bind off very loosely on the WS knitwise.

Making the Button and Button Loop

- With the crochet hook, attach the yarn with a slip stitch just inside the left front edge, about 1"/2.5 cm up from the bottom. Chain 9, or work a crochet chain long enough to fit around the chosen button, and attach it again with a slip stitch to the inside edge about 2"/5 cm up from the bottom. With yarn or matching sewing thread, sew button onto right front band to correspond to the button loop.

- Block to measurements. Weave in ends.

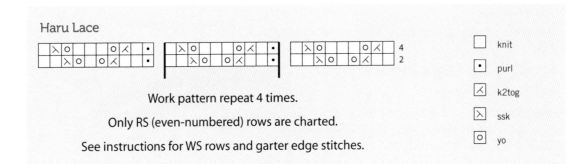

Haru Lace

Work pattern repeat 4 times.

Only RS (even-numbered) rows are charted.

See instructions for WS rows and garter edge stitches.

	knit
•	purl
⟋	k2tog
⟍	ssk
o	yo

I Heart You Dress

DESIGNED BY JUDITH DURANT

What says, "I love you" better than a bunch of hearts? The lace heart pattern used here comes from Barbara Walker's Charted Knitting Designs *(Schoolhouse Press, 1998) and is just the right size for the lower skirt and bodice.*

Size and Finished Measurements

To fit 6–12 months, 20"/51 cm chest circumference and 14"/35.5 cm long

Yarn

Berroco Comfort Sock, 50% super fine nylon, 50% super fine acrylic, 447 yds (412 m)/3.5 oz (100 g), Color 1757 True Red

Needles

US 3 (3.25 mm) circular needle 16"/40 cm long *or size you need to obtain correct gauge,* US 2½ (3 mm) double-point needles, and US 2½ (3 mm) circular needle 16"/40 cm long

Gauge

27 stitches and 42 rounds = 4"/10 cm in stockinette stitch with larger needle

Other Supplies

11 stitch markers (one in a unique color), scrap yarn for holders, US D/3 (3.25 mm) crochet hook, yarn needle, one ½"/13 mm button, sewing needle and coordinating thread

Knitting the Skirt

- With larger circular needle, cast on 240 stitches using the long-tail method (see page 294). Place the unique-colored marker for end of round and join into a round, being careful not to twist the stitches.

- ROUND 1: Knit.

- ROUND 2: Purl.

- ROUND 3: Knit.

- ROUND 4: K3, place marker, (k30, place marker) seven times, k27.

Knitting the Hearts

Note: The Lace Heart chart is worked over 25 stitches; each 30-stitch marked section has a 25-stitch heart followed by 5 knit stitches. The start of the round at center back begins with 3 knit stitches before the first heart, and the round ends with 2 knit stitches after the 25 stitches marked for the last heart. Do not consider the end-of-round marker in the following instructions.

- SETUP ROUND: Following Round 1 of the Lace Heart chart, k3, slip marker, *work 25 stitches of heart motif, knit to next marker, slip marker; repeat from * six more times, work 25 stitches of the last heart motif, k2.

- Work as established through Round 36 of the chart.

- Knit 10 rounds, removing markers between chart sections in last round. Piece measures about 5"/12.5 cm.

- DECREASE ROUND 1: *K1, k2tog; repeat from * to end of round. *You now have* 160 stitches.

- Work even in stockinette stitch until piece measures 7"/18 cm from cast on.

- DECREASE ROUND 2: *K6, k2tog; repeat from * to end of round. *You now have* 140 stitches.

- Work even in stockinette stitch until piece measures 8½"/21.5 cm from cast on, decreasing 1 stitch in the last round. *You now have* 139 stitches: 35 left back stitches, 69 front stitches, 35 right back stitches.

Knitting the Bodice

- ROUND 1: K57, place marker, work Round 1 of Lace Heart chart over 25 center front stitches, place marker, k57.

- ROUNDS 2–11: Knit to marker, slip marker, work 25-stitch heart motif as established, slip marker, knit to end of round.

Dividing for the Front and Backs

- NEXT ROUND (ROUND 12 OF LACE HEART CHART): Work as established to the end of the heart motif section, slip marker, k16, bind off 12 stitches for right underarm; knit until there are 29 stitches after bind-off gap, slip end-of-round marker, k29, place 58 stitches just worked on scrap-yarn holder for back; bind off 12 stitches for left underarm, work in established pattern to end of front stitches. *You now have* 57 front stitches.

Note: The remainder of the bodice is worked back and forth in rows. If your purl stitches tend to be looser than your knit stitches, work the WS purl rows on the smaller needle and the RS rows on the larger needle.

Knitting the Front

Note: The even-numbered rounds of the chart are now purled as WS rows.

- Work back and forth on remaining 57 stitches for the front, working heart motif as established over center 25 stitches and *at the same time* decrease 1 stitch inside an edge stitch at the beginning and end of the next 4 RS rows. *You now have* 49 stitches. Continue even through Row 36 of Lace Heart chart.

- Knit 2 rows even, ending with a WS row and removing the heart section markers in last row.

Shaping the Front Neck

- **NEXT ROW (RS):** K22 stitches and place on scrap-yarn holder for left front, bind off center 5 stitches, knit to end. *You now have* 22 right front stitches on needle.

MAKING THE RIGHT FRONT

- **ROW 1 (WS):** Purl to last 3 stitches, ssp, p1 — 1 stitch decreased.

- **ROW 2 (RS):** K1, ssk, knit to end of row — 1 stitch decreased.

- Repeat Rows 1 and 2 three more times. *You now have* 14 stitches.

- Work 8 rows even in stockinette stitch, ending with a RS row. Place stitches on a scrap-yarn holder for the right shoulder.

MAKING THE LEFT FRONT

- Place the 22 held left front stitches on the needle. With WS facing, attach yarn at neck edge.

- **ROW 1 (WS):** P1, p2tog, purl to end of row — 1 stitch decreased.

- **ROW 2:** Knit to last 3 stitches, k2tog, k1 — 1 stitch decreased.

- Repeat Rows 1 and 2 three more times. *You now have* 14 stitches.

- Work 8 rows even in stockinette stitch, ending with a RS row. Place stitches on a scrap-yarn holder for the left shoulder.

Lace Heart

25-stitch motif

Only odd-numbered (WS) rounds/rows are charted.
Knit all even-numbered (RS) rounds;
purl all even-numbered (WS) rows.

Chart rows numbered (right side): 1, 3, 5, 7, 9, 11, 13, 15, 17, 19, 21, 23, 25, 27, 29, 31, 33, 35

Legend:

Symbol	Meaning	Symbol	Meaning
(blank)	knit	sk2p	sk2p
k2tog	k2tog	M1L	M1L
ssk	ssk	M1R	M1R
o	yo	5 to 1	5 to 1 (see Pattern Essentials)
k1 tbl	k1 tbl	3-st cluster	3-st cluster (see Pattern Essentials)

117

Knitting the Right Back

- With RS facing, place the first 29 back stitches on the needle for the right back, leaving remaining 29 stitches on hold for left back. With WS facing, attach yarn at center back.

- ROW 1 (WS): Purl.

- ROW 2: K1, ssk, knit to end of row — 1 stitch decreased.

- Repeat Rows 1 and 2 three more times. *You now have* 25 stitches.

- Work even until piece is 6 rows shorter than front, ending with a RS row.

SHAPING THE RIGHT NECK

- ROW 1 (WS): Bind off 9 stitches, purl to end of row. *You now have* 16 stitches.

- ROW 2: Knit to last 3 stitches, k2tog, k1. *You now have* 15 stitches.

- ROW 3: Purl.

- ROW 4: Repeat Row 2. *You now have* 14 stitches.

- ROW 5: Purl.

- ROW 6: Knit.

- Place 14 stitches on a scrap-yarn holder for the right shoulder.

Knitting the Left Back

- Place the held 29 left back stitches on the needle. With RS facing, attach yarn at the center back.

- ROW 1 (RS): Knit to the last 3 stitches, k2tog, k1 — 1 stitch decreased.

- ROW 2: Purl.

- Repeat Rows 1 and 2 three more times. *You now have* 25 stitches.

- Work even until piece is 5 rows shorter than front, ending with a WS row.

SHAPING THE LEFT NECK

- ROW 1 (RS): Bind off 9 stitches, knit to end of row. *You now have* 16 stitches.

- ROW 2: Purl.

- ROW 3: K1, ssk, knit to end of row. *You now have* 15 stitches.

- ROWS 4 AND 5: Repeat Rows 2 and 3 once more. *You now have* 14 stitches. Leave stitches on needle.

Joining the Fronts and Backs

- Place 14 left front stitches on the needle. Hold left front and back pieces together with RS facing and join stitches with three-needle bind off (see page 299).

- Place 14 right front stitches on the needle. Hold right front and back pieces together with RS facing and join stitches with three-needle bind off.

Finishing

- With double-point needles, and beginning at the center of the underarm, pick up and knit (see page 297) 70 stitches around the armhole. *Note:* Pick-up rate is approximately 2 stitches for every 3 rows.

- Purl 1 round, knit 1 round, purl 1 round.

- Bind off knitwise.

- With double-point needles or small straight needle and RS facing, and beginning at bottom of left back opening, pick up and knit 25 stitches to the neck edge. Knit 3 rows, bind off knitwise.

- With double-point needles or small straight needle and RS facing, and beginning at right back neck edge, pick up and knit 25 stitches to the bottom of the back opening. Knit 3 rows, bind off knitwise.

- With smaller circular needle and RS facing, and beginning at left back neck edge, pick up and knit 14 stitches to shoulder seam, 12 stitches along left front neck, 3 stitches from bound-off stitches at center front, 12 stitches along right front neck to shoulder seam, and 14 stitches to right back neck edge. *You now have* 55 stitches.

- Knit 3 rows, bind off knitwise. Cut the yarn, leaving a 20"/51 cm tail. Use a crochet hook to chain 8–10 stitches, or a long-enough chain to make a loop that accommodates your button. Fasten off and attach the end of the chain to the center back edge at the bottom of the neck edging.

- With the crochet hook and RS facing, work 1 round of single crochet along the bottom edge of the skirt.

- Weave in ends. Use a steam iron to smooth all areas of the dress. Sew button to neck edge, opposite button loop, with a sewing needle and thread.

{ *Joining New Yarn* }

If you find it necessary to join a new yarn, do this at the beginning of a row so you can hide the ends in the edge of the piece. Alternatively, if your lace pattern includes small fields of stockinette or garter stitch, you could join a new yarn here and hide the thread on the back side. Just don't try to join a new thread where you're doing yarnovers and other pattern stitches — at best it will be difficult to hide the ends, at worst you'll interrupt the pattern with a change of tension.

Welcome Home Baby Blanket

DESIGNED BY ELLEN HARVEY

Wrap your newborn in this lovely lacy yet warm welcome blanket. The size is perfect for carrying or for using in a car seat or pram. Beware: This could easily become baby's security blanket.

Finished Measurements

22"/56 cm wide and 27½"/70 cm long

Yarn

Valley Yarns Valley Superwash, 100% superwash extra fine merino wool, 485 yds (443 m)/8.8 oz (250 g), Natural

Needles

US 7 (4.5 mm) straight needles *or size you need to obtain correct gauge*

Gauge

19½ stitches and 26 rows = 4"/10 cm in Traveling Leaf pattern, blocked

Other Supplies

Yarn needle

Knitting the Blanket

- Cast on 107 stitches. Work seed stitch for 5 rows, beginning and ending with a WS row.
- Keeping the first 3 and last 3 stitches in seed stitch as established, work Traveling Leaf pattern over center 101 stitches until piece measures 26¾"/68 cm from cast on, or ¾"/2 cm less than desired length.
- Work seed stitch for 5 rows.

Finishing

- Bind off all stitches. Weave in ends. Block.

PATTERN ESSENTIALS

Traveling Leaf (multiple of 12 stitches plus 5)

- **Row 1 and all odd-numbered rows (WS):** Purl.
- **Rows 2 and 4 (RS):** K2, *k1, yo, k3, k2tog, k1, ssk, k3, yo; repeat from * to last 3 stitches, k3.
- **Rows 6 and 8:** K2, *k1, ssk, k3, yo, k1, yo, k3, k2tog; repeat from * to last 3 stitches, k3.
- Repeat Rows 1–8 for pattern.

Seed Stitch (worked over an odd number of stitches)

- **Row 1:** *K1, p1; repeat from * to last st, k1.
- Repeat Row 1 for pattern.

Traveling Leaf

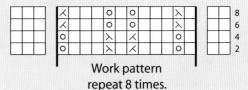

Work pattern
repeat 8 times.

Only RS (even-numbered) rows are charted.
Purl all WS (odd-numbered) rows.

☐ k on RS, p on WS

◸ k2tog

◹ ssk

⊡ yo

Granny's Little Diamond Lace Blankie

DESIGNED BY MYRNA A. I. STAHMAN

This blankie, knit circularly from the center out using a simple six-round lace diamond design, is just the right size for Granny to use when cuddling and rocking a grandchild.

Finished Measurements

30"/76 cm square, blocked

Yarn

Cascade Yarns Ecological Wool, 100% undyed Peruvian Highland wool, 478 yds (437 m)/8.8oz (250 g), Color 8010 Ecru

Needles

Set of US 6–10 (4–6 mm) double-point needles and same-size circular needle 24"/60 cm long *or size you need to obtain correct gauge* (Blankie shown was made by a relaxed knitter using size US 6 [4 mm] needles.)

Gauge

13 stitches and 21 rows = 4"/10 cm in Diamond Lace pattern, washed and blocked

Other Supplies

Stitch markers, yarn needle

Special Abbreviations

Sk2p slip 1 kwise, k2tog, pass slipped stitch over — 2 stitches decreased
S2kp slip 2 kwise, k1, pass 2 slipped stitches over — 2 stitches decreased

Knitting the Blankie

- Using double-point needles and a circular method (see page 290), cast on 8 stitches and join for working in the round, being careful not to twist stitches. Knit 1 round.

- Work Rounds 1–16 of Diamond Lace chart, working four repeats in each round, and increasing as shown. *You now have* 80 stitches: 20 stitches each in four sections.

- Work Rounds 17–22 of chart, working the 8-stitch pattern repeat once in each section. *You now have* 112 stitches: 28 stitches each in four sections.

- Changing to circular needle when appropriate, repeat Rounds 17–22 until piece is almost the desired finished size, ending with Round 22 and leaving enough yarn to work 6 rounds of the seed stitch border and the bind off.

Notes: Each time you repeat Rounds 17–22 there are enough new stitches to work the 8-stitch repeat one more time. For example, the second time you work Rounds 17–22 there are enough stitches to work the 8-stitch repeat twice, then when you repeat these rounds again there are enough stitches to work the repeat three times, and so on. The blankie shown worked Rounds 17–22 nine times for a total of 70 chart rounds, and used almost the entire skein of yarn.

Knitting the Border

- Place a marker at the end of each section if you have not already done so; take care that the markers do not slip underneath any yarnovers at the corners.

- ROUND 1: (Yo, *k1, p1; repeat from * to 2 stitches before marker, k1, yo, k1, slip marker) four times — 8 stitches increased: 2 stitches in each section.

- ROUND 2: (*K1, p1; repeat from * to 2 stitches before marker, k2, slip marker) four times.

- ROUND 3: (Yo, *p1, k1; repeat from * to 2 stitches before marker, p1, yo, k1, slip marker) four times — 8 stitches increased: 2 stitches in each section.

- ROUND 4: *P1, k1; repeat from * to end.

- ROUNDS 5 AND 6: Repeat Rounds 1 and 2 once more — 8 stitches increased: 2 stitches in each section.

- Bind off all stitches in seed stitch pattern without increasing at the corners.

Finishing

- Weave in ends. Wash and block.

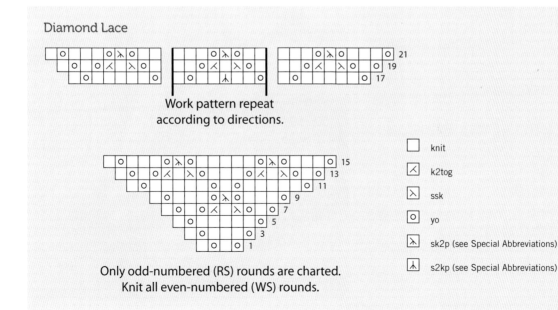

Diamond Lace

Work pattern repeat according to directions.

Only odd-numbered (RS) rounds are charted.
Knit all even-numbered (WS) rounds.

	knit
⟋	k2tog
⟍	ssk
○	yo
⟑	sk2p (see Special Abbreviations)
⟰	s2kp (see Special Abbreviations)

Lacy Pig Buddy

Designed by Julie L. Anderson

This delightful blanket buddy is a quick knit. It uses a simple yarnover technique for the body, and the rest is stockinette stitch. Embroidered eyes and nostrils make this safe for even the youngest babies.

Finished Measurements

Body: 11"/28 cm wide and 10"/25.5 cm tall
Head: approximately 5"/12.5 cm wide and 4"/10 cm tall

Yarn

Cascade 220 Superwash, 100% superwash wool, 220 yds (200 m)/3.5 oz (100 g), Color 835 Pink

Needles

US 8 (5 mm) straight needles *or size you need to obtain correct gauge* and set of four US 5 (3.75 mm) double-point needles

Gauge

20 stitches and 28 rows = 4"/10 cm in stockinette stitch on larger needles

Other Supplies

Stitch marker, polyester fiberfill or other stuffing material, yarn needle, scraps of black yarn for features

Knitting the Blanket

- Using straight needles cast on 46 stitches.
- ROWS 1 AND 2: Knit.
- ROW 3: K1, *yo, k1; repeat from * to last stitch, k1. *You now have* 90 stitches.
- ROW 4: K1, purl to last stitch, k1.
- ROW 5: K1, *k2tog; repeat from * to last stitch, k1. *You now have* 46 stitches.

124

- **ROWS 6 AND 7:** K1, *yo, k2tog; repeat from * to last stitch, k1.
- **ROWS 8 AND 9:** Knit.
- Repeat Rows 3–9 nine more times (do not repeat Rows 1 and 2). **Note:** Because the pattern repeat contains an odd number of rows the fabric will look similar on both sides and does not have defined RS and WS rows.
- **NEXT ROW:** Bind off 11 stitches, knit until there are 23 stitches on right-hand needle after previous bind off, bind off 12 stitches. Cut yarn and pull through last stitch. *You now have* 23 stitches.

Knitting the Head

- **NEXT ROW (RS):** Kfb in each stitch. *You now have* 46 stitches.
- Place 23 stitches onto each of two double-point needles by placing the first stitch onto Needle 1, the second stitch onto Needle 2, the third stitch onto Needle 1, the fourth stitch onto Needle 2, and so on. From this point on, the head is worked in the round on two needles. If you want, you can redistribute the stitches on more than two double-point needles as the head grows.
- With RS still facing, place marker and begin working in the round.
- **ROUND 1:** Knit.
- **ROUND 2:** (Kfb, k21, kfb) twice. *You now have* 50 stitches.
- **ROUND 3:** Knit.
- **ROUND 4:** (Kfb, k23, kfb) twice. *You now have* 54 stitches.
- **ROUND 5:** Knit.
- **ROUND 6:** (Kfb, k25, kfb) twice. *You now have* 58 stitches.
- **ROUNDS 7–20:** Knit.
- **ROUND 21:** (Ssk, k25, k2tog) twice. *You now have* 54 stitches.
- **ROUND 22:** Knit.
- **ROUND 23:** (Ssk, k23, k2tog) twice. *You now have* 50 stitches.
- **ROUND 24:** Knit.
- **ROUND 25:** (Ssk, k21, k2tog) twice. *You now have* 46 stitches.
- **ROUND 26:** Knit.
- **ROUND 27:** (Ssk, k19, k2tog) twice. *You now have* 42 stitches.

- **ROUND 28:** (Ssk, k17, k2tog) twice. *You now have* 38 stitches.
- **ROUND 29:** (Ssk, k15, k2tog) twice. *You now have* 34 stitches.
- **ROUND 30:** (Ssk, k13, k2tog) twice. *You now have* 30 stitches.
- **ROUND 31:** (Ssk, k11, k2tog) twice. *You now have* 26 stitches.
- Lightly stuff the head. If they are not already on two needles, place stitches on two needles with 13 stitches on each needle. Join live stitches at top of head with Kitchener stitch (see page 293). Weave in ends.

Knitting the Snout

- With double-point needles, cast on 21 stitches. Divide evenly onto three needles. Mark the first stitch and join into a round, being careful not to twist the stitches.
- **ROUNDS 1–4:** Knit.
- **ROUND 5:** Purl.
- **ROUND 6:** (K5, k2tog) three times. *You now have* 18 stitches.
- **ROUND 7:** (K4, k2tog) three times. *You now have* 15 stitches.
- **ROUND 8:** (K3, k2tog) three times. *You now have* 12 stitches.
- **ROUND 9:** (K2, k2tog) three times. *You now have* 9 stitches.
- Cut yarn, leaving an 8"/20.5 cm tail. Thread tail onto yarn needle and draw through remaining stitches; pull up snugly and secure. Stuff snout lightly and sew to middle of head. Weave in ends.

continued on next page

Knitting the Ears (make 2)

- With double-point needles, cast on 24 stitches, leaving a long tail for seaming, and divide evenly on three needles. Mark the first stitch and join into a round, being careful not to twist the stitches.

- ROUNDS 1 AND 2: Knit.

- ROUND 3: (Ssk, k8, k2tog) twice. *You now have* 20 stitches.

- ROUND 4: Knit.

- ROUND 5: (Ssk, k6, k2tog) twice. *You now have* 16 stitches.

- ROUND 6: Knit.

- ROUND 7: (Ssk, k4, k2tog) twice. *You now have* 12 stitches.

- ROUND 8: Knit.

- ROUND 9: (Ssk, k2, k2tog) twice. *You now have* 8 stitches.

- ROUND 10: (Ssk, k2tog) twice. *You now have* 4 stitches.

- Cut yarn, leaving a 6"/15 cm tail. Thread tail onto yarn needle and draw through remaining stitches; pull up snugly and secure. Use beginning tail to neatly sew the ears to the head, using the decreases along the sides of the head as a guide.

Finishing

- Using a small amount of black yarn, embroider eyes and nostrils, using the photo as a guide. Weave in all ends.

Meg's Doll Ensemble

DESIGNED BY DIANA FOSTER

Most girls can't get have too many outfits for their dolls, and this ensemble of hat, shawl, and leg warmers is sure to please. The clothes fit a standard 18-inch doll.

Finished Measurements

To fit an 18"/45.5 cm doll

Yarn

Brown Sheep Company Wildfoote Luxury Sock, 75% washable wool/25% nylon, 215 yds (197 m)/1.75 oz (50 g), Color SY800 Sonatina

Needles

US 3 (3.25mm) circular needles: two 24"/60 cm or one 40"/100 cm, or a set of four US 3 (3.25 mm) double-point needles *or size you need to obtain correct gauge*. See note below.

Gauge

28 stitches and 53 rows = 4"/10 cm in garter stitch

Other Supplies

Yarn needle, stitch marker

Note: Circular pieces may be knit with the magic loop method (see page 295) on one long circular needle, on two circulars, or on four double-point needles.

Knitting the Shawl

- Cast on 3 stitches.
- ROW 1: Yo, k3. *You now have* 4 stitches.
- ROW 2: Yo, k4. *You now have* 5 stitches.
- ROW 3: Yo, k2tog, yo, k3. *You now have* 6 stitches.
- ROW 4: Yo, k2tog, yo, knit to end of row — 1 stitch increased.
- ROWS 5–89: Repeat Row 4 eighty-five more times. *You now have* 92 stitches; piece is approximately 6¾"/17 cm long.

Knitting the Top Edging

- ROW 1 (EYELET ROW): K2, *yo, k2tog; repeat from * to end of row.
- ROWS 2 AND 3: Knit.

- Cast on 3 stitches onto left-hand needle and work 3-stitch I-cord bind off (see page 292) until only 3 I-cord stitches remain; piece is approximately 7"/18 cm long. Cut yarn and thread tail onto yarn needle; draw through last 3 stitches, pull up snugly and secure. Weave in end.

Knitting the Tie

- Cast on 3 stitches and work I-cord (see page 292) for 6"/15 cm. Cut yarn and thread tail onto yarn needle; draw through last 3 stitches, pull up snugly and secure. Weave in end. Thread I-cord through yarnover holes at each end of Eyelet Row and tie as shown.

Knitting the Hat

Cast on 70 stitches. Place marker and join into a round, being careful not to twist the stitches.

Knitting the Picot Edge

- Work in stockinette stitch for 1"/2.5 cm.
- PICOT ROUND: *Yo, k2tog; repeat from * to end of round.
- Work in stockinette stitch for 1"/2.5 cm.

Knitting the Lace

- ROUND 1: *Yo, k2tog; repeat from * to end of round.
- ROUNDS 2–4: Knit.
- Repeat Rounds 1–4 four more times, then knit every round until piece measures 3½"/9 cm from Picot Round.

Shaping the Crown

- ROUND 1: K1, *k2tog, k1; repeat from * to end of round. *You now have* 47 stitches.
- ROUND 2: Knit.
- ROUND 3: K1, *k2tog; repeat from * to end of round. *You now have* 24 stitches.
- ROUND 4: Knit.
- ROUNDS 5–7: *K2tog; repeat from * to end of round. *You now have* 3 stitches after Round 7.

Finishing

- Work 3-stitch I-cord for 2"/5 cm. Cut yarn and thread tail onto yarn needle; draw through last 3 stitches, pull up snugly and secure. Weave in end. Tie a knot at the base of the I-cord. Fold hem to WS along Picot Round and slipstitch in place to the inside. Weave in ends.

Knitting the Leg Warmers (make 2)

- Cast on 36 stitches. Place marker and join into a round, being careful not to twist the stitches.

Knitting the Bottom Rib

- ROUND 1: *(K1 tbl) twice, p2; repeat from * to end of round.
- Repeat Round 1 until piece measures 1"/2.5 cm.

Knitting the Lace

- ROUNDS 1–3: Knit.
- ROUND 4: *Yo, k2tog; repeat from * to end of round.
- Repeat Rounds 1–4 four more times, then work Rounds 1–3 once more.

Knitting the Top Rib

- Work as for bottom rib for 1"/2.5 cm.
- Bind off all stitches. Weave in ends.

it's a wrap

Scarves ∽ Cowls ∽ Shawls & Stoles

Spring Leaves Scarf

DESIGNED BY MARIN MELCHIOR

If you're new to lace knitting, this scarf is a great introduction. There are only five patterned rows, and they're easily memorized. And don't worry if your scarf doesn't look like the picture as you knit — blocking transforms its appearance. Go ahead. Wow your friends.

Finished Measurements

Approximately 9"/23 cm wide and 56"/142 cm long

Yarn

Classic Elite Silky Alpaca, 70% baby alpaca/30% silk, 460 yds (421 m)/1.75 oz (50 g), Color 2462 Cosmos

Needles

US 4 (3.5 mm) straight needles *or size you need to obtain correct gauge*

Gauge

28 stitches and 24 rows = 4"/10 cm in Spring Leaf Lace pattern, blocked

Other Supplies

Stitch markers (optional), stitch holder, yarn needle

130

Knitting the First Half of the Scarf

- Cast on 64 stitches and purl 1 WS row.

Knitting the Beginning Edge

- ROW 1 (RS): K3, ssk, k7, yo, k2, *yo, k7, s2kp, k7, yo, k2; repeat from * to last 12 stitches, yo, k7, k2tog, k3.

- ROW 2: Purl.

- ROWS 3–7: Repeat Rows 1 and 2 twice, then work Row 1 once more.

- ROW 8: P3, p2tog, purl to end. *You now have* 63 stitches.

Knitting the Spring Leaf Lace

- Keeping 3 stitches at the beginning and end of each row in stockinette stitch and working the center 57 stitches in pattern from the chart, work Rows 1–10 of Spring Leaf Lace chart 16 times (160 rows total).

Notes: The edge stitches are not shown on the chart. The pattern repeat begins as 19 stitches, increases to 25 stitches for Rows 1–6, decreases to 21 stitches after Row 7, and then decreases back to 19 stitches after Row 9. You may find it helpful to place markers between the pattern repeats.

- Cut yarn and place stitches on holder.

Knitting the Second Half of the Scarf

- Work as for the first half. Cut the yarn, leaving a very long tail — about three times the width of the scarf — for grafting.

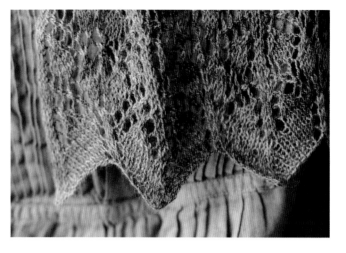

Finishing

- Join the two halves together with Kitchener stitch (see page 293). Block to desired dimensions. Weave in ends.

Spring Leaf Lace

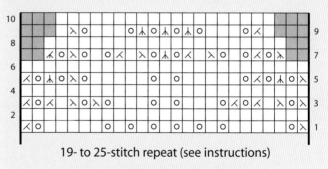

19- to 25-stitch repeat (see instructions)

Work pattern repeat 3 times.

☐ k on RS, p on WS		⋏ s2kp
⟋ k2tog		⟍ k3tog
⟍ ssk		⟋ sk2p
◯ yo		▨ no stitch

131

Christine's Alpaca Lace Scarf

DESIGNED BY MYRNA A. I. STAHMAN

This beautiful alpaca lace scarf begins with a simple lace pattern stitch in the center for the neckline. After completing the neckline lace, the tails are worked down from each end of the piece. Working both tails at the same time makes it possible to create tails of equal length while using all the yarn.

Finished Measurements

6"/15 cm wide and 56"/142 cm long, blocked

Yarn

Royal Fiber Spinnery Royal Alpaca DK, 100% North American alpaca, 250 yds (230 m)/3.2 oz (90 g), White

Needles

US 7 (4.5 mm) straight needles (two sets) *or size you need to obtain correct gauge* and a needle at least three sizes larger for binding off

Gauge

22 stitches and 26 rows = 4"/10 cm in Christine Lace pattern from chart, blocked

Other Supplies

Scrap yarn for provisional cast on, crochet hook similar in size to knitting needles for provisional cast on, yarn needle

PATTERN ESSENTIALS

Seed Stitch Border (worked over an odd number of stitches)

- **Row 1:** Slip 1 purlwise wyif, *k1, p1; repeat from * to last 4 stitches, k1, p1, k2.
- Repeat Row 1 for pattern.

Neckline Lace (multiple of 4 stitches plus 1)

- **Setup Row (WS):** Slip 1 purlwise wyif, k1, p1, k1, purl to last 4 stitches, k1, p1, k2.
- **Row 1 (RS):** Slip 1 purlwise wyif, k1, p1, k1, k2tog, yo, *k1 tbl, yo, sk2p, yo; repeat from * to last 7 stitches, k1 tbl, yo, ssk, k1, p1, k2.
- **Rows 2 and 4:** Slip 1 purlwise wyif, k1, p1, k1, purl to last 4 stitches, k1, p1, k2.
- **Row 3:** Slip 1 purlwise wyif, k1, p1, k1, k1 tbl, *yo, sk2p, yo, k1 tbl; repeat from * to last 4 stitches, k1, p1, k2.
- Repeat Rows 1–4 for pattern; do not repeat the Setup Row.

Knitting the Neckline Lace

Note: If you wind your yarn into a center-pull ball, you'll be able to work both tails at the same time, working one from the center and one from the outside of the ball.

- Using a provisional method (see pages 297–298), cast on 29 stitches. Following written instructions, work the WS Setup Row of the Neckline Lace pattern, then repeat Rows 1–4 until piece measures approximately 12"/30.5 cm, ending with an even-numbered (WS) row.

Knitting the Lace Tails

- Carefully remove the provisional cast on from the beginning of the Neckline Lace pattern and place the 29 live stitches on a needle — call this end Tail 1. Join the other end of your yarn (the one not attached to the live stitches at the end of the neckline lace).

Notes: The 4-stitch border continues as established at each side and is not shown on the chart. On both RS and WS rows, work the first 4 stitches as slip 1 purlwise wyif, k1, p1, k1, and work the last 4 stitches as k1, p1, k2.

Only RS rows are charted. On all WS rows, work 4 border stitches as established, purl to last 4 stitches, work 4 border stitches as established.

- Work 4 border stitches, work Setup Row 1 of Christine Lace chart over center 21 stitches of Tail 1, increasing to 25 stitches as shown, work 4 border stitches. *You now have 33 stitches.* Working borders at each side as established, work Setup Rows 2–4 on Tail 1.

Christine Lace

	knit
k2tog	k2tog
ssk	ssk
yo	yo
no stitch	no stitch
s2kp	s2kp
sk2p	sk2p

Chart rows numbered (bottom to top): 1, 3, 5, 7, 9, 11, with Setup 1 and Setup 3 below.

Only RS (odd-numbered) rows are charted.

See instructions for WS rows and borders.

Beaded Lace Scarf

Designed by Christine Nissley

Inspired by Estonian lace patterns, this lace scarf is highlighted by glass seed beads that are added as you knit — no prestringing necessary. The sample uses hex beads, which are extra sparkly.

Finished Measurements

10"/25.5 cm wide and 62"/157.5 cm long

Yarn

Prism Yarns Delicato Layers, 100% Tencel, 630 yds (576 m)/4 oz (113 g), Aegean

Needles

US 6 (4 mm) straight needles *or size you need to obtain correct gauge*

Gauge

29½ stitches and 20 rows = 4"/10 cm in Beaded Lace pattern from chart, blocked

Other Supplies

Stitch markers; stitch holder or spare needle same size or smaller than main needles; approximately 400 (12 g) size 8° hex beads; US 12 (1 mm) steel crochet hook, or size to fit through beads; yarn needle

---

PATTERN ESSENTIALS

Place Bead Slide a bead onto the crochet hook, remove next stitch from left-hand needle with crochet hook, push the bead down onto the stitch, return stitch to left-hand needle, then knit the beaded stitch.

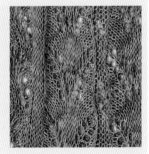

- Using the yarn attached to the live stitches at the other end of the scarf (call this Tail 2), and working border stitches at each side as established, work Setup Rows 1–4 of chart on stitches of Tail 2. *You now have 33 stitches.*

  Note: The 12-row chart repeat begins with 25 stitches, increases to 29 stitches for Rows 3–6, and then decreases back to 25 stitches for Rows 7–12.

- Repeat Rows 1–12 of chart (do not repeat the Setup Rows), working 12 rows on Tail 1 followed by 12 rows on Tail 2, until the scarf is almost as long as desired, with about 4–5 yds/3.7–4.6 m of yarn remaining for each tail, and ending after working Row 9. Work 5 rows of Seed Stitch Border, and then bind off loosely in pattern, using a much larger needle.

Finishing

- Weave in ends. Wash and block.

Knitting the Edging

- Cast on 73 stitches, placing markers after the second stitch and every 10 stitches thereafter. Slip all markers as you come to them.

- ROW 1 (RS): Slip 1 purlwise wyif, k1, *yo, k3, p3tog, k3, yo, k1; repeat from * to last stitch, k1.

- ROWS 2 AND 4 (WS): Slip 1 purlwise wyif, purl to last stitch, k1.

- ROW 3: Slip 1 purlwise wyif, k1 *yo, k1, yo, k2tog, p3tog, ssk, (yo, k1) twice; repeat from * to last stitch, k1.

- Repeat Rows 1–4 three more times, then work Rows 1 and 2 once more, removing markers on last row.

- Work 2 rows of seed stitch as follows.

- ROW 1: *K1, P1; repeat from * to last stitch, k1.

- ROW 2: *K1, p1; repeat from * to last stitch, kfb. *You now have* 74 stitches.

- Cut yarn, leaving a long tail for grafting, and place stitches on holder or spare needle. Make a second edging in the same manner; leave stitches on the main needles and do not cut yarn.

Knitting the Shawl Body

- Work Rows 1–12 of Beaded Lace chart (see page 136) 22 times (264 chart rows completed).

- Leave stitches on needle.

Finishing

- Graft live stitches at end of shawl body together with held stitches of edging piece using Kitchener stitch (see page 293). Weave in ends. Block to size.

Beaded Lace Scarf

Beaded Lace

Chart row numbers (odd, top right): 11, 9, 7, 5, 3, 1

Chart row numbers (even, bottom left): 12, 10, 8, 6, 4, 2

Legend:

☐ k on RS, p on WS	� k2tog	Ⓑ place bead
• p on RS	⊠ ssk	
○ yo	⅄ sk2p	

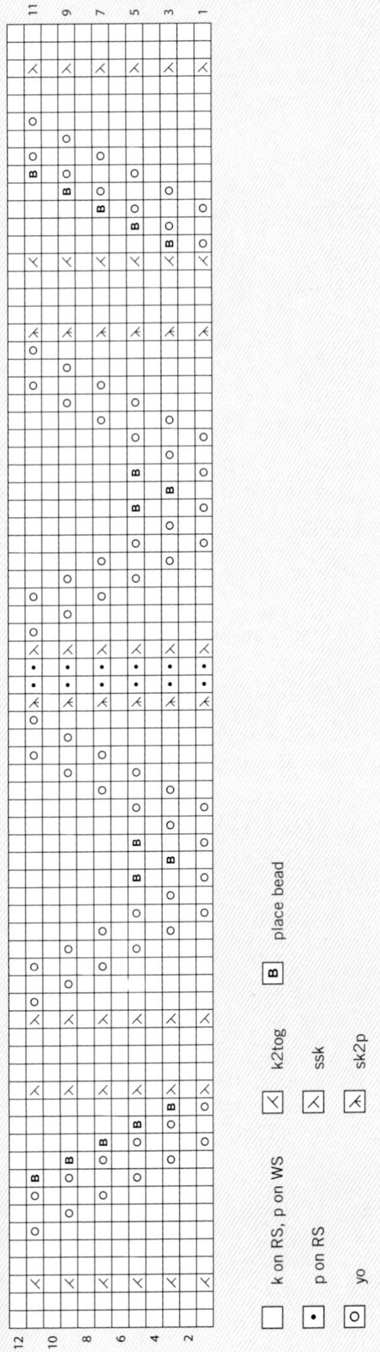

Mezzaluna Scarf

DESIGNED BY MARIANNE HOBART

With its crescent shape, this scarf can be worn wrapped around the neck or simply draped over the shoulders as a shawlette. The scarf is knit end to end, then turned 90 degrees for adding the border.

Finished Measurements

Approximately 57"/145 cm long and 10"/25.5 cm deep in center

Yarn

Cherry Tree Hill Supersock Silk, 85% superwash merino wool/15% silk, 420 yds (384 m)/4 oz (113 g), Drowning Waters *or* Fibernymph Dye Works Bedazzled, 75% superwash merino wool/20% nylon/5% Stellina, 438 yds (400 m)/3.5 oz (100 g), Sea Nymph

Needles

US 5 (3.75 mm) circular needle 32"/80 cm long *or size you need to obtain correct gauge*

Gauge

22 stitches and 36 rows = 4"/10 cm in garter stitch, blocked

Other Supplies

Yarn needle

PATTERN ESSENTIALS

Eyelet Lace (stitch count varies during shaping)

- **Row 1 (RS):** K1, *yo, k2tog; repeat from * to last stitch, k1, slip 2 purlwise wyif.
- **Row 2 (WS):** K3, *yo, p2tog; repeat from * to last stitch, k1.
- **Rows 3 and 4:** Repeat Rows 1 and 2.
- **Rows 5–14:** Work 10 rows in garter stitch (knit every row), slipping last 2 stitches of WS rows purlwise wyif.

Knitting the Scarf Body

Notes: Every RS row ends with slip 2 stitches purlwise wyif to create a nice rolled finish at the neck edge. Slip all stitches purlwise.

Beginning the Garter Wedge

- Cast on 5 stitches.
- ROW 1 (RS): K3, slip 2 wyif.
- ROWS 2 AND 4 (WS): Knit.
- ROW 3: Kfb, k2, slip 2 wyif. *You now have* 6 stitches.
- ROW 5: Knit to last 2 stitches, slip 2 wyif.
- ROWS 6 AND 8: Knit.
- ROW 7: Kfb, knit to last 2 stitches, slip 2 wyif — 1 stitch increased.
- Repeat Rows 5–8 fifteen more times, then work Rows 5 and 6 once more. *You now have* 22 stitches.

Knitting the Eyelet Lace Pattern

- Following written instructions, work Rows 1–14 of Eyelet Lace seven times, increasing 1 stitch at the beginning of Rows 7 and 11 in each repeat by working the first stitch of these rows as kfb. *You now have* 36 stitches.

- Work Rows 1–14 of Eyelet Lace twice, increasing 1 stitch at the beginning of Rows 7, 9, 11, and 13 in each repeat as before. *You now have* 44 stitches.

- Work Rows 1–14 of Eyelet Lace twice with no increases.

- Work Rows 1–14 of Eyelet Lace twice, decreasing 1 stitch at the beginning of Rows 7, 9, 11, and 13 in each repeat by working the first 2 stitches of these rows as k2tog. *You now have* 36 stitches.

Chart legend:
21
19
17
15
13
11
9
7
5
3
1

	knit
⨯	k2tog
⟋	ssk
o	yo
⟍	sk2p

Work pattern repeat 13 times.

Only odd-numbered (RS) rows are charted. See instructions for border stitches and even-numbered (WS) rows.

Mezzaluna Border

- Work Rows 1–14 of Eyelet Lace seven times, decreasing 1 stitch at the beginning of Rows 7 and 11 in each repeat as before. *You now have* 22 stitches.

- Work Rows 1–6 of Eyelet Lace once with no decreases.

Ending the Garter Wedge

- Continue in garter stitch as follows.

- **ROW 1 (RS):** K2tog, knit to last 2 stitches, slip 2 wyif — 1 stitch decreased.

- **ROWS 2 AND 4 (WS):** Knit.

- **ROW 3:** Knit to last 2 stitches, slip 2 wyif.

- Repeat Rows 1–4 fifteen more times, then work Rows 1–3 once more. *You now have* 5 stitches. Bind off all stitches knitwise. Cut yarn.

Knitting the Border

- With RS facing, attach yarn and pick up and knit (see page 297) 293 stitches along the curved edge at the end of RS rows as follows: 3 stitches at bound-off edge,

41 stitches along the beginning garter wedge, 4 stitches along Rows 1–6 of Eyelet Lace worked at end of pattern section, 10 stitches each from the next 20 full Eyelet Lace repeats (4 stitches from eyelet section and 6 stitches from garter section of each repeat), 42 stitches from the ending garter wedge, and 3 stitches at cast-on edge.

- ROW 1 (WS): Knit.

- ROW 2 (RS): K2, yo, knit to last 2 stitches, yo, k2. *You now have 295 stitches.*

- ROWS 3 AND 5: K2, purl to last 2 stitches, k2.

- ROW 4: K2, yo, k2, *yo, k2tog; repeat from * to last 3 stitches, k1, yo, k2. *You now have 297 stitches.*

- ROW 6: Repeat Row 2. *You now have 299 stitches.*

- ROW 7: Repeat Row 3.

Knitting the Lace Pattern

Note: The first and last 2 stitches of every row are knit to form a garter stitch border. Only RS (odd-numbered) rows are charted; the first and last 2 border stitches are not shown on the chart. Work all WS rows as k2, purl to last 2 stitches, k2.

- Work Rows 1–22 of the Mezzaluna Border chart. *You now have 321 stitches (including border stitches not shown on chart).* Bind off very loosely with your method of choice.

Finishing

- Weave in ends. Block in crescent shape.

Luxe Möbius Scarf

DESIGNED BY SARAH-HOPE PARMETER

A picot bind off is the perfect accent for the undulating edge of this reversible scarf. Wear it as an infinity scarf for decoration, or wrap it a few times around your neck for warmth.

139

Finished Measurements

Approximately 7"/18 cm wide and 47"/119.5 cm circumference

Yarn

Curious Creek Fibers Gombe, 100% superfine alpaca, 293 yds (268 m)/3.5 oz (100 g), Plum Thunder

Needles

US 7 (4.5 mm) circular needle 40"/100 cm long *or size you need to obtain correct gauge*

Gauge

17 stitches and 15 rows = 4"/10 cm in Möbius Lace, blocked

Other Supplies

10 stitch markers (one in a unique color), cable needle, yarn needle

Special Abbreviations

C3/3B slip 3 stitches onto cable needle and hold in back, work 3 stitches from left-hand needle as they appear (i.e., knit the knits and purl the purls), work 3 stitches from cable needle as they appear

Knitting the Scarf

- Cast on 200 stitches using the Möbius method (see page 296), not counting the stitches on the cable beneath the right-hand needle. Place the unique-colored marker for beginning of round.

- NEXT ROUND: Placing same-colored markers every 40 stitches to help with counting, work 20-stitch pattern from Round 1 of Möbius Lace chart 10 times on 200 stitches for the first half of round, slip the beginning-of-round marker, and work Round 1 of chart 10 times over 200 stitches for second half of the round, ending with the beginning-of-round marker at the tip of the left-hand needle again. *You now have* 400 stitches.

- Continuing in chart pattern, work Rounds 2–12 once, then work Rounds 1–12 once more, working the 20-stitch pattern 20 times in each round (10 times over each half of the stitches). *Note:* The cables are worked in a reversible k1, p1 rib; when working a C3/3B cable, work the stitches as they appear, either as knits or purls.

- Knit 1 round.

- Purl 1 round.

- Knit 1 round.

Finishing

- Work picot bind off as follows: *Cast on 3 stitches, bind off 7 stitches; repeat from * until all stitches are bound off. Weave in ends. Lightly steam if necessary.

Möbius Lace

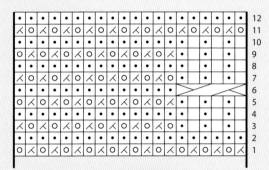

20-stitch repeat

Work according to instructions.

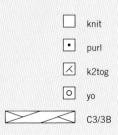

☐ knit

• purl

k2tog

○ yo

C3/3B

Emerald Lace Scarf

Designed by Rebecca Mercier

Knit in a fingering-weight yarn of mixed fibers, this scarf is useful for all seasons — simply change the color. The pattern is presented in both text and chart formats.

Finished Measurements

4½"/11.5 cm wide and 62"/157.5 cm long

Yarn

SWTC Tofutsies, 50% superwash wool/25% Soysilk/22.5% cotton/2.5% chitin, 465 yds (425 m)/3.5 oz (100 g), Color 942 Tropical TOEcan

Needles

US 5 (3.75 mm) straight needles *or size you need to obtain correct gauge* and US 6 (4 mm) straight needles

Gauge

31 stitches and 33 rows = 4"/10 cm in Emerald Lace pattern on smaller needle, blocked

Other Supplies

Yarn needle

Special Abbreviations

LT (left twist) with the right-hand needle behind the left-hand needle, knit the second stitch through the back loop and leave it on the needle, knit the first stitch, and slip both stitches from the left-hand needle

RT (right twist) K2tog, leaving stitches on left-hand needle, knit the first stitch again, and slip both stitches from the left-hand needle

Knitting the Scarf

- With larger needle, cast on 35 stitches using knitted-on cast on (see page 294). Change to smaller needle and work Rows 1–8 of Emerald Lace pattern following chart or written directions.

Note: Slip stitches purlwise.

- **ROW 1 (RS):** K1, slip 1 wyif, k1, k1 tbl, yo, k3tog, yo, k4, (k2tog, yo) twice, RT, k1, LT, (yo, ssk) twice, k4, yo, sk2p, yo, k1 tbl, k1, slip 1 wyif, k1.

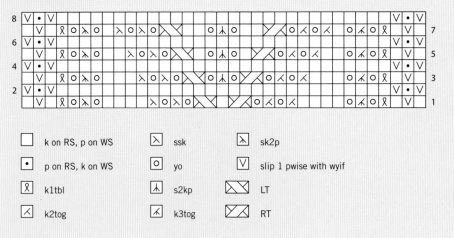

{ Use Pointy Needles }

When knitting lace, you may sometimes need to knit or purl three stitches together and it can be difficult to get your needle into the three stitches. This is easily accomplished with pointy needles made especially for lace knitting.

- **ROW 2 AND ALL EVEN-NUMBERED ROWS TO ROW 6 (WS):** Slip 1 wyif, k1, slip 1 wyif, p29, slip 1 wyif, k1, slip 1 wyif.

- **ROW 3:** K1, slip 1 wyif, k1, k1 tbl, yo, k3tog, yo, k3, (k2tog, yo) twice, RT, yo, s2kp, yo, LT, (yo, ssk) twice, k3, yo, sk2p, yo, k1 tbl, k1, slip 1 wyif, k1.

- **ROW 5:** K1, slip 1 wyif, k1, k1 tbl, yo, k3tog, yo, k2, (k2tog, yo) twice, RT, k1, yo, s2kp, yo, k1, LT, (yo, ssk) twice, k2, yo, sk2p, yo, k1 tbl, k1, slip 1 wyif, k1.

- **ROW 7:** K1, slip 1 wyif, k1, k1 tbl, yo, k3tog, yo, k1, (k2tog, yo) twice, RT, k2, yo, s2kp, yo, k2, LT, (yo, ssk) twice, k1, yo, sk2p, yo, k1 tbl, k1, slip 1 wyif, k1.

- **ROW 8:** Repeat Row 2.

- Repeat Rows 1–8 to desired length, ending with Row 8.

Finishing

- Bind off loosely. Weave in ends. Block.

Emerald Lace

	k on RS, p on WS		ssk		sk2p
	p on RS, k on WS		yo		slip 1 pwise with wyif
	k1tbl		s2kp		LT
	k2tog		k3tog		RT

River Rapids

Designed by Rae Blackledge

River Rapids is so named because the lace pattern has lots of movement. The scarf is worked in one piece from end to end.

Finished Measurements
10½"/27 cm wide and 70"/178 cm long

Yarn
Madelinetosh Prairie, 100% superwash merino wool, 840 yds (768 m)/4 oz (113 g), Mourning Dove

Needles
US 4 (3.5 mm) straight needles *or size you need to obtain correct gauge*

Gauge
30½ stitches and 37 rows = 4"/10 cm in River Rapids pattern, blocked

Other Supplies
Cable needle, yarn needle

Special Abbreviations
1/1 LC   slip 1 stitch onto a cable needle, hold in front, knit the next stitch, knit the stitch from the cable needle

PATTERN NOTES

Odd-numbered rows are WS rows. Working the edge stitches as shown, work the 18-stitch pattern repeat four times in each row.

143

Knitting the Scarf

- Cast on 80 stitches.
- Work Rows 1–4 of River Rapids chart once.
- Work Rows 5–24 of chart 32 times for scarf as shown. *Note:* To adjust the length, repeat Rows 5–24 more or fewer times until anticipated blocked measurement is ½"/13 mm shorter than desired, leaving enough yarn to work 3 more rows and the bind off.
- Work Rows 25–27 of chart once.

Finishing

- Bind off. Weave in ends. Block to measurements.

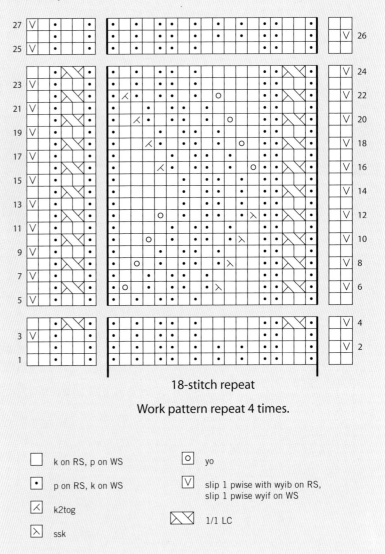

River Rapids

18-stitch repeat

Work pattern repeat 4 times.

	k on RS, p on WS		yo
•	p on RS, k on WS	V	slip 1 pwise with wyib on RS, slip 1 pwise wyif on WS
⟋	k2tog		1/1 LC
⟍	ssk		

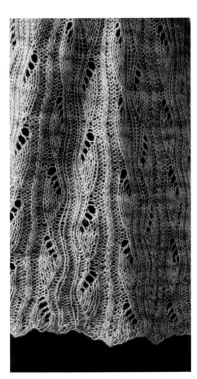

144

Butterflies Are Free

DESIGNED BY JUDITH DURANT

Ruffles are a girl's new best friend, and this scarf is loaded with them. You'll work a lower ruffle and a base, then work the next ruffle and attach it to the base, and continue until all the ruffles are added for half the scarf. Then you'll do it again for the other half and join the halves together at the center back. Warning: This is not for the faint of needles!

Finished Measurements
Base: 4"/10 cm wide and 58"/147.5 cm long; each ruffle: about 3"/7.5 cm deep

Yarn
Schaefer Yarns Audrey, 50% merino wool/50% cultivated silk, 700 yds (640 m)/4 oz (113 g), Pomegranate

Needles
Two US 1½ (2.5 mm) circular needles or two sets of US 1½ (2.5 mm) straight needles *or size you need to obtain correct gauge*

Gauge
32 stitches and 36 rows = 4"/10 cm in stockinette stitch

Other Supplies
Yarn needle

Knitting the First Half of the Scarf

Note: Knit nine ruffles for the first half.

Knitting the First Ruffle

- Using the long-tail method (see page 294), cast on 103 stitches. Knit 1 WS row. *Note:* Using this cast on and knitting 1 row forms a garter ridge on the RS, which helps prevent the ruffle from curling.

- Work Rows 1–22 of the Ruffle chart, working the repeat three times in each row, and purling all stitches in Row 22. *You now have* 37 stitches.

- Work Rows 23–32 once, then work Rows 23–31 again, ending with a RS row. Cut yarn but leave stitches on needle.

Knitting Second Ruffle

- With an empty needle, cast on and work as for first ruffle through Row 21. *You now have* 37 stitches.

- Pick up the needle with the live stitches of the first ruffle and hold the needles together with the WS of both pieces facing you, and the second ruffle behind the first.

- NEXT ROW (WS, ROW 22 OF RUFFLE CHART): *Purl 1 stitch from back needle together with 1 stitch from front needle; repeat from * until all stitches are joined. *You now have* 37 stitches on one needle.

{ *Ripping without a Lifeline* }

If you haven't used a lifeline but have to rip back more than a couple of rows, remove the knitting from the needles and rip back to the row *before* the one you want to rework. Place the stitches back on a needle and undo the last row one stitch at a time. This will ensure that you don't miss any yarnovers and keep the integrity of the pattern.

- With both ruffles now joined on the same needle, work Rows 23–32 once, then work rows 23–31 again, ending with a RS row. Cut yarn but leave stitches on needle.

Knitting Subsequent Ruffles

- Work as for second ruffle, joining each new ruffle to the live stitches of the top ruffle held on the other needle. Continue until you have nine ruffles, ending the last ruffle on Row 31 as for previous ruffles. Cut yarn but leave stitches on needle.

Knitting the Second Half of the Scarf

- Work as for first half on the other needle(s).

Joining the Halves

- Hold the needles together with RS together and WS facing out. Purl 1 stitch from back needle together with 1 stitch from front needle; *pl from back needle together with 1 stitch from front needle, slip previous stitch over the p2tog to bind off 1 stitch; repeat from * until all stitches are joined and bound off.

Finishing

- Weave in all ends. Block the scarf so that each ruffle flares out in a semicircle.

Ruffle

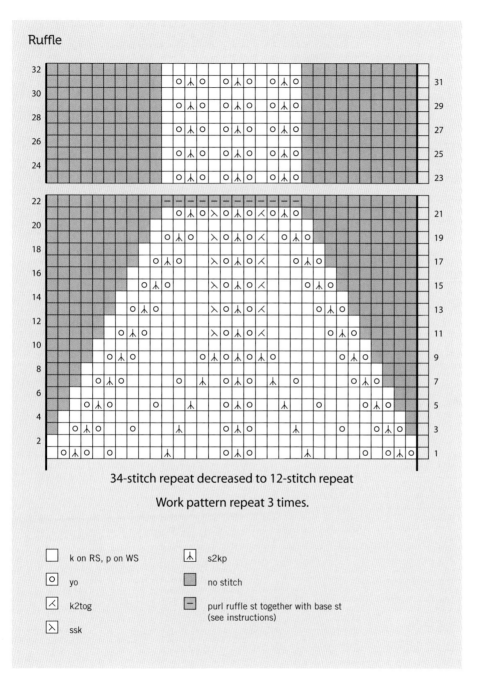

34-stitch repeat decreased to 12-stitch repeat

Work pattern repeat 3 times.

☐ k on RS, p on WS	人 s2kp
○ yo	▨ no stitch
⧄ k2tog	— purl ruffle st together with base st (see instructions)
⧅ ssk	

Lake Effect Scarf

DESIGNED BY SARAH BURTON

A garter stitch background hosts snowflakes worked in a variation of a Brioche Cascade stitch enhanced with beads. The glass beads are a wonderful complement to the wispy mohair, and they are added to slip stitches with a crochet hook.

Finished Measurements

4½"/11.5 cm wide and 62"/157.5 cm long

Yarn

Rowan Kidsilk Haze, 70% mohair/30% silk, 229 yds (210 m)/
0.88 oz (25 g), Color 592 Heavenly

Needles

US 9 (5.5 mm) straight needles *or size you need to obtain correct gauge*

Gauge

13 stitches and 36 rows = 4"/10 cm in pattern

Other Supplies

18 g (approximately 220) size 6° glass beads, US 10 (1.3 mm) steel crochet hook or size to fit through beads, yarn needle

PATTERN ESSENTIALS

brk (brioche knit, also known as a "bark")   knit the stitch slipped in the previous row together with its yarnover.

PB (Place Bead)   slide a bead onto the crochet hook, remove next stitch from left-hand needle with the crochet hook, push the bead down onto the stitch, return stitch to left-hand needle, and work the beaded stitch in pattern.

yfsl1yo (yarn forward, slip 1, yarn over)   bring the yarn forward between the needles, slip 1 stitch purlwise, bring the yarn to the back over the top of the right-hand needle to create a yarnover on top of the slipped stitch. The working yarn is now in position to knit the next stitch.

yfsl1yoyo (yarn forward, slip 1 purlwise, yarn over twice) bring the yarn forward between the needles, slip 1 stitch purlwise, bring the yarn to the back over the top of the right-hand needle, then wrap the yarn completely around the right-hand needle again to create a double yarnover. The working yarn is now in position to knit the next stitch. On the following row, drop 1 wrap of the double yarnover to create an elongated loop.

+   the + sign is used to designate the number of yarnovers on top of the slipped stitch. For example, yfsl1+yo means to bring the yarn forward (yf), slip 1 stitch plus its existing yarnover from the previous row (sl1+), then bring the yarn to the back over the top of the right-hand needle to create another yarnover on top of the slipped stitch (yo). A + sign is added for each yarnover that was slipped in an earlier row.

brk+++++1   knit the stitch together with the 5 yarnovers on top, which were slipped on previous rows; in other words, knit 6 loops together.

Knitting the Scarf

• Cast on 15 stitches loosely.

• ROW 1 (WS): K3, *PB, yfsl1yoyo, k3; repeat from * to end of row. *Note:* The slipped stitch of each ylsl1yoyo is the beaded stitch.

• ROW 2: (RS) K3, *yfsl1+yo (dropping the extra wrap of the double yo as you slip it to form an elongated loop), k3; repeat from * to end of row.

• ROW 3: K3, *yfsl1++yo, k3; repeat from * to end of row.

• ROW 4: K3, *yfsl1+++yo, k3; repeat from * to end of row.

• ROW 5: K3, *yfsl1++++yo, k3; repeat from * to end of row.

• ROW 6: K3, *brk+++++1, k3; repeat from * to end of row.

• Repeat Rows 1–6 until the scarf is desired length.

Finishing

• Bind off all stitches loosely. Weave in ends. Block.

Menat Scarf

DESIGNED BY JEAN M. CLEMENT

The ribbed neck makes this a seaman's scarf, meant to hug the neck for maximum warmth. This one is knit in both directions; it begins with a provisional cast on and is knit to one end, then the stitches are picked up for working the ribbed neck section and the other end.

Finished Measurements

8"/20.5 cm at widest point, 4½"/11.5 cm at narrowest point (with ribbing relaxed), and 46"/117 cm long

Yarn

Brooks Farm Yarn Acero, 60% superwash wool/20% silk/ 20% viscose, 420 yds (384 m)/4 oz (113 g), Color NY12

Needles

US 7 (4.5 mm) straight needles *or size you need to obtain correct gauge*

Gauge

20 stitches and 30 rows = 4"/10 cm in Lace pattern

Other Supplies

Scrap yarn for provisional cast on, US G/6 (4 mm) crochet hook, yarn needle

PATTERN ESSENTIALS

Neck Ribbing (multiple of 10 stitches plus 5)

- **Row 1 (RS):** *K5, p5; repeat from * to last 5 stitches, k5.
- **Row 2 (WS):** *P5, k5; repeat from * to last 5 stitches, p5.
- Repeat Rows 1 and 2 for pattern.

Lace (multiple of 7 stitches)

- **Row 1 and all WS rows:** Purl.
- **Row 2 (RS):** *Yo, k1, ssk, k4; repeat from * to end of row.
- **Row 4:** *K1 tbl, yo, k1, ssk, k3; repeat from * to end of row.
- **Row 6:** *K1, k1 tbl, yo, k1, sk2p, k1, yo; repeat from * to end of row.
- **Row 8:** *K2, k1 tbl, yo, s2kp, yo, k1 tbl; repeat from * to end of row.
- **Row 10:** *K3, k2tog, yo, k1 tbl, k1; repeat from * to end of row.
- **Row 12:** *K2, k2tog, yo, k1 tbl, k2; repeat from * to end of row.
- Repeat Rows 1–12 for pattern.

Lace

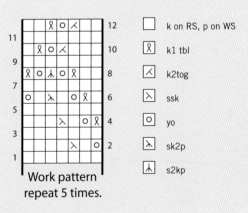

	k on RS, p on WS
ℓ	k1 tbl
⅄	k2tog
⅄	ssk
○	yo
⅄	sk2p
⅄	s2kp

Work pattern repeat 5 times.

Knitting the First Lace End

- With scrap yarn and crochet hook, cast on 41 stitches using a provisional method (see page 297). Keeping the first and last 3 stitches in garter stitch (knit every row) throughout and working Lace pattern over center 35 stitches, follow written or charted pattern to work Rows 1–12 of Lace pattern 11 times, or until piece measures 17½"/44.5 cm. Work 5 rows of garter stitch. Bind off using the sewn bind off (see page 298).

Knitting the Neck Ribbing

- Carefully remove scrap yarn from the provisional cast on and place stitches on the needle. Maintaining garter stitch border on first and last 3 stitches, work Neck Ribbing over center 35 stitches for 10"/25.5 cm, ending with a RS row.

Knitting the Second Lace End

- Maintaining garter stitch border on first and last 3 stitches, work Rows 1–12 of Lace pattern 11 times (or same number as first end). Work 5 rows of garter stitch. Bind off using the sewn bind off.

Finishing

- Weave in ends. Block scarf ends, but not neck ribbing.

Raindrops Scarf

DESIGNED BY LAURA HEIN ECKEL

This lace pattern is perfect for a scarf — it looks great on both sides! It's also quick to knit on large needles with only 27 stitches per row.

Finished Measurements

Approximately 6¾"/17 cm wide and 40"/102 cm long

Yarn

Plymouth Yarn Baby Alpaca Brush, 80% baby alpaca/20% acrylic, 110 yds (100 m)/1.75 oz (50 g), Color 1710

Needles

US 10 (6 mm) straight needles *or size you need to obtain correct gauge*

Gauge

16 stitches and 18 rows = 4"/10 cm in pattern, blocked

Other Supplies

Yarn needle

Knitting the Scarf

- Cast on 27 stitches.

  Note: Slip the first stitch of every row knitwise.

- SETUP ROWS 1 AND 2: Slip 1, knit to end of row.

- ROW 1: Slip 1, k2, *yo, sk2p, yo, k3; repeat from * to end of row.

- ROW 2: Slip 1, k2, purl to last 3 stitches, k3.

- ROWS 3–8: Repeat Rows 1 and 2 three times.

- ROW 9: Slip 1, k5, *yo, sk2p, yo, k3; repeat from * to last 3 stitches, k3.

- ROW 10: Slip 1, k2, purl to last 3 stitches, k3.

- ROWS 11–16: Repeat Rows 9 and 10 three times.
- Repeat Rows 1–16 of pattern to desired length, or until enough yarn remains for 2 more rows and the bind off, ending with Row 8 or Row 16 of pattern. *Note:* Sample was worked with 11 complete pattern repeats.

- NEXT ROW: Slip 1, knit to end of row.
- LAST ROW: Slip 1, knit to end of row.

Finishing

- Bind off loosely. Weave in ends. Block.

{ Picking Up a Missed Yarnover }

If you're knitting along and realize that you forgot to make a yarnover in the previous row, you can easily pick one up in this row (figure 1). Place the left needle from front to back under the thread that's between the needles (figure 2). This becomes the yarnover, and you can work it as instructed.

If you missed a yarnover from two rows before, you can usually still correct this without going back. If you pull the two needles away from each other, you should be able to see two parallel threads between the stitches on the needles (figure 3). Insert the right needle under both threads from front to back (figure 4). Use the left needle to lift the lower thread over the upper thread and off the needle (figure 5). Now transfer the newly made stitch to the left needle and proceed according to plan.

figure 1

figure 2

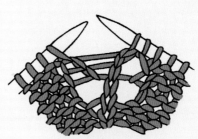

figure 3

figure 4

figure 5

Paper Lanterns Scarf

DESIGNED BY SARAH-HOPE PARMETER

The billowing shape of this scarf is reminiscent of pleated Japanese paper lanterns. The large mesh sections contrast vividly with the small yarnover bands, which are knit at a much tighter gauge.

Finished Measurements
Width varies from about 5¼" to 9"/13.5 to 23 cm, 60"/152.5 cm long

Yarn
Hand Maiden Fine Yarn Silk Twist, 65% wool/35% silk, 437 yds (400 m)/3.5 oz (100 g), Green

Needles
US 1 (2.25 mm) and US 6 (4 mm) straight needles *or sizes you need to obtain correct gauge*

Gauge
About 27 stitches = 4"/10 cm on larger needles for Section A; about 23½ stitches = 4"/10 cm on smaller needles for Section B. **Note:** Exact gauge is not crucial to this project.

Other Supplies
Yarn needle

Knitting the Scarf

- Using smaller needles, cast on 31 stitches.
- Work 8 setup rows as follows.
- ROWS 1–3: Knit.
- ROW 4: *K2tog, yo; repeat from * to last st, k1.

154

- ROWS 5–7: Knit.
- ROW 8: *Kfb; repeat from * to last stitch, k1. *You now have* 61 stitches.

Knitting Section A

- Change to larger needles.
- ROW 1: Knit.
- ROW 2: *K2tog, yo; repeat from * to last stitch, k1.
- ROW 3: Knit.
- ROW 4: K1, *yo, ssk; repeat from * to end of row.
- Repeat Rows 1–4 eight more times, then work Row 1 once more (37 rows completed).

Knitting Section B

- Change to smaller needles.
- ROW 1: *K2tog; repeat from * to last stitch, k1. *You now have* 31 stitches.
- ROWS 2–4: Knit.
- ROW 5: *K2tog, yo; repeat from * to last stitch, k1.
- ROWS 6–8: Knit.
- ROW 9: *Kfb; repeat to last stitch, k1. *You now have* 61 stitches.
- Alternate Sections A and B as desired (sample shows seven repeats of each), ending with Row 8 of the final Section B. *You now have* 31 stitches.

Finishing

- Bind off all stitches using smaller needles. Weave in ends. Block to desired measurements.

Chantilly Lace Scarf

DESIGNED BY REBECCA MERCIER

Chantilly bobbin lace made in France during the seventeenth century was usually worked in black silk. This modern version is knitted in a lovely French blue silk-and-wool yarn. The lace pattern naturally forms a scalloped beginning and end.

155

Finished Measurements
6"/15 cm wide and 66"/167.5 cm long

Yarn
Jagger Spun Zephyr 2/18, 50% Chinese tussah silk/50% fine merino wool, 630 yds (576 m)/2 oz (57 g), Aegean Blue

Needles
US 5 (3.75 mm) straight needles *or size you need to obtain correct gauge*

Gauge
32 stitches and 30 rows = 4"/10 cm in Chantilly Lace pattern, blocked

Other Supplies
Yarn needle

Knitting the Scarf

- Cast on 48 stitches. Work Rows 1–10 of Chantilly Lace following chart or written instructions to desired length (scarf shown has 50 repeats).

Finishing

- Bind off loosely. Weave in ends. Block.

PATTERN ESSENTIALS

Chantilly Lace (multiple of 14 stitches plus 6)

Note: Slip stitches purlwise.

- **Row 1 and all odd-numbered rows to Row 9 (WS):** Slip 1 wyif, k1, slip 1 wyif, p to last 3 stitches, slip 1 wyif, k1, slip 1 wyif.
- **Row 2 (RS):** K1, slip 1 wyib, k1, *yo, k3, k2tog, ssk, k3, yo, k4; repeat from * to last 3 stitches, k1, slip 1 wyib, k1.
- **Row 4:** K1, slip 1 wyib, k1, *k1, yo, k3, k2tog, ssk, k3, yo, k3; repeat from * to last 3 stitches, k1, slip 1 wyib, k1.
- **Row 6:** K1, slip 1 wyib, k1, *k2, yo, k3, k2tog, ssk, k3, yo, k2; repeat from * to last 3 stitches, k1, slip 1 wyib, k1.
- **Row 8:** K1, slip 1 wyib, k1, *k3, yo, k3, k2tog, ssk, k3, yo, k1; repeat from * to last 3 stitches, k1, slip 1 wyib, k1.
- **Row 10:** K1, slip 1 wyib, k1, *k4, yo, k3, k2tog, ssk, k3, yo; repeat from * to last 3 stitches, k1, slip 1 wyib, k1.
- Repeat Rows 1–10 for pattern.

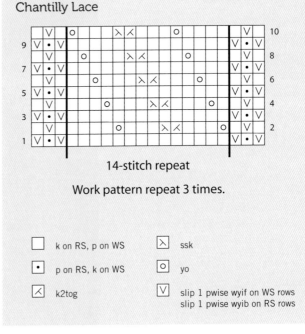

Chantilly Lace

14-stitch repeat

Work pattern repeat 3 times.

☐ k on RS, p on WS

• p on RS, k on WS

◩ k2tog

◪ ssk

○ yo

Ⅴ slip 1 pwise wyif on WS rows
slip 1 pwise wyib on RS rows

Broomstick Lace Scarf

DESIGNED BY KARLIE ROBINSON

Some may consider lace too formal for everyday wear, but not so with this scarf. By working one row of the four-row pattern using a large "broomstick" needle, the project knits up quickly, and the result is so light and airy it's the perfect accessory for cool spring outings. The best part is that the lace is created without a complex chart, and there isn't a yarnover to be found.

Finished Measurements
Approximately 6"/15 cm wide and 40"/102 cm long

Yarn
Habu Textiles A-174 Cotton Gima, 100% cotton, 265 yds (242 m)/1 oz (28 g), Color 25 Lemon

Needles
Two US 6 (4 mm) straight needles *or size you need to obtain correct gauge* and one US 17 (12.75 mm) straight needle

Gauge
32 stitches = 4"/10 cm in garter stitch on smaller needles

Other Supplies
Yarn needle

PATTERN ESSENTIALS

Broomstick Lace
(multiple of 4 stitches)

- **Rows 1 and 2:** With smaller needle, knit.
- **Row 3:** With larger needle, knit.
- **Row 4:** With smaller needle, *k4tog but do not remove stitches from the left-hand needle, work (p1, k1, p1) all into the same 4 stitches of the k4tog, and then drop the stitches off the left-hand needle; repeat from * to end of row.
- Repeat Rows 1–4 for pattern.

157

Knitting the Scarf

- Using smaller needles, cast on 48 stitches. Work Rows 1–4 of Broomstick Lace pattern until piece is desired length, ending with Row 4 of pattern. Knit 2 rows with smaller needle.

Finishing

- Bind off. Weave in ends.

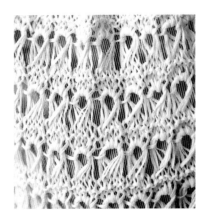

Cleopatra Scarf

DESIGNED BY LINDSAY LEWCHUK

This handsome cotton scarf combines lace with cabled edges. Tassels provide the perfect finishing touch.

Finished Measurements
6¼"/16 cm wide and 70"/178 cm long, excluding tassels

Yarn
Wolle's Yarn Creations Color Changing Cotton, 100% cotton, 480 yds (438 m)/3.88 oz (110 g), Black Cherry

Needles
US 3 (3.25 mm) straight needles *or size you need to obtain correct gauge*

Gauge
30 stitches and 38 rows = 4"/10 cm in Cleopatra Lace pattern

Other Supplies
Cable needle, 9"/23 cm × 4½"/11.5 cm cardboard rectangle for making tassels, yarn needle

Special Abbreviations
C3/4B slip 4 stitches onto cable needle and hold in back, k3 from left-hand needle, k4 from cable needle
C3/4F slip 3 stitches onto cable needle and hold in front, k4 from left-hand needle, k3 from cable needle
C4/4B slip 4 stitches onto cable needle and hold in back, k4 from left-hand needle, k4 from cable needle
C4/4F slip 4 stitches onto cable needle and hold in front, k4 from left-hand needle, k4 from cable needle

Knitting the Scarf

Notes: The four-strand yarn as purchased transitions from black at one end to red at the other end. To work the scarf as pictured, separate one strand from the other three, reverse its direction, and wind the four strands together again — the yarn now transitions from three strands of black and one strand of red at one end to three strands of red and one strand of black at the other end.

Knitting the First Point

- Set aside about 12–14 yds/11–13 m of yarn from the starting end of the skein for a tassel (enough to wrap about 50 times around the cardboard tassel form).

- Cast on 6 stitches. Purl 1 WS row. Work Rows 1–48 of Cleopatra Lace chart A. *You now have* 47 stitches.

Knitting the Center of the Scarf

- Work Rows 1–40 of Cleopatra Lace chart B 13 times, then work Rows 1–10 once more.

Knitting the Second Point

- Work Rows 1–40 of Cleopatra Lace chart C. *You now have* 6 stitches after Row 39. Bind off all stitches.

Making the Tassels (make 2)

- Fold a cardboard rectangle in half to make a 4½"/11.5 cm square. Using yarn reserved at the beginning, wrap yarn around the cardboard 50 times. Slide an extra piece of yarn between the layers of cardboard underneath all strands and tie tightly around the yarn at the "head" of the tassel. Wrap an extra piece of yarn around the "neck" of the tassel about ½"/13 mm down from the top of the tassel and tie securely. Make a second tassel in the same manner using the yarn left over after the end of the second point. Attach one tassel to each point of the scarf, matching the colors.

Cleopatra Lace A

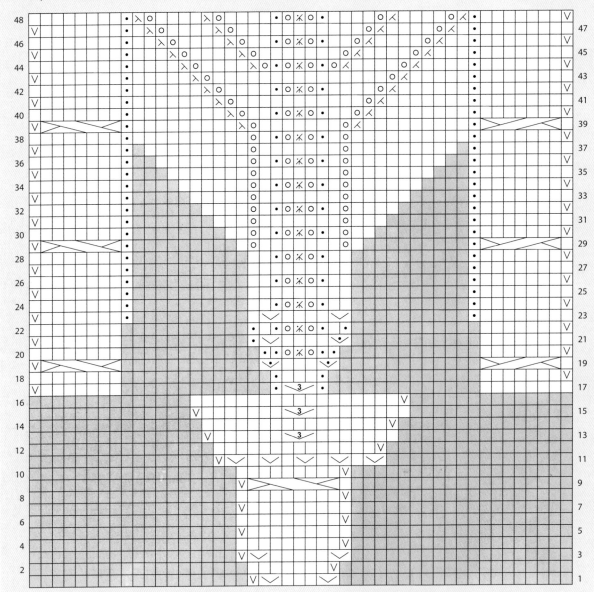

Cleopatra Lace B

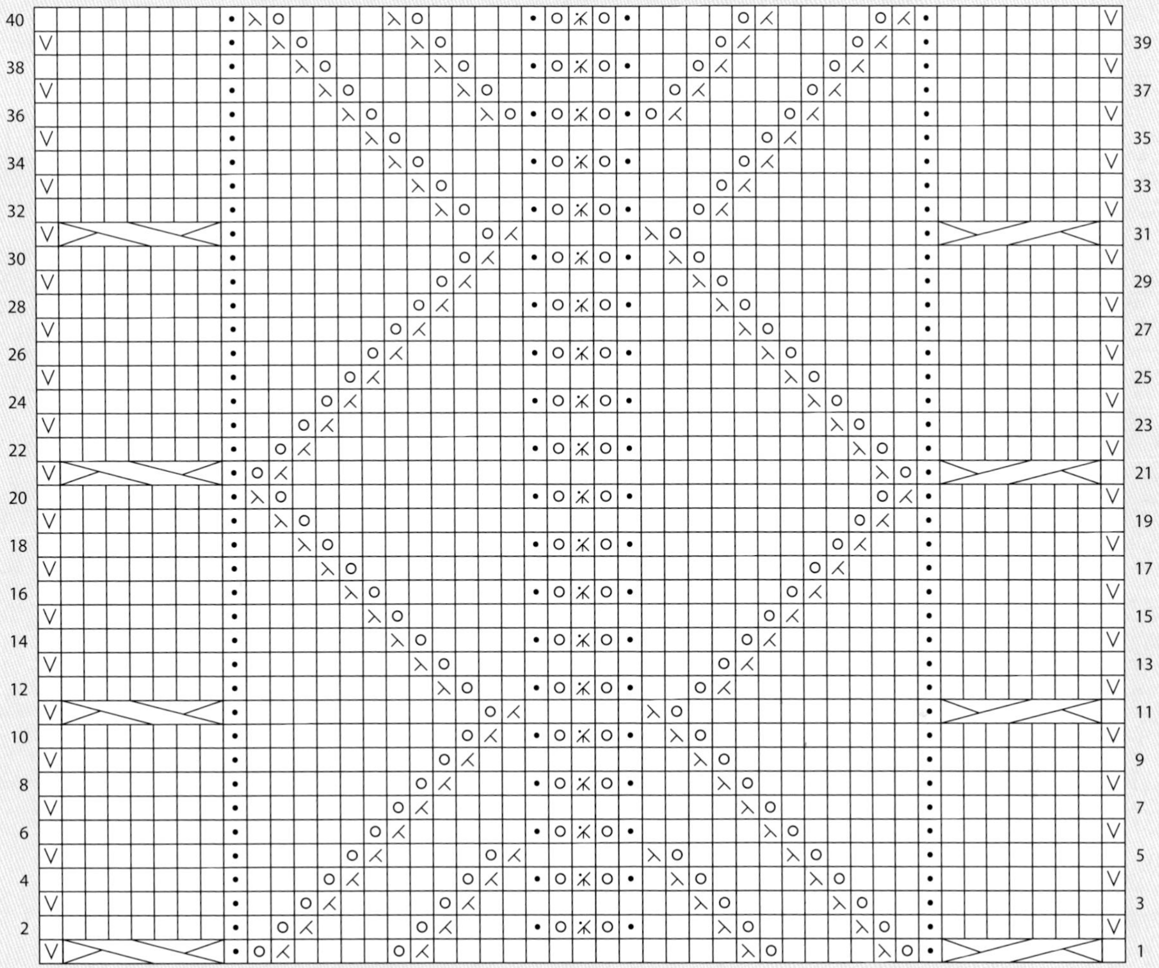

knit on RS, p on WS

• p on RS, k on WS

k2tog on RS, p2tog on WS

ssk on RS, ssp on WS

o yo

k3tog on WS

V slip 1 pwise: wyib on RS, wyif on WS

no stitch

kfb

pfb

3 knit into front, back, front of same st

C3/4F

C3/4B

C4/4F

C4/4B

161

Cleopatra Lace C

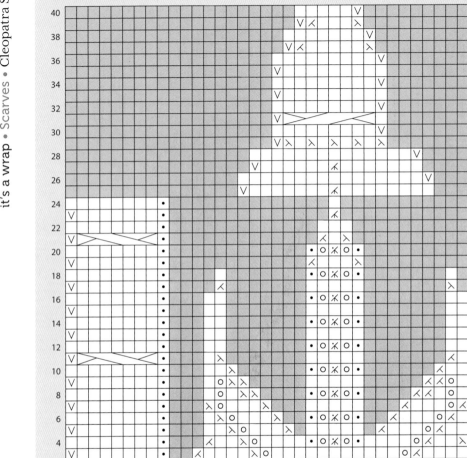

knit on RS, p on WS

• p on RS, k on WS

⟋ k2tog on RS, p2tog on WS

⟍ ssk on RS, ssp on WS

○ yo

⟌ k3tog on RS

⟍ k3tog on WS

∨ slip 1 pwise: wyib on RS, wyif on WS

no stitch

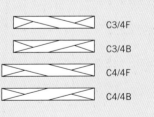

C3/4F

C3/4B

C4/4F

C4/4B

{ Following Charts }

If you have a fear of charts, now is the time to free yourself from that fear. Because charts mimic the pattern that they represent, it is much easier to find your place on a chart than in a long string of written words should you get distracted. Each symbol used in charts represents a specific stitch or combination of stitches, and they are designed to look like the finished stitch; for example, a yarnover is represented by a large circle and a k2tog is represented by a right-leaning symbol.

Because knitting progresses from the bottom up, you'll begin following a chart on the bottom-most row, and since we work from right to left, the first stitch of the row is the rightmost stitch in the bottom row. When knitting back and forth, follow all right-side chart rows from right to left and follow all wrong-side chart rows from left to right. When knitting in the round, all rows are right-side rows and you'll follow all rows from right to left.

A good way to keep track of where you are is to use a Post-it note on the chart — place the note just above the chart row you're currently working and move it up when you've finished each row. Placing the note above the knitting allows you to see all the chart rows that you've already knit, and this should look very similar to the work in your hands.

A Spray of Lace

DESIGNED BY PAULA PAPOOJIAN

A lovely lace spray pattern is flanked by seed stitch borders for a simply handsome design. The pattern is presented in both text and chart form.

Finished Measurements
5"/12.5 cm wide and 60"/152.5 cm long

Yarn
Harrisville Designs New England Shetland, 100% wool, 217 yds (198 m)/1.75 oz (50 g), Color 22 Plum

Needles
US 6 (4 mm) straight needles *or size you need to obtain correct gauge*

Gauge
18 stitches and 28 rows = 4"/10 cm in Lace Spray pattern, blocked

Other Supplies
Yarn needle, blocking wires (optional)

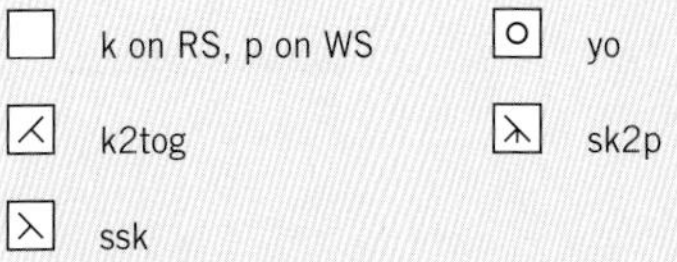

PATTERN ESSENTIALS

Lace Spray (worked over 17 stitches)

- **Row 1 and all odd-numbered rows (WS):** Purl.
- **Row 2 (RS):** Ssk, yo, k2, k2tog, yo, k1, yo, sk2p, yo, k1, yo, ssk, k2, yo, k2tog.
- **Row 4:** Ssk, k3, yo, k2tog, yo, k3, yo, ssk, yo, k3, k2tog.
- **Row 6:** Ssk (k2, yo) twice, k2tog, k1, ssk, (yo, k2) twice, k2tog.
- **Row 8:** Ssk, k1, yo, k3, yo, k2tog, k1, ssk, yo, k3, yo, k1, k2tog.
- Repeat Rows 1–8 for pattern.

Seed Stitch (worked over odd number of stitches)

- **Row 1:** *K1, p1; repeat from * to last st, k1.
- Repeat Row 1 for pattern.

Lace Spray

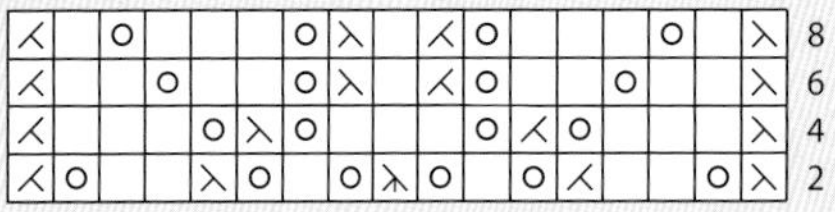

Only RS (even-numbered) rows are charted.

Purl all WS (odd-numbered) rows.

☐   k on RS, p on WS   ⊡   yo

⟋   k2tog   ⅄   sk2p

⟍   ssk

Knitting the Scarf

- Cast on 23 stitches. Work 4 rows seed stitch, ending with a RS row. Keeping the first and last 3 stitches in seed stitch, follow text or chart to work Rows 1–8 of Lace Spray pattern 50 times or until piece measures about ½"/13 mm less than desired length. Work 4 rows seed stitch.

Finishing

- Bind off knitwise. Weave in ends. Wash and stretch block with wires, if desired, for the full effect.

Ostrich Plumes Scarf

DESIGNED BY JENISE REID

Variegated yarn adds to the wavy movement of the purl ridges in the lace pattern and enhances the scalloped edges of the scarf. This piece is light enough to be worn as a headband or hair tie.

Finished Measurements

9"/23 cm wide and 54"/137 cm long

Yarn

Knit Picks Shadow Lace, 100% merino wool, 440 yds (402 m)/1.75 oz (50 g), Queen Anne Tonal

Needles

US 8 (5 mm) straight needles *or size you need to obtain correct gauge*

Gauge

27 stitches and 14½ rows = 4"/10 cm in Ostrich Lace pattern, lightly blocked

Other Supplies

Yarn needle

166

Knitting the Scarf

- Cast on 61 stitches. Knit 4 rows.

- Work Ostrich Lace pattern as follows.

- **ROW 1 (RS):** K2, *(k1, yo) five times, (ssk) four times, k3tog, (k2tog) four times, (yo, k1) four times, yo; repeat from * to last 3 stitches, k3.

- **ROWS 2–4:** K2, purl to last 2 stitches, k2.

- **ROWS 5–32:** Repeat Rows 1–4 seven times.

- **ROW 33:** K2, (k2tog) five times, (yo, k1) nine times, yo, (ssk) four times, k3tog, (k2tog) four times, (yo, k1) nine times, yo, (ssk) five times, k2.

- **ROWS 34–36:** K2, purl to last 2 stitches, k2.

- **ROWS 37–64:** Repeat Rows 33–36 seven times.

- **ROWS 65–128:** Repeat Rows 1–64 once more.

- **ROWS 129–190:** Repeat Rows 1–62 once more.

- Knit 4 rows.

Finishing

- Bind off loosely. Weave in ends. Block to desired measurements.

Choose Your Look Scarf

DESIGNED BY MINDY VASIL

Options abound with this project: change the width, change the length of the zigzags, and choose picots or fringe for the ends. The pattern is easy to learn, and the scarf works up quickly.

Finished Measurements

Wide scarf: 7¼"/18.5 cm wide and 57"/145 cm long, excluding fringe
Narrow scarf: 5¾"/14.5 cm wide and 69"/175 cm long

Yarn

Lion Brand Yarn Wool-Ease, 80% acrylic/20% wool, 197 yds (180 m)/3 oz (85 g), Color 140 Rose Heather (wide scarf) or 104 Blush Heather (narrow scarf)

Needles

US 10 (6 mm) straight needles or size you need to obtain correct gauge

Gauge

16 stitches and 20 rows = 4"/10 cm in Zigzag pattern, blocked

Other Supplies

Yarn needle

Knitting the Scarf

- Measure out 10 yds/9 m of yarn and set aside for edging.

- Cast on 23 stitches for narrow scarf or 29 stitches for wide scarf.

- SETUP ROW 1 (RS): Knit.

- SETUP ROW 2 (WS): K2, purl to last 2 stitches, k2.

- Repeat Setup Rows 1 and 2 once more.

- Work short or long Zigzag pattern (see Notes above) until you're almost out of yarn, leaving enough for 2 more rows and binding off, and ending with Row 6 or Row 12 of the short Zigzag pattern, or Row 14 or Row 28 of the long Zigzag pattern.

- NEXT ROW (RS): Knit.

- NEXT ROW (WS): K2, purl to last 2 stitches, k2.

- Repeat the last 2 rows once more.

- Bind off all stitches. Weave in ends. Block if desired (see Finishing).

PATTERN ESSENTIALS

Picot Bind Off *Knit into the first stitch without dropping the original stitch off the needle and add the new stitch to the left-hand needle, k2, bind off 1 stitch by slipping the first stitch over the second stitch, k1, bind off 1 stitch, move the stitch on the right-hand needle back to the left-hand needle; repeat from * until all stitches are bound off.

Zigzag (multiple of 6 stitches plus 5)

- **Row 1 (RS):** K2, *k2tog tbl, k2, yo, k2; repeat from * to last 3 stitches, k3.
- **Row 2 (WS):** K2, purl to last 2 stitches, k2.
- **Row 3:** K5, *yo, k2, k2tog, k2; repeat from * to end of row.
- **Row 4:** K2, purl to last 2 stitches, k2.

Notes: For a short Zigzag pattern, work Rows 1 and 2 three times, then work Rows 3 and 4 three times. Repeat these 12 rows for pattern. For a long Zigzag pattern, work Rows 1 and 2 seven times, then work Rows 3 and 4 seven times. Repeat these 28 rows for pattern.

Finishing

- Using the yarn that was set aside at the beginning, work the Picot or Fringe Edging (see below).

- *For the Picot Edging:* With RS facing, pick up and knit (see page 297) 1 stitch for each cast-on or bound-off stitch along one short end of scarf (23 or 29 stitches). Purl 1 WS row. With RS facing, work Picot Bind Off. Repeat for the other short end of scarf.

- *For the Fringe Edging:* Cut one 3"/7.5 cm piece of yarn for each cast-on or bound-off stitch times two (46 or 58 pieces). Fold each yarn piece in half and thread the folded loop through one of the cast-on or bound-off stitches along one short end of the scarf, pull the cut ends through the loop, and tug lightly to tighten. Place one fringe in this manner in each cast-on or bound-off edge stitch along both short ends of scarf. Trim fringe evenly.

Symmetria Scarf

DESIGNED BY HENNA MARKKANEN

Knit in two pieces, each starting from a scarf end, the two halves are joined at the center back with Kitchener stitch. With multiple patterns, this is a great piece for honing your lace-knitting skills.

Finished Measurements
14"/35.5 cm wide and 69"/175 cm long, blocked

Yarn
Regia Lace, 71% new wool, 29% nylon, 656 yds (600 m)/3.5 oz (100 g), Color 06579 Carnelian **Note:** Scarf uses approximately 547 yds/500 m.

Needles
US 7 (4.5 mm) straight needles *or size you need to obtain correct gauge*

Gauge
16 stitches and 22 rows = 4"/10 cm in pattern, blocked

Other Supplies
Scrap yarn for holder, yarn needle

PATTERN ESSENTIALS

Make 2 out of 1 Knit into the front and back of same stitch — 1 stitch increased.

Make 2 out of 3 K2; return second stitch to left-hand needle, k2tog tbl — 1 stitch decreased.

Knitting the Scarf

- Cast on 57 stitches loosely and knit 1 row. Working the garter stitch border (see Pattern Notes) at each side, work Rows 1–23 of Symmetria chart A, working the 10-stitch repeat four times in each row, and ending with RS Row 23. Slipping the first stitch of each row as established, knit 3 rows (27 rows completed).

- Maintaining the garter stitch border at each side, work Rows 1–161 of charts B and C, then work WS Row 162, working the 20-stitch charted repeat twice in each row (189 rows total completed). After working Row 162, place stitches on holder.

- Repeat all instructions for second half of scarf.

Finishing

- Graft the scarf halves together with Kitchener stitch (see page 293). Weave in ends. Block.

PATTERN NOTES

The scarf has a 3-stitch garter border at each side, which is not shown on the charts. On both RS and WS rows, work the first 3 stitches as slip 1 purlwise wyif, k2, and work the last 3 stitches as k3. Only RS rows are charted; purl all the stitches between the 3-stitch garter borders on WS rows unless otherwise instructed.

The stitch counts of the charts do not remain constant from row to row. When checking the count, remember that the Make 2 out of 1 and Make 2 out of 3 symbols represent 2 stitches, even though they occupy only one square of the chart. You may find it easier to check the number of stitches after completing the next RS row *after* a row that contains these multistitch symbols, when the stitch count has been restored to 57 stitches again.

Symmetria A

Work pattern repeat 4 times.

Only RS (odd-numbered) rows are charted.

See instructions for WS rows and garter borders.

Symmetria B

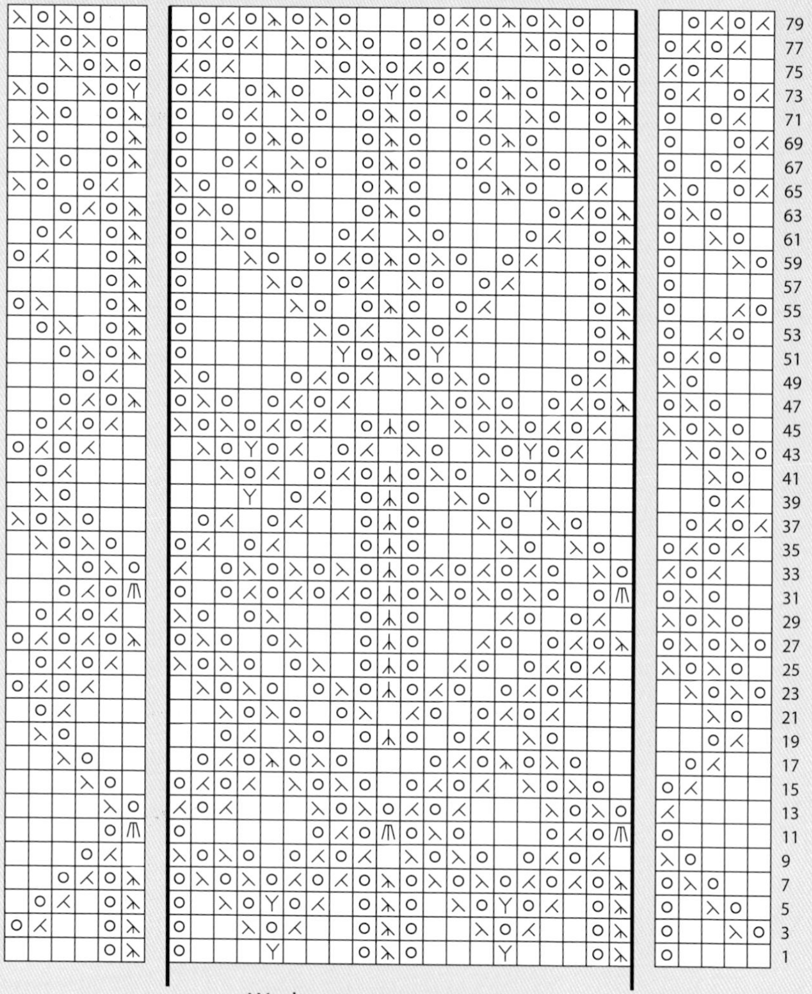

Work pattern repeat 2 times.

☐ knit	○ yo	sk2p
k2tog	Y make 2 out of 1	slip 2tog kwise, k1, pass 2 slipped sts over k st
ssk	⋀ make 2 out of 3	

continued on next page

171

Symmetria C

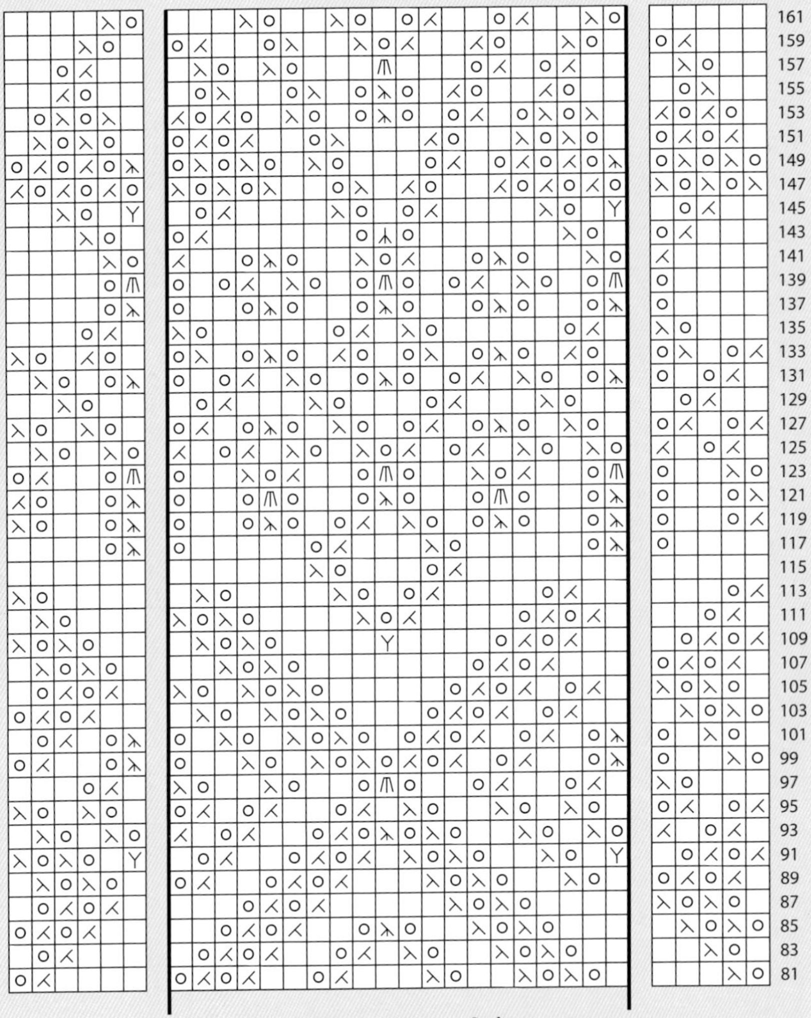
161
159
157
155
153
151
149
147
145
143
141
139
137
135
133
131
129
127
125
123
121
119
117
115
113
111
109
107
105
103
101
99
97
95
93
91
89
87
85
83
81

Work pattern repeat 2 times.

- knit
- k2tog
- ssk
- yo
- make 2 out of 1
- make 2 out of 3
- sk2p
- slip 2tog kwise, k1, pass 2 slipped sts over k st

April Showers Cowl

DESIGNED BY MEG STRONG

Here's a lovely cowl of ample width to provide warmth while remaining light and airy. Wear the cowl simply draped around the neck, wrap it for a snug fit, or allow it to drape over one shoulder — anything goes.

Finished Measurements

39"/99 cm circumference and 13"/33 cm deep

Yarn

Madelinetosh Tosh Lace, 100% super-wash merino wool, 950 yds (868 m)/4 oz (114 g), Mica

Needles

US 6 (4 mm) straight needles and one extra for three-needle bind off *or size you need to obtain correct gauge*

Gauge

24 stitches and 28 rows = 4"/10 cm in stockinette stitch with yarn doubled; 27 stitches and 28 rows = 4"/10 cm in lace pattern with yarn doubled

Other Supplies

Scrap yarn for provisional cast on, yarn needle

Knitting the Cowl

Note: Yarn is used doubled throughout.

- With yarn doubled, cast on 89 stitches using a provisional method (see pages 297–298).

- ROW 1 (WS): Slip 1 purlwise wyif, p1, k1, *p5, k1; repeat from * to last 2 stitches, p2.

- ROW 2 (RS): Slip 1 purlwise wyib, k1, p1, *k1, yo, k2, k2tog, p1; repeat from * to last 2 stitches, k2.

continued on next page

- **ROW 3:** Repeat Row 1.
- **ROW 4:** Slip 1 purlwise wyib, k1, p1, *k2tog, k2, yo, k1, p1; repeat from * to last 2 stitches, k2.
- Repeat Rows 1–4 to desired length, ending with Row 4.

Finishing

- Carefully remove provisional cast on and place live stitches on a needle. Join the beginning and ending stitches together with the three-needle bind off (see page 299). Weave in ends. Block to desired measurements.

Mari Lace Cowl

DESIGNED BY GINA HOUSE

An airy and relaxed Möbius cowl, Mari Lace is reversible and versatile: it can be worn as one big loop, doubled up around the neck, or even wrapped over the head like a hood. Simple to knit and a joy to wear.

Finished Measurements

66"/167.5 cm circumference and 8"/20.5 cm deep

Yarn

Tess' Designer Yarns Superwash Merino Lace, 100% superwash wool, 500 yds (457 m)/1.75 oz (50 g), Magenta

Needles

US 4 (3.5 mm) straight needles *or size you need to obtain correct gauge* and US 5 (3.75 mm) straight needles

Gauge

30 stitches and 40 rows = 4"/10 cm in lace pattern on smaller needles

Other Supplies

US E/4 (3.5 mm) crochet hook, 1 yd/1 m scrap lace yarn for cast on, yarn needle

Knitting the Cowl

- With smaller needles, cast on 60 stitches using a provisional cast-on method (see pages 297–298).

- ROW 1: Slip 1 purlwise wyif, yo, k2tog, *k1, yo, k2tog; repeat from * to end of row.

- Repeat Row 1 until piece measures 5"/12.5 cm.

- NEXT ROW (GARTER RIDGE ROW): Slip 1 purlwise wyif, knit to end of row.

- Repeat the Garter Ridge Row five more times (6 Garter Ridge Rows total).

- Work 5"/12.5 cm of lace (Row 1) followed by 6 Garter Ridge Rows seven more times (eight times total). *Note:* Work fewer repeats for a shorter cowl.

- Repeat Row 1 for another 5"/12.5 cm.

- Work 4 Garter Ridge Rows.

Making the Möbius

- Remove the provisional cast on and carefully place the live stitches on a smaller needle. Fold the piece in half to bring the needles together, and insert a 180-degree twist in the fabric. Join the ends together with the three-needle bind off (see page 299) using a larger needle. Cut yarn, leaving a 4"/10 cm tail. Secure the last stitch by pulling the tail through.

Finishing

- Weave in all ends. Soak in wool wash and warm water. Block gently to desired dimensions and let air-dry. *Note:* Each lace section blocks out nicely to 8"/20.5 cm wide.

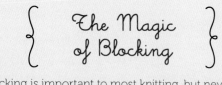

{ The Magic of Blocking }

Blocking is important to most knitting, but never more so than with lace. What comes off your needles is often a wrinkled mass of little shape with undefined patterning. Once blocked, a piece will usually be significantly larger than it was and when all those eyelets are opened up you'll see the lovely airy pattern.

If you're knitting a garment that needs to fit, such as a hat or a sweater, be sure to fully block your swatch before measuring for gauge — otherwise your finished piece could be too large to wear.

These pieces have exactly the same number of stitches, knit in the same lace pattern. Only one was blocked!

175

Silver Lamé Cowl

DESIGNED BY IZUMI OUCHI

The openwork lace used in this cowl is beautifully accented by the shimmer of Lurex and the halo of mohair. The cowl can be knit to a smaller or larger circumference by working fewer or more repeats of the lace pattern.

Finished Measurements
Approximately 40"/102 cm circumference and 9"/23 cm deep, blocked

Yarn
S. Charles Luna, 71% super kid mohair/20% silk/9% Lurex, 232 yds (212 m)/0.88 oz (25 g), Color 21 Silver Mist

Needle
US 7 (4.5 mm) circular needle 24"/60 cm long *or size you need to obtain correct gauge*

Gauge
18 stitches and 25 rounds = 4"/10 cm in Silver Lamé Lace pattern, blocked

Other Supplies
Stitch marker, yarn needle

Knitting the Cowl

- Cast on 182 stitches. Place marker and join into a round, being careful not to twist the stitches. Purl 1 round.

- Work Rounds 1–8 of Silver Lamé Lace chart seven times or to desired length, ending with Round 8.

- Purl 1 round.

Finishing

- Bind off purlwise. Weave in ends. Block.

Silver Lamé Lace

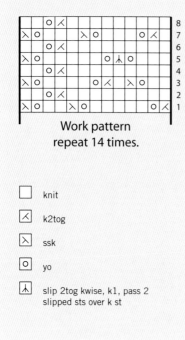

Work pattern
repeat 14 times.

☐ knit

◩ k2tog

◪ ssk

☑ yo

◿ slip 2tog kwise, k1, pass 2
slipped sts over k st

Jade Sapphire Cowl

DESIGNED BY LYNN M. WILSON

Luxurious cashmere yarn and a lovely, well-balanced lace design are perfect together. The edges of this cowl are finished with a knitted-on I-cord, and you can have some fun choosing just the right buttons.

Finished Measurements

Approximately 23"/58.5 cm circumference and 9½"/24 cm deep

Yarn

Jade Sapphire Mongolian Cashmere 4-Ply, 100% cashmere, 200 yds (183 m)/1.9 oz (55 g), Color 42 Olive Twist

Needles

US 5 (3.75 mm) straight needles *or size you need to obtain correct gauge*

Gauge

17 stitches and 34 rows = 4"/10 cm in pattern

Other Supplies

Yarn needle, three ⅞"/2.2 cm buttons, sewing needle and coordinating thread (optional)

PATTERN ESSENTIALS

Garter Slip Stitch (worked over an odd number of stitches)

Note: Slip all stitches pwise.

- **Row 1 (RS):** Knit.
- **Row 2 (WS):** Slip first 3 stitches wyif, knit to last 3 stitches, slip last 3 stitches wyif.
- **Row 3:** K4, *slip 1 wyib, k1; repeat from * to last 3 stitches, k3.
- **Row 4:** Slip first 3 stitches wyif, k1, *slip 1 wyif, k1; repeat from * to last 3 stitches, slip last 3 stitches wyif.
- **Row 5:** Knit.
- **Row 6:** Slip first 3 stitches wyif, knit to last 3 stitches, slip last 3 stitches wyif.
- **Row 7:** K5, *slip 1 wyib, k1; repeat from * to last 4 stitches, k4.
- **Row 8:** Slip first 3 stitches wyif, k2, *slip 1 wyif, k1; repeat from * to last 4 stitches, k1, slip last 3 stitches wyif.
- Repeat Rows 1–8 for pattern.

Lace (multiple of 10 stitches plus 5)

- **Row 1 and all odd-numbered rows (WS):** Slip first 3 stitches wyif, purl to last 3 stitches, slip 3 wyif.
- **Row 2 (RS):** K5, (k2tog, yo) twice, *k3, yo, ssk, k1, (k2tog, yo) twice; repeat from * to last 6 stitches, k6.
- **Row 4:** K6, k2tog, yo, k3, *(yo, ssk) twice, k1, k2tog, yo, k3; repeat from * to last 4 stitches, k4.
- **Row 6:** K4, yo, ssk, k4, *(yo, ssk) three times, k4; repeat from * to last 5 stitches, yo, ssk, k3.
- **Row 8:** K5, yo, ssk, k2, *(yo, ssk) four times, k2; repeat from * to last 6 stitches, yo, ssk, k4.
- **Row 10:** Repeat Row 6.
- **Row 12:** Repeat Row 4.
- **Row 14:** Repeat Row 2.
- **Row 16:** K4, *(k2tog, yo) three times, k4; repeat from * to last stitch, k1.
- **Row 18:** K3, *(k2tog, yo) four times, k2; repeat from * to last 2 stitches, k2.
- **Row 20:** Repeat Row 16.
- Repeat Rows 1–20 for pattern.

• • •

Wrap Stitch With yarn in back, slip 1 purlwise, bring yarn forward, slip the stitch back to left-hand needle, bring yarn back, slip the wrapped stitch to right-hand needle.

Knitting the Cowl

Knitting the Button Band

- Cast on 25 stitches and work Rows 1–8 of Garter Slip Stitch pattern twice, then work Rows 1 and 2 once more.

- **NEXT ROW (RS, INCREASE ROW):** K3, M1L, *k1, M1L; repeat from * to last 3 stitches, k3. *You now have 45 stitches; piece measures about 1½"/4 cm.*

Knitting the Lace

- Following either the written instructions or the chart, work Rows 1–20 of Lace pattern eight times or until piece measures approximately 3¼"/8.5 cm less than desired finished length; then work Rows 1–15 one more time. *Note: By ending after working Row 15, the Lace pattern mirrors the pattern at the opposite end. If this does not work with your desired finished measurement, end having just worked any WS row.*

Knitting the Buttonhole Band

- **ROW 1 (RS, DECREASE ROW):** K2, *k2tog; repeat from * to last 3 stitches, k3. *You now have 25 stitches.*

- **ROW 2:** Slip first 3 stitches wyif, knit to last 3 stitches, slip 3 wyif.

- **ROWS 3–10:** Work Rows 1–8 of Garter Slip Stitch pattern.

- **ROW 11 (RS, FIRST BUTTONHOLE ROW):** K4, (Wrap Stitch, k1, pass Wrap Stitch over knit stitch, bind off next 2 stitches, k3) three times. *You now have 16 stitches.*

- **ROW 12 (WS, SECOND BUTTONHOLE ROW):** Slip 3 wyif, *k1, turn work and cast on 4 stitches using either the knitted-on (see page 294) or cable method (see page 290), turn work, k1, pass last cast-on stitch over knit stitch, k2; repeat from * three times, ending last repeat slip 3 wyif instead of k2. *You now have* 25 stitches.

- **ROWS 13 AND 14:** Work Rows 3 and 4 of Garter Slip Stitch pattern.

- **NEXT ROW (RS):** K2tog, knit to last 2 stitches, ssk. *You now have* 23 stitches.

- Bind off knitwise; cut yarn.

Finishing

- Weave in ends, block as needed. Mark button placement on button band to correspond to buttonholes, and attach buttons using either yarn or sewing needle and coordinating thread.

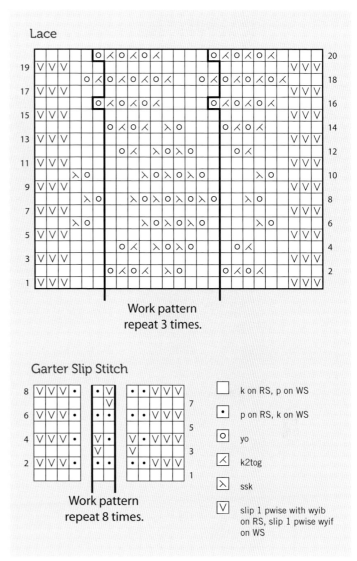

Lace

Work pattern repeat 3 times.

Garter Slip Stitch

Work pattern repeat 8 times.

	k on RS, p on WS
•	p on RS, k on WS
o	yo
⊼	k2tog
⊼	ssk
V	slip 1 pwise with wyib on RS, slip 1 pwise wyif on WS

Flying Gulls Cowl

DESIGNED BY TERRY COLLARD

Here's an example of a simple garter stitch lace worked in the round — every other round is purled. The lace pattern naturally forms points that make a decorative bottom edge.

Finished Measurements

Approximately 20"/51 cm circumference and 8¼"/21 cm deep (to tip of points)

Yarn

Harrisville Designs New England Shetland, 100% wool, 217 yds (198 m)/ 1.75 oz (50 g), Color 59 Chicory

Needle

US 6 (4 mm) circular needle 16"/40 cm long *or size you need to obtain correct gauge*

Gauge

22½ stitches and 35 rounds = 4"/10 cm in Lace pattern

Other Supplies

Stitch markers (one in a unique color), yarn needle

PATTERN ESSENTIALS

Lace
(multiple of 14 stitches plus 1)

- **Round 1:** *K1, yo, k5, s2kp, k5, yo; repeat from * to last stitch, k1.
- **Round 2 and all even-numbered rounds:** Purl.
- **Round 3:** *K2, yo, k4, s2kp, k4, yo, k1; repeat from * to last stitch, k1.
- **Round 5:** *K3, yo, k3, s2kp, k3, yo, k2; repeat from * to last stitch, k1.
- **Round 7:** *K4, yo, k2, s2kp, k2, yo, k3; repeat from * to last stitch, k1.
- **Round 9:** *K5, yo, k1, s2kp, k1, yo, k4; repeat from * to last stitch, k1.
- **Round 11:** *K6, yo, s2kp, yo, k5; repeat from * to last stitch, k1.
- **Round 12:** Purl.
- Repeat Rounds 1–12 for pattern.

Knitting the Cowl

- Cast on 113 stitches. Place unique-colored marker and join into a round, being careful not to twist the stitches.

- Work Round 1 of Lace pattern, placing a marker between each of the 14-stitch repeats and before the final k1 at end of round.

- Work Rounds 2–12, then work Rounds 1–12 five or six more times to desired length; the cowl shown was worked with six total repeats.

Finishing

- Bind off loosely purlwise. Weave in ends and block.

Violeta Cowl

DESIGNED BY J. M. ELLIS

This super luxurious cowl is knitted with Buffalo Gold Lux and can be worn crunched down around your neck or pulled up over your head to keep your ears warm.

Finished Measurements

Approximately 22"/56 cm circumference and 13"/33 cm deep

Yarn

Buffalo Gold Lux, 45% bison down/20% cashmere/20% silk/15% Tencel, 330 yds (302 m)/1.4 oz (40 g), DL2 Tumbleweed

Needle

US 5 (3.75 mm) circular needle 24"/60 cm long *or size you need to obtain correct gauge*

Gauge

26 stitches and 28 rounds = 4"/10 cm in Violeta Lace pattern

Other Supplies

Stitch marker, yarn needle

PATTERN ESSENTIALS

Violeta Lace (multiple of 9 stitches)

- **Round 1:** *Yo, ssk, k7; repeat from * to end of round.
- **Round 2 and all even-numbered rounds:** Knit.
- **Round 3:** *K1, yo, ssk, k4, k2tog, yo; repeat from * to end of row.
- **Round 5:** *K1, yo, k2tog, k4, k2tog, yo; repeat from * to end of row.
- **Round 7:** *K4, yo, ssk, k3; repeat from * to end of row.
- **Round 9:** *K2, k2tog, yo, k1, yo, ssk, k2; repeat from * to end of row.
- **Round 11:** *K2, k2tog, yo, k1, yo, k2tog, k2; repeat from * to end of row.
- **Round 12:** Knit.
- Repeat Rounds 1–12 for pattern.

  Note: The decreases in Rounds 5 and 11 deliberately do not mirror each other.

Knitting the Cowl

- Cast on 144 stitches loosely. Place marker and join into a round, being careful not to twist the stitches.
- ROUNDS 1–5: Knit.
- ROUND 6: Purl.
- ROUNDS 7 AND 8: Knit.
- Work Rounds 1–12 of Violeta Lace pattern until piece measures 12"/30.5 cm with lower edge rolled, ending with Round 6 or 12.
- Knit 2 rounds.
- Work K2, P2 rib for 6 rounds.

Finishing

- Bind off loosely in pattern. Weave in ends. Block.

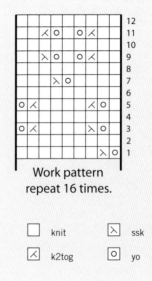

Violeta Lace

Work pattern repeat 16 times.

☐ knit ⟋ k2tog ⟍ ssk ○ yo

Islandwood Cowl

DESIGNED BY MOLLY KENT

Worked in the round from the top down with alternating Lily of the Valley and Herringbone panels, this cowl has gradual increases for a flattering tapered shape. It also features bobbles, which look lovely in this variegated yarn.

Finished Measurements

16"/41 cm flaring to 22"/56 cm circumference and 8"/20.5 cm deep

Yarn

Madelintosh Tosh DK, 100% merino wool, 225 yds (206 m)/3.5 oz (100 g), Mourning Dove

Needles

US 7 (4.5 mm) circular needle 16"/40 cm long or set of US 7 (4.5 mm) double-point needles *or size you need to obtain correct gauge*

Gauge

16 stitches and 24 rows = 4"/10 cm in stockinette stitch; chart patterns average 18–20 stitches = 4"/10 cm

Other Supplies

Stitch marker, yarn needle

PATTERN ESSENTIALS

Bobble Work k1, yo, k1, yo, k1 all in the same stitch. *You now have 5 stitches made from 1 stitch.* Pass the first 4 stitches of the bobble over the last knit stitch one at a time — 5 bobble stitches have been decreased to 1 stitch.

Knitting the Cowl

- Cast on 80 stitches. Place marker and join into a round, being careful not to twist the stitches.

- ROUND 1: *P1, work Round 1 of Herringbone chart over 13 stitches, p2, work Round 1 of Lily of the Valley chart over 23 stitches, p1; repeat from *.

- ROUNDS 2–15: Purling the stitches outside the chart sections, continue in established patterns. *Note:* For the Herringbone chart, after finishing Round 6, repeat Rounds 1–6 for pattern thereafter.

- ROUND 16: *M1RP, p1, continue Herringbone chart over 13 stitches, p1, M1RP, p1, work Round 16 of Lily of the Valley chart over 23 stitches increasing them to 25 stitches as shown, p1; repeat from *. *You now have* 88 stitches.

- ROUNDS 17–30: Purling the stitches outside the chart sections, continue in established patterns.

- ROUND 31: *(M1RP, p1) twice, continue Herringbone chart over 13 stitches, p1, (M1RP, p1) twice, continue Lily of the Valley chart over 25 stitches, p1; repeat from *. *You now have* 96 stitches.

- ROUND 32: *P4, continue Herringbone chart over 13 stitches, p5, work Round 32 of Lily of the Valley chart over 25 stitches increasing them to 27 stitches as shown, p1; repeat from *. *You now have* 100 stitches.

- ROUNDS 33–48: Purling the stitches outside the chart sections, continue in established patterns, ending with Round 6 of Herringbone chart and Round 48 of Lily of the Valley chart.

Finishing

- Bind off loosely. Weave in ends. Block.

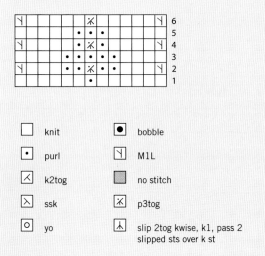

Herringbone

						knit				bobble

knit

purl

k2tog

ssk

yo

bobble

M1L

no stitch

p3tog

slip 2tog kwise, k1, pass 2 slipped sts over k st

Lily of the Valley

Pitched Cowl

DESIGNED BY KATHERINE VAUGHAN

The simple lace pattern used for the Pitched Cowl pulls the fabric right and then left, giving it a rippled effect. This effect is accentuated by the self-striping yarn.

Finished Measurements

22½"/57 cm circumference and 7½"/ 19 cm deep

Yarn

Noro Chirimen, 60% cotton/24% silk/ 16% wool, 137 yds (125 m)/1.75 oz (50 g), Color 8

Needle

US 8 (5 mm) circular needle 24"/60 cm long *or size you need to obtain correct gauge*

Gauge

18 stitches and 27 rounds = 4"/10 cm in Lace pattern

Other Supplies

Stitch marker, yarn needle

PATTERN ESSENTIALS

Lace (multiple of 16 stitches worked in the round)

- **Round 1 and all odd-numbered rounds:** Knit.
- **Rounds 2, 4, 6, and 8:** *(K2tog, yo) four times, p8; repeat from * to end of round.
- **Rounds 10, 12, 14, and 16:** *P8, (yo, ssk) four times; repeat from * to end of round.
- Repeat Rounds 1–16 for pattern.

Knitting the Cowl

- Cast on 96 stitches. Place marker and join into a round, being careful not to twist stitches. Purl 1 round, knit 1 round, purl 1 round.

- Following chart or written instructions, work Rounds 1–16 of Lace pattern twice, then work Rounds 1–9 once more. Purl 1 round, knit 1 round, purl 1 round.

Finishing

- Bind off knitwise. Weave in ends. Block.

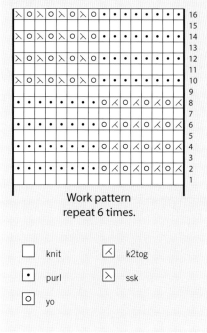

Pitched Cowl Lace

Work pattern repeat 6 times.

☐ knit	⟋ k2tog
• purl	⟍ ssk
○ yo	

Absolu Lace Cowl

DESIGNED BY BRIGITTE LANG

The lace stitch featured here is simple to do, and even beginning knitters can tackle it. The yarn, from a black-colored angora rabbit, is as light as a feather.

Finished Measurements

Approximately 23"/58.5 cm circumference and 8"/20.5 cm deep

Yarn

Anny Blatt Absolu Angora, 100% angora, 177 yds (162 m)/0.88 oz (25 g), Color 157 Caviar

Needle

US 6 (4 mm) circular needle 16"/40 cm long *or size you need to obtain correct gauge*

Gauge

22 stitches and 36 rounds = 4"/10 cm in pattern, slightly stretched

Other Supplies

Stitch marker, yarn needle

PATTERN ESSENTIALS

Lace (multiple of 5 stitches)

- **Rounds 1–3:** *K3, p2; repeat from * to end of round.
- **Round 4:** *Yo, k3tog tbl, yo, p2; repeat from * to end of round.
- **Rounds 5–7:** *K3, p2; repeat from * to end of round.
- Repeat Rounds 1–7 for pattern.

Knitting the Cowl

- Cast on 130 stitches. Place marker and join into a round, being careful not to twist the stitches. Work Rounds 1–7 of Lace pattern 10 times.

Finishing

- Bind off loosely in pattern. Weave in ends.

Mirabel Shawl

DESIGNED BY RAE BLACKLEDGE

Mirabel is knit from the neck down with shoulder shaping. Although it does have lace patterning on both the right- and wrong-side rows, it has six plain knit and purl rows between each group of four lace rows, giving the knitter a bit of a rest.

Finished Measurements

48"/122 cm wide and 24"/61 cm deep

Yarn

Interlacements Lotus, 100% silk, 500 yds (457 m)/4 oz (113 g), The Blues

Needles

US 4 (3.5 mm) straight needles *or size you need to obtain correct gauge*

Gauge

20 stitches and 28 rows = 4"/10 cm in chart patterns, blocked

Other Supplies

Scrap yarn, crochet hook (same size as knitting needles), eight stitch markers, yarn needle, blocking wires and pins

PATTERN ESSENTIALS

Centered Double Decrease On RS rows, work s2kp: Slip 2 stitches together knitwise, k1, pass the slipped stitches over the knit stitch — 2 stitches decreased. On WS rows, work s2pp: Slip 2 stitches, one at a time, knitwise, return them to left-hand needle in their "turned" orientation, insert the right-hand needle tip through the back loops of the turned stitches and slip them to the right-hand needle, p1, pass the slipped stitches over the purl stitch — 2 stitches decreased.

Knitting the Shawl

- Using scrap yarn, use the crochet over the needle provisional method (see page 297) to cast on 4 stitches.

- Knit 1 row.

- Knit a garter stitch strip for 60 rows as follows: Slip 1 purlwise wyif, k3. *You now have* a strip with 30 slipped chain selvedge stitches on each side.

Knitting Chart A

- **NEXT ROW (RS, COUNTS AS ROW 1 OF CHART A):** Slip 1 purlwise wyif, k2, place marker, yo, k1 (last stitch of garter strip), pick up and knit (see page 297) 1 stitch in each of next 6 chain selvedge stitches, yo, *place marker, pick up and knit 1 stitch in next chain selvedge stitch, place marker, yo, pick up and knit 1 stitch in each of next 7 chain selvedge stitches, yo; repeat from * two more times, unravel the provisional cast on and place 3 stitches from the base of the provisional cast on onto the left-hand needle, place marker, k3 stitches from cast on. *You now have* 45 stitches.

- Slipping markers as you come to them, work Rows 2–12 of chart A. *You now have* 85 stitches.

Knitting Chart B

Notes: The 3 edge stitches at each side and the single stitches that separate the pattern sections are not shown on chart B. Continue the edge stitches as established by working the first 3 stitches of every row as slip 1 purlwise wyif, k2, and working the last 3 stitches as k3. Work the single stitches that separate the pattern sections in stockinette.

- **NEXT ROW (RS, COUNTS AS ROW 1 OF CHART B):** Work 3 edge stitches, slip marker, *work Row 1 of chart B over 19 stitches increasing them to 21 stitches as shown and working the marked 10-stitch repeat only once, slip marker, k1 (separating stitch), slip marker; repeat from * two more times, work Row 1 of chart B over 19 stitches increasing them to 21 stitches as shown and working the marked 10-stitch repeat only once, slip marker, work 3 edge stitches.

- Work Rows 2–20 of chart B. *You now have* 165 stitches: 3 edge stitches at each side, four pattern sections with 39 stitches each, and 3 single stitches separating the pattern sections.

- Work Rows 1–20 of chart B once more, working the 10-stitch marked repeat three times in each pattern section. *You now have* 245 stitches: 3 edge stitches at each side, four pattern sections with 59 stitches each, and 3 single stitches separating the pattern sections.

Note: On the next row, the first and last separating stitches are worked into the pattern on each side of the center separating stitch, which continues to mark the center of the shawl to the end.

- **NEXT ROW (RS, COUNTS A ROW 1 OF CHART B):** Work 3 edge stitches, slip marker, *work Row 1 of chart B over 119 stitches increasing them to 121 stitches as shown, removing markers on each side of separating stitch and working the marked 10-stitch repeat 11 times,** slip marker, k1 (center stitch), slip marker; repeat from * to ** once more, slip marker, work 3 edge stitches.

- Work Rows 2–20 of chart B. *You now have* 285 stitches: 3 edge stitches at each side, two pattern sections with 139 stitches each, and 1 center stitch.

- Work Rows 1–20 of chart B once more, working the marked 10-stitch repeat 13 times in each pattern section. *You now have* 325 stitches: 3 edge stitches at each side, two pattern sections with 159 stitches each, and 1 center stitch.

- Work Rows 1–10 of chart B once more, working the marked 10-stitch repeat 15 times in each pattern section. *You now have* 345 stitches: 3 edge stitches at each side, two pattern sections with 169 stitches each, and 1 center stitch.

Knitting Chart C

Note: The 3 edge stitches at each side and the center stitch are not shown on chart C; continue to work them as established.

- **NEXT ROW (RS, COUNTS AS ROW 1 OF CHART C):** Work 3 edge stitches, slip marker, *work Row 1 of chart C over 169 stitches increasing them to 171 stitches as shown and working the marked 10-stitch repeat 15 times,** slip marker, k1 (center stitch), slip marker; repeat from * to ** once more, slip marker, work 3 edge stitches.

- Work Rows 2–10 of chart C, removing all markers in the last row. *You now have* 365 stitches.

Finishing

- **BIND OFF AS FOLLOWS:** K1, *return last stitch worked to left-hand needle, k2tog tbl; repeat from * until all stitches are bound off.

- Weave in ends and block.

□	k on RS, p on WS
⊡	p on RS, k on WS
⟋	k2tog
⟍	ssk
○	yo
⅄	s2kp on RS, s2pp on WS (see Pattern Essentials)
⋎	slip 1 pwise wyif on RS
⋁	slip 1 pwise wyif on WS
⊞	pick up and knit 1 selvedge st
▦	no stitch

Mirabel C

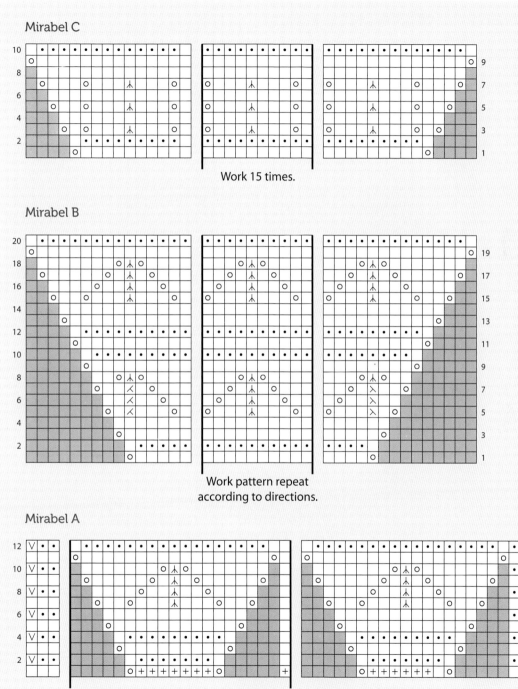

Work 15 times.

Mirabel B

Work pattern repeat
according to directions.

Mirabel A

Work 3 times.

Mary's Shawl

DESIGNED BY MARINA ORRY

A simple combination of stockinette stitch, decreases, and yarnovers is all there is to this lovely shawl. Worked back and forth on a circular needle, it's a great project for beginning lace knitters.

Finished Measurements

60"/152.5 cm wide and 20½"/52 cm deep

Yarn

Filitaly-Lab Piura, 65% alpaca, 25% nylon, 10% merino wool, 436 yds (399 m)/ 1.75 oz (50 g), Color 811

Needles

US 8 (5 mm) circular needle 24"/60 cm long *or size you need to obtain correct gauge* and US 11 (8 mm) needle for bind off

Gauge

14½ stitches and 26 rows = 4"/10 cm in stockinette, blocked

Other Supplies

Stitch markers, yarn needle

Knitting the Stockinette Section

- With circular needle, cast on 3 stitches, place marker, cast on 1 stitch, place marker, cast on 3 stitches. *You now have* 7 stitches.

- ROW 1 (RS): K2, yo, knit to first marker, slip marker, yo, knit to second marker, yo, slip marker, knit to last 2 stitches, yo, k2 — 4 stitches increased: 1 stitch at each end of marked center section and 1 stitch inside each 2-stitch border.

- **ROW 2 (WS):** Purl.

- Repeat Rows 1 and 2 thirty-six more times, ending with WS Row 2. *You now have* 155 stitches: 75 center stitches between markers and 40 stitches at each side.

Knitting the Lace Section

- **ROW 1 (RS):** K2, yo, k1, repeat (k2tog, yo) to 1 stitch before first marker, k1, slip marker, yo, k1, repeat (k2tog, yo) to 2 stitches before second marker, k2, yo, slip marker, k1, repeat (yo, k2tog) to last 3 stitches, k1, yo, k2 — 4 stitches increased.

- **ROWS 2 AND 4:** Purl.

- **ROW 3:** K2, yo, k1, repeat (k2tog, yo) to 2 stitches before first marker, k2, slip marker, yo, k1, repeat (k2tog, yo) to 2 stitches before second marker, k2, yo, slip marker, k1, repeat (yo, k2tog) to last 4 stitches, k2, yo, k2 — 4 stitches increased.

- Repeat Rows 1–4 ten more times, then work Rows 1–3 once more to end with a RS row. *You now have* 251 stitches: 123 center stitches between markers and 64 stitches at each side.

Finishing

- Using larger needle, loosely bind off all stitches purlwise on next WS row. Weave in ends. Block.

Isobel Shawl

DESIGNED BY RAE BLACKLEDGE

Isobel combines lace, cables, and cluster stitches and has a lovely scalloped edge. There is patterning on most rows, so you need to stay focused while knitting this one.

Finished Measurements

52"/132 cm wide and 26"/66 cm deep

Yarn

Alpaca with a Twist Fino, 70% alpaca/30% silk, 875 yds (800 m)/3.5 oz (100 g), Color 2002 Dry Grape

Needles

US 3 (3.25 mm) circular needle *or size you need to obtain correct gauge* and circular needles one and three sizes larger

Gauge

17 stitches and 32 rows = 4"/10 cm in chart E pattern on smallest needle, blocked

Other Supplies

16 stitch markers (4 color A, 12 color B), cable needle, yarn needle

PATTERN ESSENTIALS

- **1/1 RC** Slip 1 stitch to cable needle, hold in back, knit next stitch, knit stitch from cable needle.

- **2 (3, 5, 7)-Stitch Cluster** *Bring yarn to front, slip 2 (3, 5, 7) stitches purlwise, bring yarn to back, return slipped stitches to left-hand needle; repeat from * once more, pull yarn snug to gather slipped stitches together, purl 2 (3, 5, 7).

Knitting the Shawl

- With largest needle, cast on 375 stitches loosely, placing markers as follows:

- Cast on 22, place marker A, (cast on 22, place marker B) six times, cast on 23, place marker A, cast on 21, place marker A, (cast on 22, place marker B) six times, cast on 23, place marker A, cast on 22.

Note: The A markers indicate the boundaries between Charts A, B, C, and D, and the B markers indicate the internal repeats of Chart D. See charts on pages 196 through 199.

- Switch to the middle-size needle. Slipping markers as you come to them, establish Row 1 of chart patterns as follows: Work 22 stitches chart A, increasing them to 24 stitches; work 155 stitches chart D (working pattern repeat five times), increasing them to 169 stitches; work 21 stitches chart B, increasing them to 23 stitches; work 155 stitches chart D (working pattern repeat five times), increasing them to 169 stitches; work 22 stitches chart C, increasing them to 24 stitches.

- *You now have* 409 stitches: 24 stitches chart A, 23 stitches chart B, 24 stitches chart C, and two chart D sections with 169 stitches each.

- Continue working charts as established through Row 14, shifting the B markers between the internal chart D repeats as shown in Row 14 in order to work the clusters on the correct stitches. *You now have* 277 stitches: 8 stitches chart A, 7 stitches chart B, 8 stitches chart C, and two chart D sections with 127 stitches each.

- NEXT ROW (RS, ROW 15 OF CHARTS): Switch to smallest-size needles. Work first 7 stitches of chart A, decreasing them to 6 stitches, temporarily slip last stitch of chart A to right-hand needle, remove marker A, return slipped stitch to left-hand needle, replace marker A; work slipped stitch and first stitch of chart D together as ssk as shown on chart, work in pattern to last stitch of chart D (shifting the B markers as shown by the heavy repeat lines), temporarily slip last stitch to right-hand needle, remove marker A, return slipped stitch to left-hand needle and work last stitch of chart D and first stitch of chart B together as k2tog as shown on chart, replace marker A.

Work next 5 stitches of chart B decreasing them to 4 stitches, temporarily slip last stitch of chart B to right-hand needle, remove marker A, return slipped stitch to left-hand needle, replace marker A.

Work slipped stitch and first stitch of chart D together as ssk as shown on chart, work in pattern to last stitch of chart D (shifting the B markers as shown by the heavy repeat lines), temporarily slip last stitch to right-hand needle, remove marker A, return slipped stitch to left-hand needle and work last stitch of chart D and first stitch of chart C together as k2tog as shown on chart, replace marker A.

Work last 7 stitches of chart C decreasing them to 6 stitches.

You now have 270 stitches: 6 stitches chart A, 4 stitches chart B, 6 stitches chart C, and two chart D sections with 127 stitches each.

- Continue working charts as established through Row 22. *You now have* 258 stitches: 6 stitches chart A, 4 stitches chart B, 6 stitches chart C, and two chart D sections with 121 stitches each.

- Work Rows 23–34 of chart D, and *at the same time,* for charts A, B, and C repeat Rows 21 and 22 six times. *You now have* 234 stitches: 6 stitches chart A, 4 stitches chart B, 6 stitches chart C, and two chart D sections with 109 stitches each.

Note: From here to end of shawl, continue to repeat Rows 21 and 22 for charts A, B, and C.

- Change to smallest needle.

- NEXT ROW (RS): Keeping A markers in place, work 6 stitches chart A; *work Row 1 of chart E over 109 stitches (working pattern repeat 13 times) decreasing them to 107 stitches and removing all B markers;** work 4 stitches chart B; repeat from * to ** once more, work 6 stitches chart C. *You now have* 230 stitches: 6 stitches chart A, 4 stitches chart B, 6 stitches chart C, and two chart E sections with 107 stitches each.

- Continue working charts as established through Row 24 of chart E. *You now have* 186 stitches: 6 stitches chart A, 4 stitches chart B, 6 stitches chart C, and two chart E sections with 85 stitches each.

- Continuing charts as established, work Rows 1–24 of chart E three more times. *Note:* Each time you work chart E the stitch count decreases by 24 stitches and you work the 6-stitch pattern repeat four fewer times. For example, the next time you work Chart E there will be enough stitches to work the 6-stitch repeat nine times, then five times when you work the chart again, and then only one 6-stitch repeat the last time you work the chart.

You now have 42 stitches: 6 stitches chart A, 4 stitches chart B, 6 stitches chart C, and two chart E sections with 13 stitches each.

- NEXT ROW (RS): Work 6 stitches chart A, *work Row 1 of chart F over 13 stitches decreasing them to 11 stitches,** work 4 stitches chart B; repeat from * to ** once more, work 6 stitches chart C. *You now have* 38 stitches: 6 stitches chart A, 4 stitches chart B, 6 stitches chart C, and two chart F sections with 11 stitches each.

- Continuing charts as established, work Rows 2–11 of chart F, ending with RS Row 21 for charts A, B, and C. *You now have* 18 stitches: 6 stitches chart A, 4 stitches chart B, 6 stitches chart C, and two chart F sections with 1 stitch each.

- Work short rows as follows to eliminate the 4 center chart B stitches.

- ROW 1 (WS): Slip 1 purlwise wyif, p1, k1, p2, k1, p2tog, turn, leaving remaining stitches unworked at end of needle — 1 stitch decreased.

- ROW 2 (RS): Slip 1 purlwise wyib, p1, RC, p1, k2, turn.

- ROWS 3–8: Repeat Rows 1 and 2 three more times. *You now have* 14 stitches.

Finishing

- Cut yarn and thread tail onto yarn needle. Arrange stitches evenly on two needles (7 stitches on each needle) and use Kitchener stitch (see page 293) to graft the remaining stitches together.

- Weave in ends. Block.

Isobel C

Isobel B

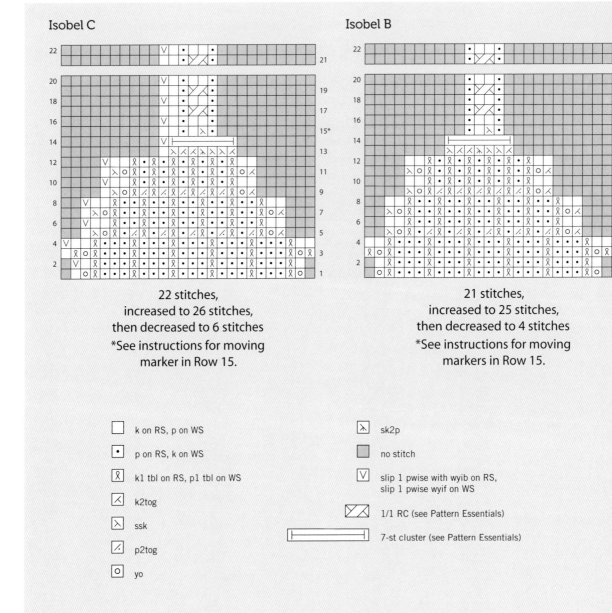

22 stitches,
increased to 26 stitches,
then decreased to 6 stitches
*See instructions for moving
marker in Row 15.

21 stitches,
increased to 25 stitches,
then decreased to 4 stitches
*See instructions for moving
markers in Row 15.

☐ k on RS, p on WS

• p on RS, k on WS

ℚ k1 tbl on RS, p1 tbl on WS

◺ k2tog

◿ ssk

◹ p2tog

⊙ yo

⋌ sk2p

▨ no stitch

∨ slip 1 pwise with wyib on RS,
slip 1 pwise wyif on WS

▱ 1/1 RC (see Pattern Essentials)

⊏⊐ 7-st cluster (see Pattern Essentials)

Isobel A

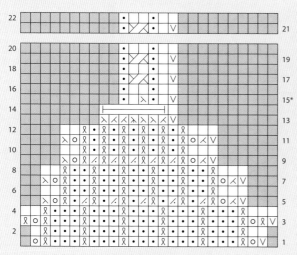

22 stitches,
increased to 26 stitches,
then decreased to 6 stitches
*See instructions for moving
marker in Row 15.

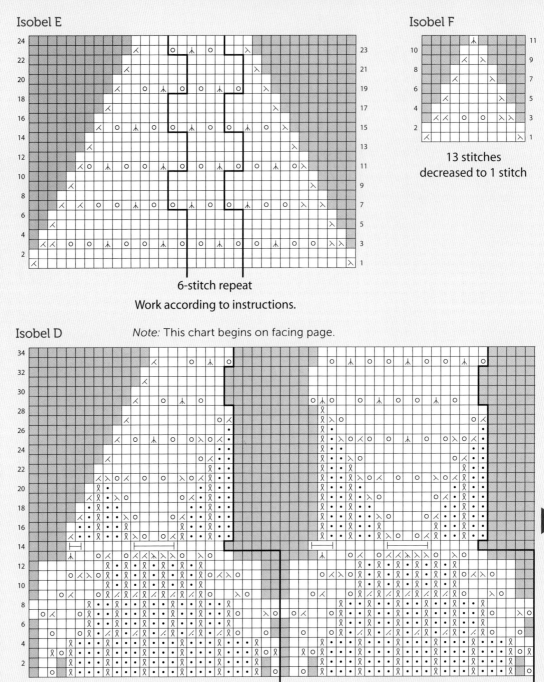

Isobel E

Isobel F

13 stitches
decreased to 1 stitch

6-stitch repeat

Work according to instructions.

Isobel D

Note: This chart begins on facing page.

22-stitch repeat
increased to 27-stitch repeat,
then decreased to 18-stitch repeat
Work pattern repeat 5 times.
*See instructions for moving markers in Row 15.

☐	k on RS, p on WS	
•	p on RS, k on WS	
ℛ	k1 tbl on RS, p1 tbl on WS	
⟋	k2tog	
⟍	ssk	
⟋	p2tog	
○	yo	
⟑	s2kp	
⟑	sk2p	
▧	no stitch	
⊢⊣	2-st cluster (see Pattern Essentials)	
⊢—⊣	3-st cluster (see Pattern Essentials)	
⊢——⊣	5-st cluster (see Pattern Essentials)	

(continued on facing page)

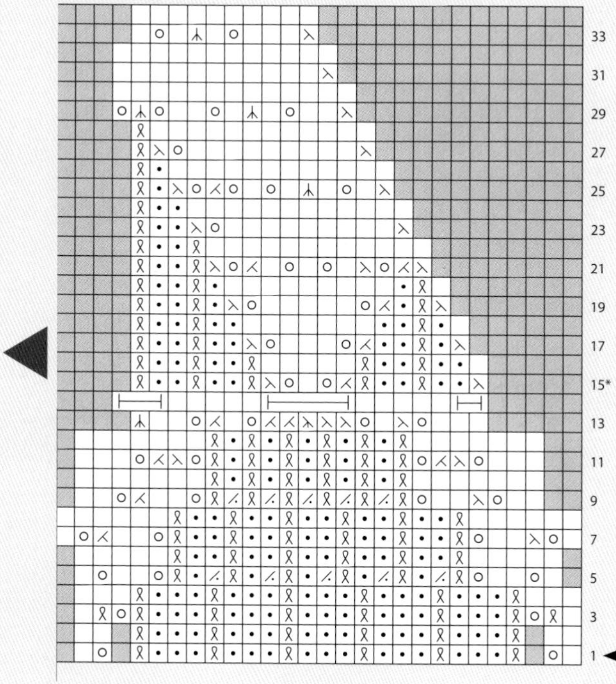

33
31
29
27
25
23
21
19
17
15*
13
11
9
7
5
3
1 ← begin here

Crashing Waves Shawl

DESIGNED BY ANGELA MYERS

This delightfully open lace shawl is knit with fingering-weight yarn on a large needle and uses less than 400 yards. Knit from the top down with a knitted-on border, it can be worked in any blockable yarn.

Finished Measurements
48"/122 cm wide and 25"/63.5 cm deep

Yarn
Three Irish Girls Carys BFL Sock, 100% superwash blue faced Leicester wool, 490 yds (448 m)/4 oz (113 g), Snow Queen

Needle
US 8 (5 mm) circular needle 32"/40 cm long *or size you need to obtain correct gauge*

Gauge
24 stitches (one Body chart repeat) = 6¾"/17 cm wide, blocked

Other Supplies
Stitch markers, yarn needle

Knitting the Shawl

• Cast on 3 stitches. Knit 5 rows.

• **PICKUP ROW (RS):** K3, then without turning the work, pick up and knit (see page 297) 3 stitches from the selvedge at the end of the row (1 stitch for each garter ridge), then pick up and knit 3 stitches from the cast-on edge. *You now have* 9 stitches.

• **ROW 1 (WS):** Purl.

• **ROW 2:** (K2, yo) twice, place marker, k1 (center stitch), place marker, (yo, k2) twice. *You now have* 13 stitches.

• **ROW 3:** K2, purl to last 2 stitches, k2.

Working the Setup Rows

Notes: The 2-stitch garter border continues as established at each side and is not shown on the charts. Only RS rows are charted; work all WS rows as k2, purl to the last 2 stitches, k2, working (k1, p1) in each double yarnover of the previous row. Slip marker on each side of center stitch every row. See charts on pages 202 and 203.

- NEXT ROW (RS): K2 (edge stitches), work Row 1 of Setup chart over next 4 stitches increasing them to 6 stitches, slip marker, k1 (center stitch), slip marker, work Row 1 of Setup chart over next 4 stitches increasing them to 6 stitches, k2 (edge stitches). *You now have* 17 stitches.

- NEXT ROW (WS): K2, purl to last 2 stitches working (k1, p1) in each double yo, k2.

- NEXT ROW: K2, work Row 3 of Setup chart over 6 stitches increasing them to 8 stitches, slip marker, k1, slip marker, work Row 3 of Setup chart over 6 stitches increasing them to 8 stitches, k2. *You now have* 21 stitches.

- Continue in this manner, working edge stitches and WS rows as established, until Row 24 of Setup chart has been completed. *You now have* 61 stitches.

Working the Body Chart

- Continuing as outlined above, work Rows 1–48 of Body chart once, working the chart as it appears on each side of the center stitch (that is, work the 24-stitch main pattern only once on each side of the center stitch). *You now have* 157 stitches.

- Work Rows 1–24 of the Body chart once more, working the 24-stitch repeat three times on each side of the center stitch. *You now have* 205 stitches: 1 center stitch and 102 stitches at each side (100 pattern stitches and 2 edge stitches).

Knitting the Edging

- With RS facing, use the backward loop method (see page 290) to cast on 7 stitches onto the left-hand needle. Work 6 rows as follows.

- ROWS 1 AND 3 (RS): K6, knit last edging stitch together with next body stitch, turn.

- ROWS 2 AND 4 (WS): Slip 1 purlwise wyif, knit to end of row.

- ROW 5: K1, (yo, k2tog) twice, yo, k1, k2tog (last edging stitch with next body stitch), turn. *You now have* 8 edging stitches and have joined 3 body stitches total.

- ROW 6: Slip 1 purlwise wyif, purl to end of row.

Notes: For the Edging and Point charts, knit the last stitch of every RS row together with the next body stitch, then turn. Work all WS rows as slip 1 purlwise wyif, purl to end.

- Work Rows 1–24 of the Edging chart seven times. *You now have* 15 body stitches remaining before the center stitch (118 body stitches total) and 8 edging stitches.

- Work Rows 1–62 of the Point chart once, removing center stitch markers as you come to them. *You now have* 87 body stitches and 8 edging stitches.

- Work Rows 1–24 of Edging chart seven more times. *You now have* 3 body stitches and 8 edging stitches.

- Work 6 more rows as follows.

- ROW 1 (RS): K1, (yo, ssk) twice, yo, k4tog (last 3 edging stitches with next stitch from body), turn. *You now have* 2 body stitches and 7 edging stitches.

- ROW 2 (WS): Slip 1 purlwise wyif, purl to end of row.

- ROWS 3 AND 5: K6, knit last edging stitch together with next body stitch, turn. *You now have* 7 edging stitches and no body stitches after completing Row 5.

- ROWS 4 AND 6: Slip 1 purlwise wyif, knit to end of row.

Finishing

- Bind off loosely knitwise. Weave in ends. Block as desired.

Body

Note: This chart begins on facing page.

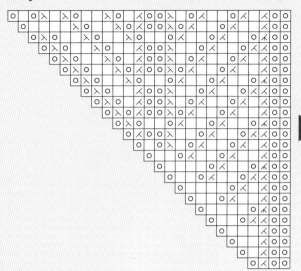

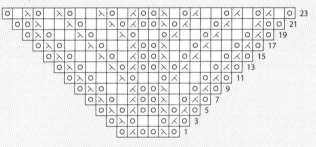

Setup

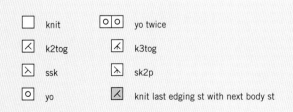

Only odd-numbered (RS) rows are charted.
See instructions for edge stitches and even-numbered (WS) rows.

	knit		o o	yo twice
	k2tog			k3tog
	ssk			sk2p
	yo			knit last edging st with next body st

(continued on facing page)

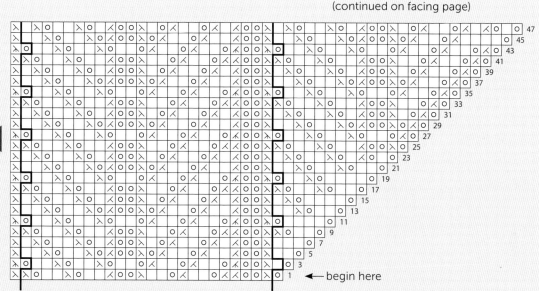

← begin here

24-stitch main pattern

Only odd-numbered (RS) rows are charted.
See instructions for border stitches and
even-numbered (WS) rows.

Point

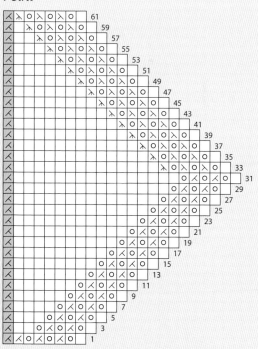

Only odd-numbered (RS) rows are charted.
See instructions for even-numbered (WS) rows.

Edging

Only odd-numbered (RS) rows are charted.
See instructions for even-numbered (WS) rows.

Indian Paintbrush Shawl

DESIGNED BY VERA SANON

According to Native American legend, the Indian paintbrush flower was used to paint the sky. It is a lovely flower and, translated to a lace insert, makes a lovely shawl. The shawl is knit from the top down in a semicircle.

Finished Measurements
48"/122 cm wide and 22"/56 cm deep

Yarn
Cascade Yarns Heritage 150 Sock Yarn, 75% superwash merino wool/25% nylon, 492 yds (450 m)/5.25 oz (150 g), Color 5637

Needle
US 7 (4.5 mm) circular needle 32"/80 cm or 40"/100 cm long *or size you need to obtain correct gauge*

Gauge
18 stitches and 29 rows = 4"/10 cm in stockinette stitch, blocked

Other Supplies
16 stitch markers (eight color 1, eight color 2), yarn needle

PATTERN NOTES

Maintain a 3-stitch garter border at the beginning and end of every row. Color 1 stitch markers are placed to mark the increases that are worked every fourth row inside the borders and between the four shawl sections. Color 2 stitch markers are placed to mark the lace patterns centered in each section. Slip markers on all rows unless otherwise instructed.

Knitting the Shawl

- Cast on 3 stitches.

- ROW 1 (RS): Kfb, k1, kfb. *You now have 5 stitches.*

- ROWS 2, 4, AND 6 (WS): Knit.

- ROW 3: Kfb, k3, kfb. *You now have 7 stitches.*

- ROW 5: Kfb, k5, kfb. *You now have 9 stitches.*

- ROW 7: K3, (yo, k1) three times, yo, k3. *You now have 13 stitches.*

- ROW 8 AND ALL EVEN-NUMBERED ROWS THROUGH ROW 34 (WS): K3, purl to last 3 stitches, k3.

- ROW 9: Knit.

- ROW 11: K3, *yo, k1; repeat from * to last 3 stitches, yo, k3. *You now have 21 stitches.*

- ROW 13: Knit.

- ROW 15: K3, place marker 1, (yo, k3, yo, place marker 1, k1, place marker 1) three times, yo, k3, yo, place marker 1, k3. *You now have 29 stitches.*

- ROW 17: Knit.

- ROW 19: K3, (slip marker 1, yo, knit to next marker 1, yo, slip marker 1, k1) three times, slip marker 1, yo, knit to next marker 1, yo, slip marker 1, k3. *You now have 37 stitches.*

- ROW 21: Knit.

- ROWS 23–34: Repeat Rows 19–22 three times. *You now have 61 stitches at the end of Row 34.*

- ROW 35: Repeat Row 19. *You now have 69 stitches: 3 border stitches at each side, 15 stitches each in four sections, and three 1-stitch marked divisions between sections.*

- ROW 36: K3, purl to last 3 stitches, k3.

Knitting the Lace Patterns

- NEXT ROW (RS): K3, slip marker 1, (k1, place marker 2, work Row 1 of chart A over center 13 stitches of section, place marker 2, k1, slip marker 1, k1, slip marker 1) three times, k1, place marker 2, work Row 1 of chart A over center 13 stitches of last section, place marker 2, k1, slip marker 1, k3.

- NEXT ROW AND ALL WS ROWS TO END OF CHARTS: K3, purl to last 3 stitches, k3.

- Continue working lace pattern as instructed below and *at the same time* beginning on the next RS row (Row 3 of chart A), increase every fourth row next to the Color 2 markers as follows.

- INCREASE ROW (RS): K3, (slip marker 2, yo, knit to next marker 1, slip marker 1, work next row of lace pattern, slip marker 1, knit to next marker 2, yo, slip marker 2, k1) three times; slip marker 2, yo, knit to next marker 1, slip marker 1, work next row of lace pattern, slip marker 1, knit to next marker 2, yo, slip marker 2, k3 — 8 stitches increased. Work all increased stitches in stockinette stitch on the following rows.

- Work Rows 4–8 of chart A once, working Increase Row on Row 7. Work Rows 1–8 of chart A four more times, working Increase Row on Rows 3 and 7 of each repeat, and removing marker 2 in final row. *You now have* 149 stitches: 3 border stitches at each side, 35 stitches each in four sections, and three 1-stitch marked divisions between sections.

- Establish pattern from Chart B and place new marker 2 on next row as follows.

- NEXT ROW (RS): K3, slip marker 1, (k10, place marker 2, work Row 1 of chart B over center 15 stitches of section, place marker 2, k10, slip marker 1, k1, slip marker 1) three times, k10, place marker 2, work Row 1 of chart B over center 15 stitches of last section, place marker 2, k10, slip marker 1, k3.

- Work Rows 2–12 of chart B once, then work Rows 1–12 two more times, and *at the same time* work Increase Row on Rows 3, 7, and 11 of each repeat, then remove marker 2 in final row. *You now have* 221 stitches: 3 border stitches at each side, 53 stitches each in four sections, and three 1-stitch marked divisions between sections.

- Establish pattern from chart C and place new marker 2 on next row as follows.

- **NEXT ROW (RS):** K3, slip marker 1, (k18, place marker 2, work Row 1 of chart C over center 17 stitches of section, place marker 2, k18, slip marker 1, k1, slip marker 1) three times, k18, place marker 2, work Row 1 of chart C over center 17 stitches of last section, place marker 2, k18, slip marker 1, k3.

- Work Rows 2–28 of chart C once, and *at the same time* work Increase Row on Rows 3, 7, 11, 15, 19, 23, and 27 of chart. *You now have* 277 stitches: 3 border stitches at each side, 67 stitches each in four sections, and three 1-stitch marked divisions between sections.

Finishing

- Removing markers in first row, knit all stitches for 6 rows. Bind off with the loosest or stretchiest bind off you know. Weave in ends. Block to measurements.

Indian Paintbrush C

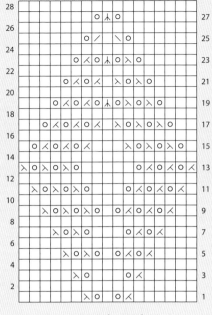

17-stitch panel

Indian Paintbrush B

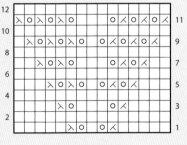

15-stitch panel

Indian Paintbrush A

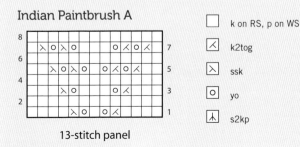

13-stitch panel

☐	k on RS, p on WS
⟋	k2tog
⟍	ssk
o	yo
⟑	s2kp

206

Julep's Beaded Shawl

DESIGNED BY MEG MYERS

*This crescent-shaped wrap begins with a lace border that has beads placed on both right-
and wrong-side rows using a crochet hook. The stockinette section is shaped with short
rows and finished with a row of beads below the slim garter stitch border at the top.*

Finished Measurements

Approximately 32"/81.5 cm along inner edge, 72"/183 cm along outer edge, and 11"/28 cm deep at center back

Yarn

Classic Elite Yarns Silky Alpaca Lace, 70% alpaca/30% silk, 440 yds (402 m)/ 1.75 oz (50 g), Color 2438 Cameroon

Needles

US 3 (3.25 mm) circular needle 24"/ 60 cm long *or size you need to obtain correct gauge* and one circular needle two sizes larger than gauge needle 24"/60 cm long

Gauge

24 stitches and 40 rows = 4"/10 cm in stockinette stitch with smaller needle, blocked

Other Supplies

Steel crochet hook small enough to fit through beads, 14 g size 8° seed beads (shown with Miyuki Delica 8° hex metallic purple/gold), locking stitch marker, yarn needle, T-pins for blocking

PATTERN NOTE

Although a circular needle is used to accommodate the large number of stitches, work back and forth in rows.

PATTERN ESSENTIALS

Place Bead Slide a bead onto the crochet hook, remove next stitch from left-hand needle with the crochet hook, push the bead down onto the stitch, return stitch to left-hand needle and knit the beaded stitch on RS rows and purl the beaded stitch on WS rows.

Wrap and Turn On RS rows, wyib slip next stitch from left- to right-hand needle, bring yarn to front, slip stitch back to left-hand needle, turn. On WS rows, wyif slip next stitch from left- to right-hand needle, bring yarn to back, slip the stitch back to left-hand needle, turn.

Knitting the Wrap

- With larger needle, cast on 391 stitches using the long-tail method (see page (294).

- Change to smaller needle and work Rows 1–35 of Julep's Lace chart, using crochet hook to place beads as indicated. *You now have* 313 stitches. Place a locking marker in the center stitch (156 stitches on each side of the marked stitch); this marker is in the stitch itself, and not on the needle between stitches.

- EYELET ROW (RS): K3, ssk, (yo, k2tog) 75 times, yo, sk2p, yo, (ssk, yo) 75 times, k2tog, k3. *You now have* 311 stitches (155 stitches on each side of the marked center stitch).

- NEXT ROW (WS): K3, place bead and purl beaded stitch, purl to last 4 stitches, place bead and purl beaded stitch, k3.

Setting Up for Short Rows

- Cut yarn. With RS facing, slip 155 stitches purlwise from left- to right-hand needle without working them. Beginning with the center stitch, attach the yarn, ready to work a RS row.

- ROW 1 (RS): K3, wrap and turn.

Julep's Lace (continued on facing page)

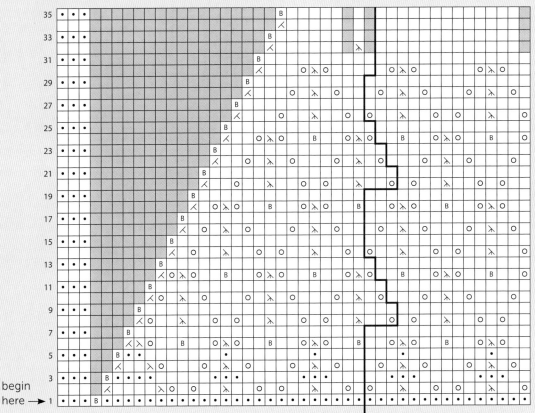

16-stitch repeat
decreased to 14-stitch repeat

Work pattern repeat 21 times.

- **ROW 2 (WS):** P5, wrap and turn.

  Note: As you work each wrapped stitch, always pick up the wrap and work it together with the stitch it wraps as a single stitch.

- **ROW 3:** Knit to wrapped stitch of previous RS row, ssk (wrapped stitch, its wrap, and the stitch after it), k2, wrap and turn — 1 stitch decreased.

- **ROW 4:** Purl to wrapped stitch of previous WS row, p2tog (wrapped stitch, its wrap, and stitch after it), p2, wrap and turn — 1 stitch decreased.

- Repeat Rows 3 and 4 thirty-six more times. *You now have* 237 stitches, with 1 wrapped stitch and 4 unworked stitches at each end of the row.

- **NEXT ROW (RS):** Knit to the wrapped stitch, ssk, knit to end of row.

- **NEXT ROW (WS):** K3, purl to wrapped stitch, p2tog, k3. *You now have* 235 stitches.

Note: This chart begins on facing page.

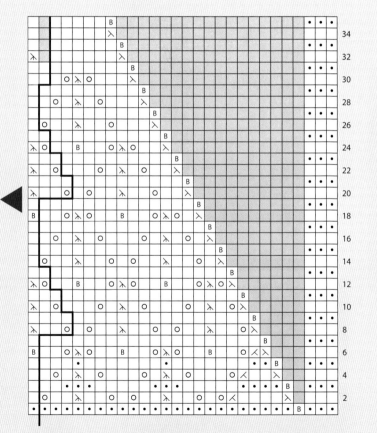

☐	k on RS, p on WS
•	p on RS, k on WS
⟋	k2tog
⟍	ssk
○	yo
⅄	sk2p
B	place bead; k on RS, p on WS
▨	no stitch

209

Placing the Edging Beads

- **NEXT ROW (RS):** K3, place bead and knit beaded stitch, ssk, *k1, place bead and knit beaded stitch; repeat from * to last 5 stitches, slip 1 knitwise wyib, place bead and knit beaded stitch, slip last 2 stitches back to left-hand needle, k2tog, k3. *You now have 233 stitches.*

- Knit 3 rows.

- With larger needle, loosely bind off all stitches knitwise on the RS.

Finishing

- Wet-block the shawl, pinning the lace section open. Weave in ends.

{ *Using Lifelines* }

One fear many knitters have about knitting lace is dropping stitches. While picking up stitches is easy in stockinette or other simple stitch patterns, with lace it's nearly impossible to pick up a dropped stitch. So for insurance, many of us use lifelines.

Thread a piece of smooth contrasting yarn that is longer than your knitting row onto a yarn needle. When you've successfully finished a few rows, thread the cord through all the stitches on the needle (but don't pass through the stitch markers!) and leave the ends hanging out on each side of the row. (If you're the nervous type, use a lifeline that is twice the width of your knitting and tie the ends together.) Now continue knitting your lace pattern. If you drop a stitch in the next few rows that you can't pick up, simply rip back to the row with the lifeline and place the stitches back on the needle. If you place a lifeline every eight rows, you'll never have to re-knit more than that!

Cortona Kerchief

DESIGNED BY JULIE BLAGOJEVICH

Cortona is a lacy neckerchief designed to be worn with the point in the front. You'll begin at the longest edge and decrease to the point, making chain stitches along the edges to accommodate the edging that is added when the piece is finished.

Finished Measurements
Approximately 34"/86 cm wide and 13"/33 cm deep

Yarn
Lana Grossa Lace Lux, 67% viscose/ 33% virgin merino wool, 339 yds (310 m)/ 1.75 oz (50 g), Color 004 Bronze

Crochet Hook
US 7 (4.5 mm) *or size you need to obtain correct gauge*

Gauge
18 stitches and 16 rows = 4"/10 cm in pattern from body of kerchief

Other Supplies
Yarn needle

PATTERN ESSENTIALS

Picot Chain 3, then work single crochet in 3rd chain from hook (the first of the 3 chain stitches).

Crocheting the Kerchief

- Chain 139.

- ROW 1: Dc in 4th ch from hook and in each chain across. The first 3 skipped chains count as the first dc. *You now have* 137 dc.

- ROW 2: Ch 1, turn; sc in first dc; *ch 3, sc in 3rd ch from hook (picot made); skip next dc, sc in next dc; repeat from * to end of row. **Note:** Make the final sc in the top of the ch-3 from the previous row.

- ROW 3: Ch 4, turn; skip the first 4 stitches (first sc, first picot, 2nd sc, and 2nd picot), slip stitch in next sc; push the ch-4 just made behind the 4 skipped stitches; ch-4 (counts as dc and ch 1), skip next picot, dc in next sc; *ch 1, skip next picot, dc in next sc; repeat from * ending with dc in 5th stitch from row end. Leave the last 4 stitches (2 picots and 2 sc) unworked. *You now have* 129 stitches.

- ROW 4: Ch 1, turn; sc in 1st dc; *make picot, sc in next dc; repeat from * to end of row. **Note:** Make the final sc in the 3rd ch of the ch-4 from the previous row.

- ROW 5: Repeat Row 3. *You now have* 121 stitches.

- ROW 6: Repeat Row 4.

- ROWS 7–34: Repeat Rows 3 and 4 fourteen times with the following stitch counts at row ends:

- ROWS 7 AND 8: 113 stitches.

- ROWS 9 AND 10: 105 stitches.

- ROWS 11 AND 12: 97 stitches.

- ROWS 13 AND 14: 89 stitches.

- ROWS 15 AND 16: 81 stitches.

- ROWS 17 AND 18: 73 stitches.

- ROWS 19 AND 20: 65 stitches.

- ROWS 21 AND 22: 57 stitches.

- ROWS 23 AND 24: 49 stitches.

- ROWS 25 AND 26: 41 stitches.

- ROWS 27 AND 28: 33 stitches.

- ROWS 29 AND 30: 25 stitches.

- ROWS 31 AND 32: 17 stitches.

- ROWS 33 AND 34: 9 stitches.

- ROW 35: Ch 3, turn; skip the first 2 stitches (first sc and first picot), slip stitch in next sc; push the ch-3 just made behind the skipped stitches; ch 4 (counts as dc and ch 1), skip next picot, dc in next sc, ch 1, skip next picot, dc in next sc. Leave remaining 2 stitches unworked. *You now have* 5 stitches.

- ROW 36: Ch 1, turn; sc in first dc, make picot, sc in next dc, make picot, sc in top of ch-3 at row end.

- ROW 37: Ch 4, turn; skip first 4 stitches (sc, picot, sc, and picot), slip stitch in final sc in the row; tuck the ch-4 just made behind the skipped stitches.

Chaining the Left Side

- With RS of kerchief facing you, work down the left side of the triangle as follows.

- Loosely slip stitch into the stitches at the end of the picot row and the dc row (Rows 35 and 36) and slip stitch in the next sc (in Row 35). Ch 3; attach the chain with a slip stitch in the sc at the end of Row 35; tuck the ch-3 behind the skipped stitches, essentially moving the chains to the WS of the kerchief. You have now duplicated the ch-3 at the start of Row 35 on the right-hand side of the triangle with a ch-3 on the left-hand side.

- Loosely slip stitch into the stitches at the end of the picot row and the dc row. Slip stitch in the next sc (in the row below). Ch 4; attach this chain with a slip stitch in the sc at the end of the row; tuck this chain behind the skipped stitches, essentially moving the chain to the WS of the kerchief. You have now duplicated the ch-4 on the right-hand side of the triangle with a ch-4 on the left-hand side.

- Continue along row ends in this way until you complete the very last row end with a ch-4, tucking each chain behind the skipped stitches as before. *You now have* a ch-4 space at the top point of the triangle, one ch-3 space at each side just below the top point, and 16 ch-4 spaces along each side.

Adding Picots to the Top

- With RS still facing and beginning at lower left-hand side of kerchief, work along row ends of the first 2 rows as ch 1, sc in same place, make picot, sc in row end; make picot, sc in first foundation chain, make picot, sc in same stitch (corner made). Make picot, rotate kerchief so foundation edge is across the top, and work along foundation chains as sc in next stitch, *make picot, skip next foundation ch, sc in next ch; repeat from * to next corner. Work (sc, picot, sc) as for previous corner. Now work along row ends on the remaining side of the first 2 rows as make picot, sc in row end, make picot, slip stitch in final stitch of the row ends.

Crocheting the Edging

- The edging is worked into the ch-4 and ch-3 spaces you created earlier. With RS facing, slip stitch in first ch-4 space behind row end. Work edging as follows.

- ROW 1: Slip stitch in first ch-4 space, ch 3 (counts as 1st dc), work (3 dc, ch 2, 4 dc) all in same ch-4 space. In each of the remaining 15 ch-4 spaces working toward the kerchief point, work (4 dc, ch 2, 4 dc). In the next ch-3 space, work (3 dc, ch 2, 3 dc). In the ch-4 space at the point, work (4 dc, ch 2, 4 dc). In the next ch-3 space work (3 dc, ch 2, 3 dc). In the next 16 ch-4 spaces, work (4 dc, ch 2, 4 dc).

- ROW 2: Ch 1, turn. Along first side, *work 1 sc in each of next 4 dc, work (sc, ch 6, sc) all in ch-2 space, work 1 sc in each of next 4 dc; repeat from * 15 more times. In next group, work 1 sc in each of next 3 dc, work (sc, ch 6, sc) all in ch-2 space, work 1 sc in each of next 3 dc. At the point, work 1 sc in each of next 4 dc, work (sc, ch 6, sc) all in ch-2 space, work 1 sc in each of next 4 dc. Along second side, *work 1 sc in each of next 4 dc, work (sc, ch 6, sc) all in ch-2 space, work 1 sc in each of next 4 dc; repeat from * 15 more times.

- ROW 3: Ch 1, turn. *Loosely slip stitch in each sc to next ch-6 space, then work (sc, picot, sc, picot, sc, picot, sc, picot, sc) all in same ch-6 space, repeat from * until last ch-6 space has been worked, then loosely slip stitch in each sc to end of row.

- ROW 4: Ch 3, turn. Slip stitch in first picot, work (ch 2, slip stitch in next picot) three times; *ch 3, slip stitch in next picot, work (ch 2, slip stitch in next picot) three times; repeat from * ending with ch 3 and join with a slip stitch to the beginning slip stitch in Row 3.

Finishing

- Fasten off. Weave in ends. Block.

Snowdrop Shawlette

DESIGNED BY AMANDA CARRIGAN

The border takes center stage on this triangular shawl. The sample used every bit of a 328-yard/300-meter ball of yarn, but if you have more, you can easily make the shawl larger by working more repeats.

Finished Measurements

37"/94 cm across top edge, 19"/48.5 cm deep, blocked

Yarn

Diamond Yarns Luxury Cashmere/Silk Lace Weight, 70% cashmere/30% silk, 328 yds (300 m)/0.88 oz (25 g), Winter White
Note: The designer recommends you work with a skein that has at least 372 yds/340 m.

Needle

US 6 (4 mm) circular needle 24"/60 cm long *or size you need to obtain correct gauge*

Gauge

18 stitches = 4"/10 cm in pattern, blocked

Other Supplies

Stitch markers, yarn needle

PATTERN ESSENTIALS

- **1 into 3** Work (k1, yo, k1) all in same stitch — 3 stitches made from 1 stitch.

- **3 into 9** Insert right-hand needle into next 3 stitches as if to k3tog, and without removing stitches from the left-hand needle work (k1, yo) four times, k1 all in same 3-stitch bundle, then slip all 3 stitches from needle — 9 stitches made from 3 stitches.

Knitting the Shawl Body

- Cast on 3 stitches.
- ROW 1 (WS): Knit.
- ROW 2 (RS): Kfb, k1, kfb. *You now have* 5 stitches.
- ROW 3: Knit.
- ROW 4: Kfb, k3, kfb. *You now have* 7 stitches.
- ROW 5: Knit.
- ROW 6: K3, yo, k1 tbl, yo, k3. *You now have* 9 stitches.
- ROW 7: K3, p3, k3.
- ROW 8: K3, yo, k1, yo, place marker, k1 tbl (center stitch), yo, k1, yo, k3. *You now have* 13 stitches.
- ROW 9: K3, purl to last 3 stitches, k3.
- ROW 10: K3, yo, k1, (1 into 3), k1, yo, slip marker, k1 tbl (center stitch), yo, k1, (1 into 3), k1, yo, k3. *You now have* 21 stitches.
- ROW 11: K3, purl to last 3 stitches, k3.
- ROW 12: K3, yo, k1, (1 into 3), *k3tog, (1 into 3); repeat from * to 1 stitch before center stitch, k1, yo, slip marker, k1 tbl (center stitch), yo, k1, **(1 into 3), k3tog; repeat from ** to last 5 stitches, (1 into 3), k1, yo, k3 — 8 stitches increased: 1 stitch on each side of center stitch, 1 stitch inside each 3-stitch garter edge, and 2 stitches each in first and last (1 into 3) stitch of row.

Note: The first time you work Row 12 there will only be enough stitches to work the repeated sections from * to * and from ** to ** once each. Every time you repeat Rows 11 and 12 thereafter, enough stitches will have been increased to work each repeated section once more.

- Repeat Rows 11 and 12 twenty-nine more times, then work Row 11 again to end with a WS row. *You now have* 261 stitches; the final Row 12 contains 31 (1 into 3) clusters on each side of the center stitch.

Notes: The body of the shawl can be adjusted as desired as long as you finish with the number of (1 into 3) clusters on each side of the center stitch equal to a multiple of 3 plus 1 (e.g., 34, 37, or 40 clusters). Each additional cluster is paired with a k3tog decrease to make a unit of 4 stitches, so adding 3 clusters at each side (six 4-stitch units total) increases the stitch count by 24 stitches. For example, 34 clusters on each side of the center stitch give a total of 285 stitches.

Knitting the Border

Note: The border instructions are written for a shawl body that ends with 261 stitches. If you increased the size of the shawl body, work the Setup Row with one extra repeat of the border chart on each side of the center stitch for every 24 stitches added.

- SETUP ROW (RS): Work Row 1 of Border chart as follows to establish pattern. Work 8 stitches before the marked repeat once, increasing them to 14 stitches. Work the 12-stitch repeat 10 times, working gold-shaded stitches as shown and increasing each repeat to 14 stitches, and ending 2 stitches before the center stitch. For the next repeat *only*, work the gold-shaded stitches on the chart as k5, then work the following 3 stitches as (3 into 9); the center stitch is the middle stitch of the k5, and the last 8 stitches have increased to 14 stitches. Work the 12-stitch repeat 10 times, working gold-shaded stitches as shown and increasing each repeat to 14 stitches, and ending before the last 5 stitches. Work 5 stitches after the marked repeat once. *You now have* 313 stitches.
- Working stitches outside the repeat as shown and working the pattern repeat 21 times in each row, work Rows 2–20 of Border chart. *You now have* 515 stitches.

Finishing

- Bind off as follows on next RS row: *K2tog, slip stitch back to left-hand needle; repeat from * until 1 stitch remains, then fasten off last stitch.
- Weave in ends and block.

Border

Note: This chart begins on facing page.

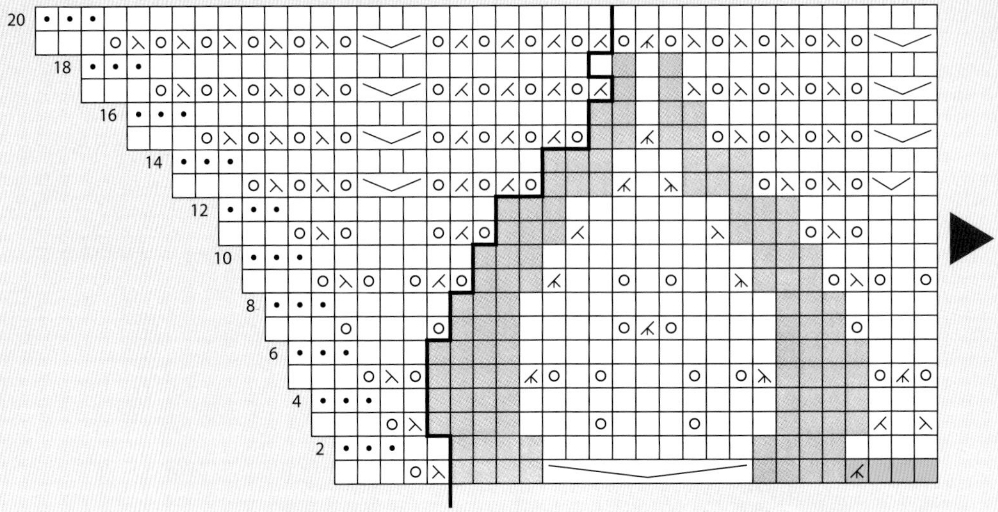

12-stitch repeat
increased to 22-stitch repeat

See instructions for gold-shaded stitches.

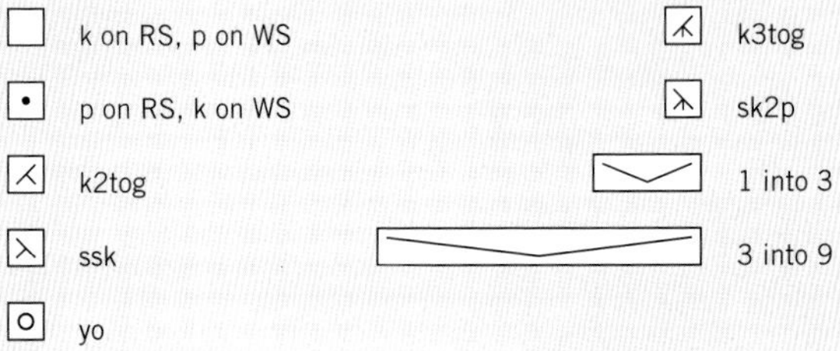

☐ k on RS, p on WS	⟋	k3tog
• p on RS, k on WS	⟍	sk2p
⟋ k2tog	⌄	1 into 3
⟍ ssk	⌄⌄	3 into 9
○ yo		

(continued on facing page)

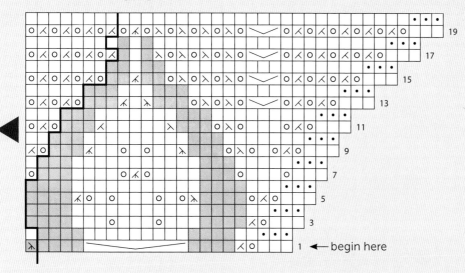

← begin here

Grapevine Shawl

DESIGNED BY HEATHER BROADHURST

This top-down triangle shawl features mirrored variations on the Ivy pattern from Barbara Walker's Third Treasury of Knitting Patterns *(Schoolhouse Press, 1998) transitioning into the Traveling Vine pattern from* A Treasury of Knitting Patterns *(Schoolhouse Press, 1998), which extends out from the center spine of the shawl. The Traveling Vine pattern is identified as French in origin, as is the grape used to produce the colorway's namesake wine, Syrah.*

Finished Measurements
41"/104 cm across longest edge and 21"/53.5 cm deep at center back

Yarn
Curious Creek Fibers Gombe, 100% super fine alpaca, 293 yds (268 m)/3.5 oz (100 g), Petite Syrah

Needle
US 7 (4.5 mm) circular needle 24"/60 cm long *or size you need to obtain correct gauge*

Gauge
16–18 stitches (two pattern repeats) and 21 rows = 4"/10 cm in pattern from charts B and C, blocked

Other Supplies
Stitch markers, yarn needle

Special Abbreviations
LB (left border) on RS rows, work last 3 stitches as k1, yo, k2tog; on WS rows, knit first 3 stitches
RB (right border) on RS rows, work first 3 stitches as ssk, yo, k1; on WS rows, knit last 3 stitches

Knitting the Shawl

• Cast on 9 stitches. Purl 1 WS row.

Setting Up the Rows

• **ROW 1 (RS):** RB, yo, k1, yo, k1 (center stitch), yo, k1, yo, LB. *You now have* 13 stitches.

PATTERN NOTES

The first and last 3 stitches are worked in 3-stitch border patterns as noted at left. The border stitches are not shown in the charts. The center stitch is worked as k1 on both RS and WS rows and is shown in chart A, but not shown in charts B and C.

• **ROW 2 (WS):** LB, p3, k1, p3, RB.

• **ROW 3:** RB, yo, k3, yo, k1, yo, k3, yo, LB. *You now have 17 stitches.*

• **ROW 4:** LB, p5, k1, p5, RB.

• **ROW 5:** RB, yo, k5, yo, k1, yo, k5, yo, LB. *You now have 21 stitches.*

• **ROW 6:** LB, p7, k1, p7, RB.

• **ROW 7:** RB, yo, k7, yo, k1, yo, k7, yo, LB. *You now have 25 stitches.*

• **ROW 8:** LB, p9, k1, p9, RB.

Grapevine A

Legend:

- ☐ k on RS, p on WS
- • p on RS, k on WS
- ⟋ k2tog on RS, p2tog on WS
- ⟍ ssk on RS, p2tog tbl on WS
- ○ yo
- ▨ no stitch

Working Chart A

- **NEXT ROW (RS):** RB, work Row 1 of chart A over center 19 stitches increasing them to 23 stitches as shown, LB. *You now have* 29 stitches.

- **NEXT ROW (WS):** LB, work Row 2 of chart A over center 23 stitches, RB.

- Working the first and last 3 stitches in border patterns, work Rows 3–10 of chart A. *You now have* 45 stitches.

Working Charts B and C

Note: Each pattern repeat in charts B and C increases to 9 stitches after completing a RS row, and then decreases back to an 8-stitch repeat after completing a WS row.

- **NEXT ROW (RS):** RB, work Row 1 of chart B over next 19 stitches working marked pattern repeat once, k1 (center stitch), work Row 1 of chart C over next 19 stitches working marked pattern repeat once, LB.

- **NEXT ROW (WS):** LB, work Row 2 of chart C, k1 (center stitch), work Row 2 of chart B, RB.

- Working border patterns and center stitch as established, work Rows 3–48 of charts B and C. *You now have 141 stitches: 3 border stitches at each side, 1 center stitch, and 67 stitches each in charts B and C.*

- Working border patterns and center stitch as established, work Rows 1–41 of charts B and C once more, working the marked pattern repeat seven times for each chart. *You now have 247 stitches: 3 border stitches at each side, 1 center stitch, and 120 stitches each in charts B and C.*

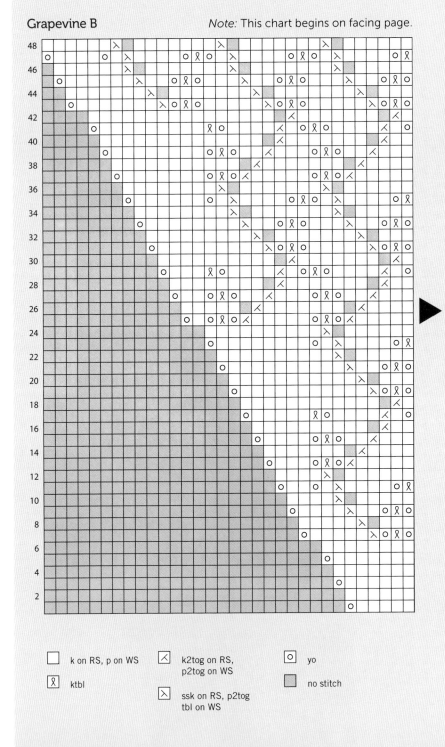

Grapevine B

Note: This chart begins on facing page.

| ☐ | k on RS, p on WS | ⟋⟍ | k2tog on RS, p2tog on WS | ○ | yo |
| ℘ | ktbl | ⟍ | ssk on RS, p2tog tbl on WS | ▨ | no stitch |

(continued on facing page)

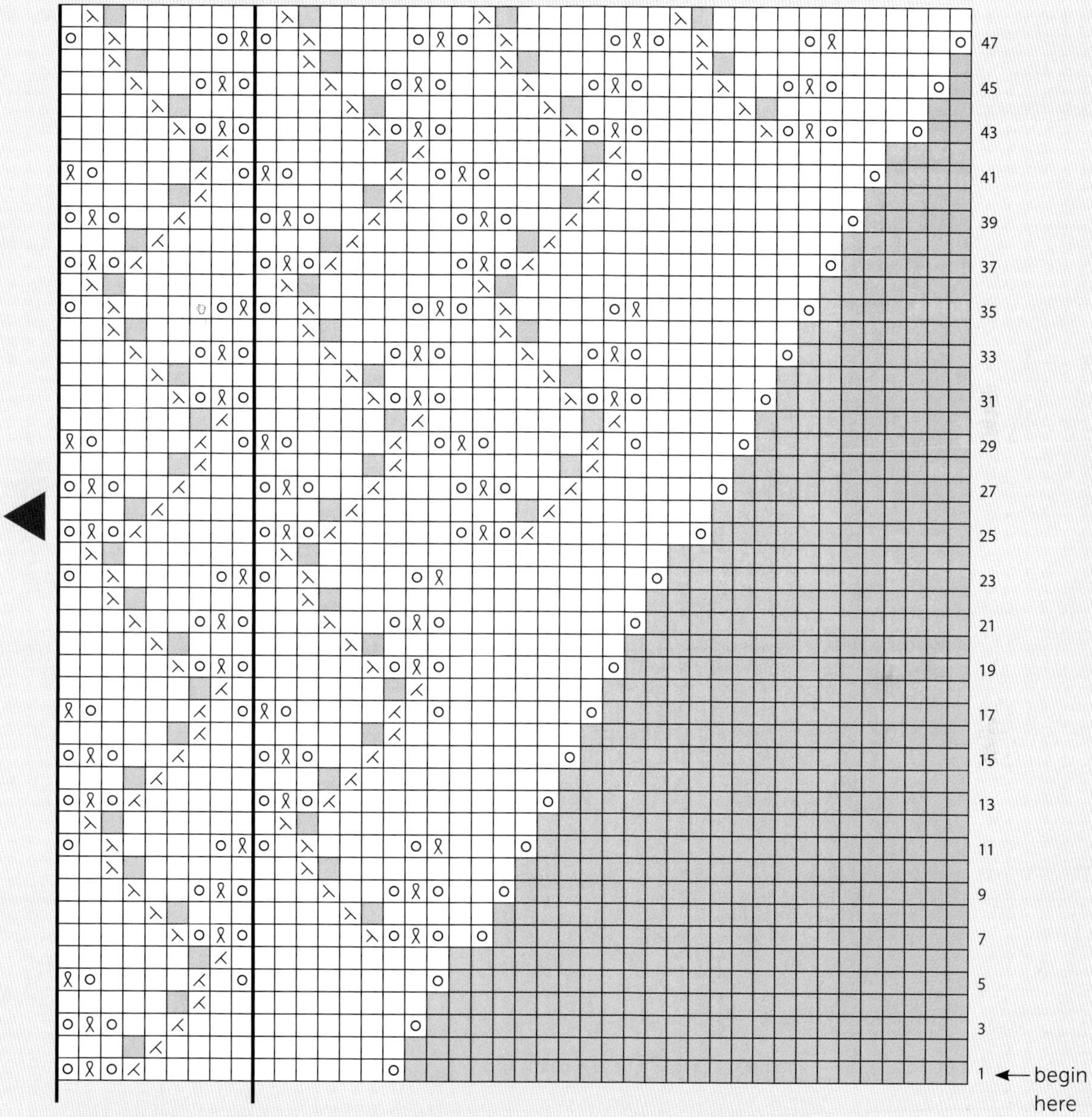

8- to 9-stitch repeat

Work pattern repeat
according to directions.

Working the Garter Stitch Edge

- **ROW 1 (WS):** LB, knit to last 3 stitches, RB.

- **ROW 2 (RS):** RB, yo, knit to center stitch, yo, k1, yo, knit to last 3 stitches, yo, LB. *You now have 251 stitches.*

- **ROW 3:** Repeat Row 1.

- **ROW 4:** Knit.

Finishing

- Bind off all stitches loosely.

- Use cast-on tail to sew the first and last stitches of the cast-on row together, forming a small keyhole in the center of the top edge. Weave in ends. Block lightly.

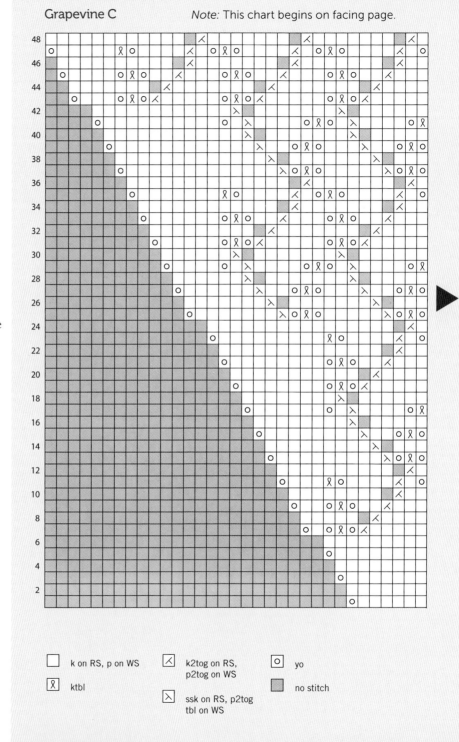

Grapevine C   *Note:* This chart begins on facing page.

	k on RS, p on WS		k2tog on RS, p2tog on WS		yo
	ktbl		ssk on RS, p2tog tbl on WS		no stitch

(continued on facing page)

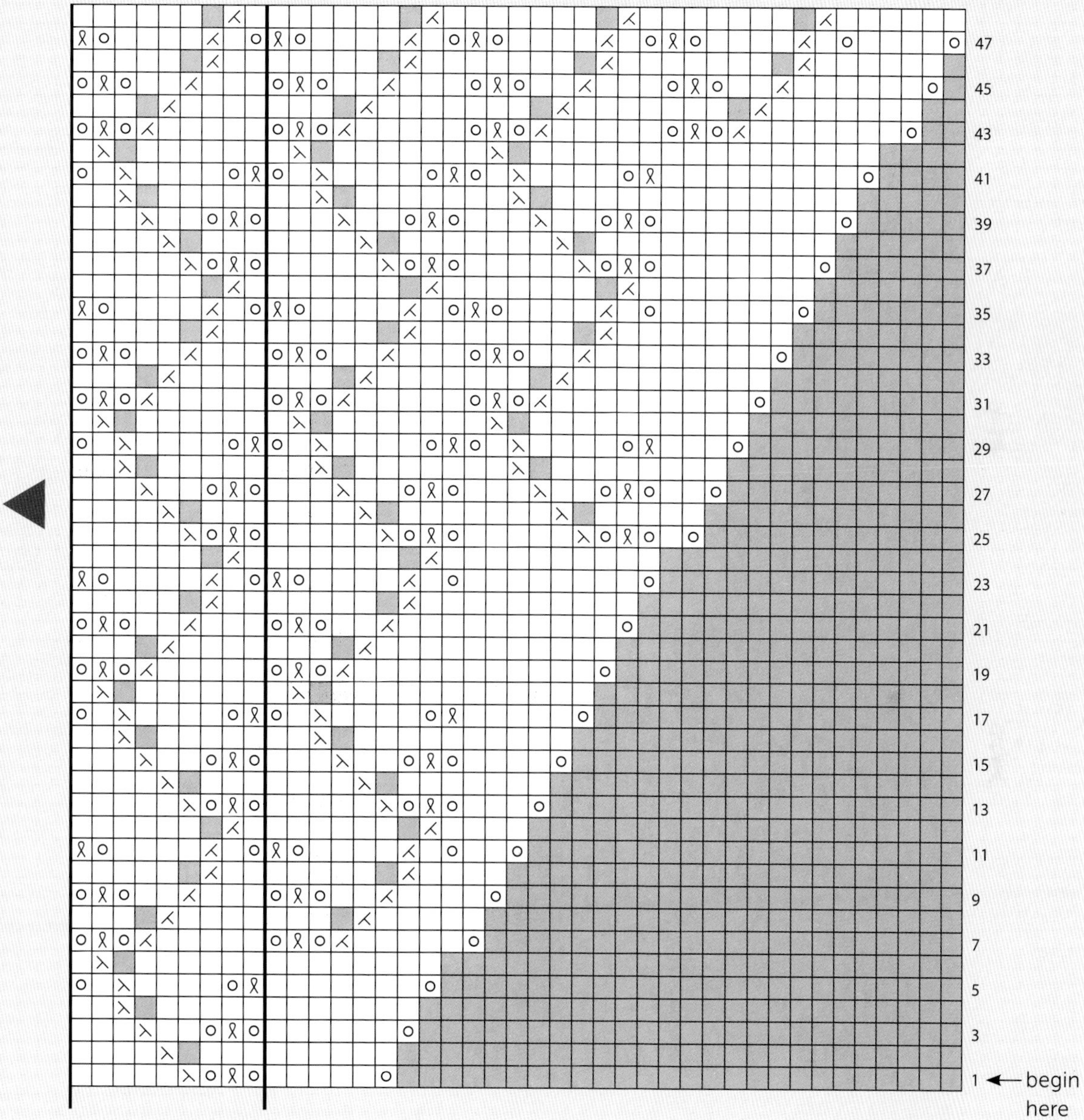

8- to 9-stitch repeat

Work pattern repeat
according to directions.

Simply Sweet Shawl

DESIGNED BY SHARON BALLSMITH

Light as a feather, this sweet and very open shawl is crocheted with an easy-to-remember lace pattern. The top edge features soft clusters, and the bottom is edged with openwork scallops between picots. This is a go-anywhere shawl.

Finished Measurements

62"/157.5 cm wide and 19"/48.5 cm deep

Yarn

Patons Lace, 80% acrylic/10% mohair/10% wool, 498 yds (455 m)/3 oz (85 g), Color 33008 Vintage

Crochet Hooks

US I/9 (5.5 mm) *or size you need to obtain correct gauge* and US H/8 (5 mm)

Gauge

5 V-stitches plus 2 dc and 8 rows of gauge swatch = approximately 4"/10 cm square using larger hook

Other Supplies

Locking stitch marker, yarn needle, blocking wires and pins

Special Abbreviations

bb   back bar
edc   extended double crochet
trcl   treble cluster
V-st   V-stitch

Crocheting a Gauge Swatch

- **ROW 1:** With larger hook ch 19, V-st in bb of 5th ch from hook (last 3 chs count as dc), (skip 2 chs, V-st in bb of next ch) four times, skip next ch, dc in bb of last ch, turn. *You now have* 1 dc at each end of row with 5 V-stitches in between.

PATTERN ESSENTIALS

Beginning Treble Cluster Ch 4, *yo twice, insert hook in place indicated, yo and pull up loop, (yo and draw through 2 loops) twice; repeat from * once more, yo and draw through all 3 loops on hook.

Ending Treble Cluster *Yo twice, insert hook in place indicated, yo and pull up loop, (yo and draw through 2 loops) twice; repeat from * two more times, yo and draw through all 4 loops on hook.

Extended Double Crochet Yo, insert hook in place indicated, yo and pull up loop (3 loops on hook), yo and draw through 1 loop, (yo and draw through 2 loops) twice.

Picot (Slip stitch, ch 2, sc in 2nd ch from hook, slip stitch) in place indicated.

Point Shell Dc in 1st dc of point V-st, V-st in ch-1 space of point V-st, dc in next dc of point V-st.

Point V-stitch V-st at bottom point of shawl.

V-stitch (Dc, ch 1, dc) in place indicated.

- **ROW 2:** Ch 3 (counts as 1st dc), V-st in ch-1 space of each V-st across, dc in top of last ch-3. *You now have* 1 dc at each end of row with 5 V-sts in between.

- **ROWS 3–8:** Repeat Row 2 six more times. Fasten off and measure.

Crocheting the Shawl

Notes: Shawl is worked from the center of the top edge out. The point shell consists of the point V-stitch and 1 dc on each side; it is worked on even-numbered rows.

- **ROW 1:** With larger hook, ch 5 (last 4 chs count as ch-4 of next beginning trcl), work (beginning trcl, 2 edc, 5 dc, 2 edc, ending trcl) in 5th ch from hook, turn. *You now have* 1 beginning trcl, 4 edc with 5 dc in center of these 4 stitches, 1 ending trcl.

- **ROW 2:** (Beginning trcl, 2 edc) in 1st trcl, skip next stitch, V-st in next stitch, skip next stitch, dc in next stitch, V-st in next stitch (point V-st made); place marker in ch-1 space of V-st, dc in next stitch, skip next st, V-st in next stitch, skip next stitch, (2 edc, ending trcl) in last trcl, turn. *You now have* 1 trcl and 2 edc at each end of row, 1 marked point shell at center (consisting of a V-st with 1 dc on each side), and 1 V-st between the edc and point shell at each side.

- **ROW 3:** (Beginning trcl, 2 edc) in 1st trcl, skip next edc, V-st in next edc, V-st in ch-1 space of next V-st, V-st in 1st dc of point shell, V-st in ch-1 space of point V-st (removing marker and replacing it in ch-1 space of new V-st), V-st in last dc of point shell, V-st in ch-1 space of next V-st, V-st in next edc, skip next edc, (2 edc, ending trcl) in last trcl, turn. *You now have* 1 trcl and 2 edc at each end of row, 1 point V-st with marker at center, and 3 V-sts between edc and point V-st at each side.

- **ROW 4:** (Beginning trcl, 2 edc) in 1st trcl, skip next edc, V-st in next edc, V-st in ch-1 space of each V-st to marked point V-st, point shell in point V-st (removing and replacing marker), V-st in ch-1 space of each V-st to next edc, V-st in edc, skip next edc, (2 edc, ending trcl) in last trcl, turn. *You now have* 1 trcl and 2 edc at each end of row, 1 point shell with marker in center, and 1 V-st has been increased between edc and point shell at each side.

- **ROW 5:** (Beginning trcl, 2 edc) in 1st trcl, skip next edc, V-st in next edc, V-st in ch-1 space of each V-st to point shell, V-st in 1st dc of point shell, V-st in ch-1 space of point V-st (removing and replacing marker), V-st in last dc of point shell, V-st in ch-1 space of each V-st to next edc, V-st in edc, sk next edc, (2 edc, end trcl) in last trcl, turn. *You now have* 1 trcl and 2 edc at each end of row, 1 point V-st with marker in center, and 2 V-sts have been increased between edc and point V-st at each side.

continued on next page

• **ROWS 6–31:** Repeat Rows 4 and 5 thirteen times. Do not fasten off. *You now* have 1 trcl and 2 edc at each end of row, 1 point V-st with marker in center, and 45 V-sts between edc and point V-st at each side.

Crocheting the Edging

• **ROW 32:** (Beginning trcl, 2 edc) in 1st trcl, skip next edc, (dc, ch 3, dc) in next edc, *dc in ch-1 space of next V-st, (dc, ch 3, dc) in ch-1 space of following V-st; repeat from * 44 more times ending at last V-st, dc in ch-1 space of last V-st, (dc, ch 3, dc) in next edc, skip next edc, (2 edc, end trcl) in last trcl, turn. *You now have* 1 trcl and 2 edc at each end of row, and 47 ch-3 spaces.

• Change to smaller hook.

• **ROW 33:** (Beginning trcl, 2 edc) in 1st trcl, skip next edc, picot in next edc, *skip next dc, 9 sc in next ch-3 space, skip next dc, picot in next dc; repeat from * 45 more times ending at last (dc, ch 3, dc), skip next dc, 9 sc in next ch-3 space, skip next dc, picot in next edc, skip next edc, (2 edc, end trcl) in last trcl, turn. *You now have* 1 trcl and 2 edc at each end of row, 47 scallops of 9 sc, and 48 picots (1 at each end of scallops and remaining 46 between each pair of scallops).

Finishing

• Fasten off and weave in yarn ends. Block to desired measurements.

Melifera Shawl

DESIGNED BY AMANDA CARRIGAN

The Melifera Shawl is knit from the bottom up using the openwork Honeybee Pattern with Faggoting from Barbara Walker's Second Treasury of Knitting Patterns (Schoolhouse Press, 1998). The sample is 22 bees high in the center column; with more yarn you could continue the pattern to make a larger shawl.

Finished Measurements

61"/155 cm wide and 23"/58.5 cm deep, blocked

Yarn

Rico Design Superba Klassik, 75% superwash wool/25% nylon, 459 yds (420 m)/3.5 oz (100 g), Color 508 Burgundy

Needles

US 6 (4 mm) straight needles *or size you need to obtain correct gauge*

Gauge

18 stitches and 24 rows = 4"/10cm in pattern, blocked

Other Supplies

Yarn needle, blocking wires and pins

Special Abbreviations

p1 wrn2   purl 1, wrapping yarn around the needle twice. This forms an elongated stitch when the extra wrap is dropped on the next row; the double wrap still counts as 1 stitch.

PATTERN ESSENTIALS

Pick Up Dropped Yarnovers Drop the quadruple yarnover of the previous row, *insert the right-hand needle tip underneath all four loose strands of the last 4 dropped yarnovers from front to back and draw up a loop,** yo, then repeat from * to ** once more — 3 stitches made from dropped yarnover bundle.

Knitting the Shawl

- Cast on 6 stitches.
- ROW 1 (RS): Knit.
- ROW 2 (WS): Purl.
- ROW 3: K3, yo, k3. *You now have* 7 stitches.
- ROW 4: P1 wrn2, p2, yo, work (k1, p1) in yo of previous row, yo, p2, pl wrn2. *You now have* 10 stitches (counting each pl wrn2 as 1 stitch).
- ROW 5: Knit first stitch dropping extra wrap, k2, yo, k4, yo, k2, knit last stitch dropping extra wrap. *You now have* 12 stitches.
- ROW 6: P1 wrn2, p2, yo, p6, yo, p2, pl wrn2. *You now have* 14 stitches.
- ROW 7: K1 dropping extra wrap, k2, yo, k8, yo, k2, k1 dropping extra wrap. *You now have* 16 stitches.
- ROW 8: P1 wrn2, p2, yo, pl10, yo, p2, pl wrn2. *You now have* 18 stitches.

Beginning the Lace Pattern

Notes: The 3-stitch border continues as established at each side and is not shown on the charts. On RS rows, begin k1 dropping extra wrap, k2 and end k2, k1 dropping the extra wrap. On WS rows, begin pl wrn2, k2 and end k2, pl wrn2. These elongated loops at the edges are important; without them, the edges will be too tight and will curl.

The number of stitches in each bee section of the charts does not remain constant. Count each bee section as 12 stitches, even if it is on a row where the number has temporarily been increased or decreased. You may find

it helpful to check your count after completing all 6 rows of the bee pattern when each bee section has been restored to 12 stitches.

- ROW 1 (RS): Work 3 border stitches, work Row 1 of chart A over center 12 stitches decreasing to 11 stitches as shown, work 3 border stitches.

- **ROWS 2–24:** Keeping border stitches as established, continue in pattern from chart, increasing at each side as shown. *You now have* 66 stitches: 60 chart stitches and 3 border stitches at each side.

- **ROW 25:** Work 3 border stitches, work Row 25 of chart B over center 60 stitches, working 18-stitch pattern repeat three times, work 3 border stitches.

- **ROWS 26–42:** Keeping border stitches as established, continue in pattern from chart. *You now have* 102 stitches: 96 chart stitches and 3 border stitches at each side.

- **ROWS 43–132:** Repeat Rows 25–42 of chart B five more times. *You now have* 282 stitches: 276 chart stitches and 3 border stitches at each side.

- *Note:* Each time you repeat chart B there will be enough new stitches to work the 18-stitch repeat two additional times. For example, the second time you work Rows 25–42 there will be enough stitches to work the 18-stitch repeat five times, then when you repeat the chart again there will be enough stitches to work the repeat seven times, and so on.

- Keeping border stitches as established, work remaining stitches in stockinette stitch for 3 more rows *without* increasing.

Finishing

- Bind off loosely. Weave in ends and block.

   Note: For a larger shawl, repeat Rows 25–42 of chart B until enough yarn remains for 4 or 5 rows, ending with Row 30, Row 36, or Row 42 of chart. Then work the last 3 stockinette stitch rows and bind off.

Melifera B   *Note:* This chart begins on facing page.

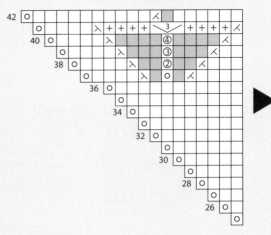

Melifera A   *Note:* This chart begins on facing page.

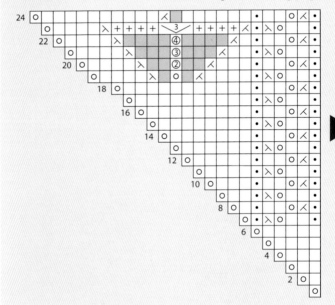

(continued on facing page)

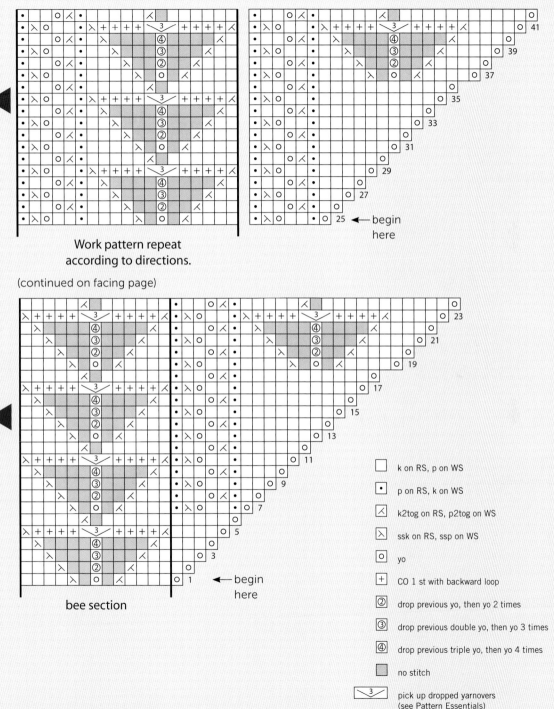

Work pattern repeat
according to directions.

(continued on facing page)

bee section

← begin
here

← begin
here

	k on RS, p on WS
•	p on RS, k on WS
⟋	k2tog on RS, p2tog on WS
⟍	ssk on RS, ssp on WS
O	yo
+	CO 1 st with backward loop
②	drop previous yo, then yo 2 times
③	drop previous double yo, then yo 3 times
④	drop previous triple yo, then yo 4 times
	no stitch
⟍3⟋	pick up dropped yarnovers (see Pattern Essentials)

Trellis Leaf Stole

DESIGNED BY JUDITH DURANT

Faced with an irresistible hank of Madelinetosh yarn, the challenge here was to find a lace pattern that would make the most of the yards available. The very open Trellis Framed Leaf pattern from Barbara Walker's Treasury of Knitting Patterns *(Schoolhouse Press, 1998) did the trick and allowed for a stole ample enough to fully wrap the shoulders.*

Finished Measurements

Approximately 61"/155 cm wide and 15"/38 cm deep

Yarn

Madelinetosh Prairie, 100% superwash merino wool, 840 yds (768 m)/4.2 oz (120 g), Charcoal
Note: The yarn label states that the skein weighs 100 g; it actually weighed 120 g, and every bit was used.

Needles

US 2½ (3 mm) straight needles *or size you need to obtain correct gauge*

Gauge

27 stitches and 34 rows = 4"/10 cm in Trellis Leaf Lace pattern, blocked

Other Supplies

Yarn needle, stitch holder

PATTERN NOTES

All but approximately 12"/30.5 cm of the yarn was used. If you doubt your yardage, knit fewer repeats in each half or work the stole in a single piece from one end to the other.

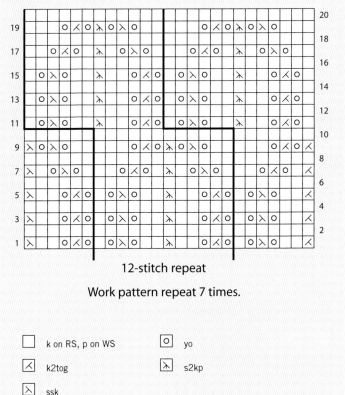

Trellis Leaf Lace

12-stitch repeat

Work pattern repeat 7 times.

	k on RS, p on WS		yo
	k2tog		s2kp
	ssk		

Knitting the Stole

- Cast on 105 stitches.

- ROWS 1–4: Knit.

- ROW 5 (RS): K5, *yo, k2tog; repeat from * to last 4 stitches, k4.

- ROWS 6 AND 7: Knit.

Knitting the Lace Pattern

- Keep the first and last 4 stitches of every row in garter stitch (knit every row); these stitches are not shown on the chart. Working the center 97 stitches in the chart pattern, work Rows 1–20 of Trellis Leaf Lace chart 13 times (260 chart rows total). **Note:** Row 1 is a WS row.

- Place stitches on stitch holder. Make a second piece the same as the first, leaving stitches on the needle.

Finishing

- Return the held stitches of the first half to a needle and graft the two halves together with Kitchener stitch (see page 293). Weave in ends. Wash and block to measurements.

{ Using Blocking Wires and Pins }

Long thin wires called blocking wires help to ensure even edges when blocking a large lace piece, such as a shawl. You'll need to use pins with the wires and block onto a surface that you can pin into, such as a blocking board or a blocking mat. If your shawl has straight edges, simply run the wires through the edges and then pin the wires out so that the shawl is the desired size.

If your shawl has an edging with points you can do one of two things. You can run the wires through the straight edges and pin out the points. Or you can run the wires through the points and pin the wires. The latter method will ensure even points.

Moss and Leaves Stole

DESIGNED BY KERRI SHANK

This delightful lace sampler is as much fun to knit as it is to wear. The wide end of the stole is beaded, which adds beauty as well as practicality in the form of a little added weight.

Finished Measurements

58"/147.5 cm wide, 15"/38 cm deep at beginning, and 25"/63.5 cm deep at end

Yarn

Madelinetosh Tosh Lace, 100% superwash merino wool, 950 yds (869 m)/4 oz (113 g), Badlands

Needles

US 2 (2.75 mm) straight needles *or size you need to obtain correct gauge*

Gauge

32 stitches and 42 rows = 4"/10 cm in Irish Moss Stitch, blocked

Other Supplies

Stitch markers, 10 g size 8° seed beads, approximately twenty-five 4 mm fire-polished beads, small steel crochet hook to fit through beads, yarn needle

PATTERN ESSENTIALS

Place Bead Slide a bead onto the crochet hook, remove next stitch from left-hand needle with the crochet hook, push the bead down onto the stitch, return stitch to left-hand needle and work the beaded stitch in pattern.

Note: The two types of beads used in the stole shown were mixed together and applied randomly.

233

Knitting the Stole

- Cast on 123 stitches using the long-tail method (see page 294).

- Work Rows 1–4 of chart A (Irish Moss Stitch) 18 times (72 rows total), ending with Row 4.

- NEXT ROW (RS): Work first 7 stitches in Irish Moss Stitch as established, place marker, work Row 1 of chart B (First Transition) on center 109 stitches, place marker, work last 7 stitches in Irish Moss Stitch as established.

- Keeping the first and last 7 stitches in Irish Moss Stitch as established, work Rows 2–18 of chart B.

- Keeping the first and last 7 stitches in Irish Moss Stitch as established, and working chart C (Little Fern) on center 109 stitches, repeat Rows 1–8 of chart 13 times, then work Rows 1–7 once more.

- NEXT ROW (WS, COUNTS AS ROW 8 OF PATTERN): Work 7 stitches in Irish Moss Stitch, purl to last 9 stitches, p2tog, work 7 stitches in Irish Moss Stitch. *You now have* 122 stitches and have completed 112 chart C rows.

- Keeping the first and last 7 stitches in Irish Moss Stitch as established, work Rows 1–16 of chart D (Second Transition) on center 108 stitches.

Note: In Rows 7 and 15 there are 2 yarnovers next to each other when the chart repeats, and the purl symbols in Rows 8 and 16 indicate where to work (p1, k1) in a double yarnover of the previous row. The yarnovers at the beginning and end of the chart pattern in Rows 7 and 15 are not doubled, and both of these single yarnovers can be worked as p1 on Rows 8 and 16.

- Keeping the first and last 7 stitches in Irish Moss Stitch as established, and working chart E (Vines) on center 108 stitches, repeat Rows 1–4 of the chart 38 times (152 chart E rows), ending with Row 4.

- NEXT ROW (RS): Work first 7 stitches in Irish Moss Stitch as established, *work Row 1 of chart F (Third Transition) on 36 stitches, increasing them to 38 stitches; repeat from * two more times, work last 7 stitches in Irish Moss Stitch as established. *You now have* 128 stitches.

Note: The vine and leaf panels of chart F are separated by slightly darker vertical gridlines.

- Keeping the first and last 7 stitches in Irish Moss Stitch as established, work Rows 2–32 of chart F.

- NEXT ROW (RS): Work first 7 stitches in Irish Moss Stitch as established, *work Row 33 of chart F over 38 stitches, increasing them to 40 stitches; repeat from * two more times, work last 7 stitches in Irish Moss Stitch as established. *You now have* 134 stitches.

- Keeping the first and last 7 stitches in Irish Moss Stitch as established, work Rows 34–48 of chart F.

- NEXT ROW (RS): Work first 7 stitches in Irish Moss Stitch as established, work Row 1 of chart G (Falling Leaves) on center 120 stitches, increasing to 121 stitches (the final yo of the row does not have a corresponding decrease), work last 7 stitches in Irish Moss Stitch as established. *You now have* 135 stitches.

- Keeping first and last 7 stitches in Irish Moss Stitch as established, work Rows 2–16 of chart G, outlining random leaf motifs with beads.

Note: The optional "place bead" symbols are only suggestions for bead placement, and you should not work all of them; the sample stole has only seven randomly beaded leaves in the chart G section.

- Repeat Rows 17–32 three times, then work Row 17–31 once more, ending with a RS row (79 chart G rows total), and outlining leaf motifs with beads as desired. Do not cut yarn.

Knitting the Edging

- Cast on 5 stitches at end of last RS row using the cable cast-on method (see page 290). Turn work so WS is facing, work new stitches as k5, turn. Repeat Rows 1–8 of chart H (Small Points) 34 times, placing beads as indicated and knitting the last edging stitch at the end of every even-numbered WS row together with 1 stole stitch as shown on chart.

Note: Each repeat of the edging joins 4 stole stitches, or 136 stitches for 34 repeats. Because the stole only has 135 stitches, compensate by working 1 row of the edging without joining; work the last edging stitch of this row as p1, then turn.

- *You now have* 5 edging stitches and all stole stitches have been joined.

Finishing

- Bind off loosely. Weave in ends and block to finished measurements.

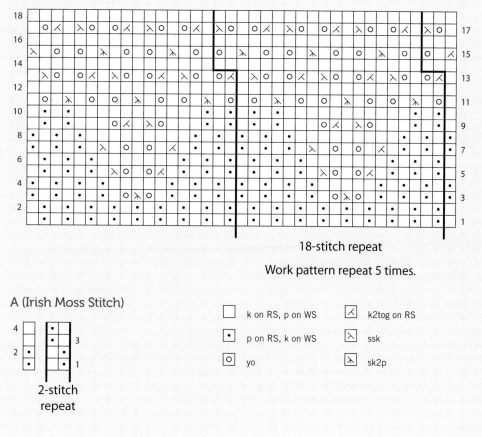

B (First Transition)

18-stitch repeat

Work pattern repeat 5 times.

A (Irish Moss Stitch)

2-stitch repeat

	k on RS, p on WS		k2tog on RS
	p on RS, k on WS		ssk
	yo		sk2p

E (Vines)

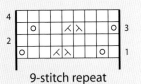

9-stitch repeat

Work pattern repeat 12 times.

C (Little Fern)

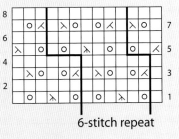

6-stitch repeat

Work pattern repeat 17 times.

D (Second Transition)

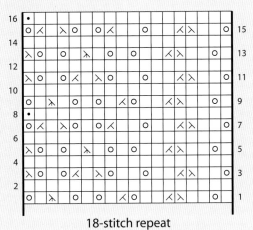

18-stitch repeat

Work pattern repeat 5 times.

	k on RS, p on WS		sk2p
	p on RS, k on WS		s2kp
	yo		no stitch
	k2tog on RS	B	place bead (see Pattern Essentials)
	ssk		

F (Third Transition)

36-stitch repeat
increased to 40-stitch repeat
Work pattern repeat 3 times.

G (Falling Leaves)

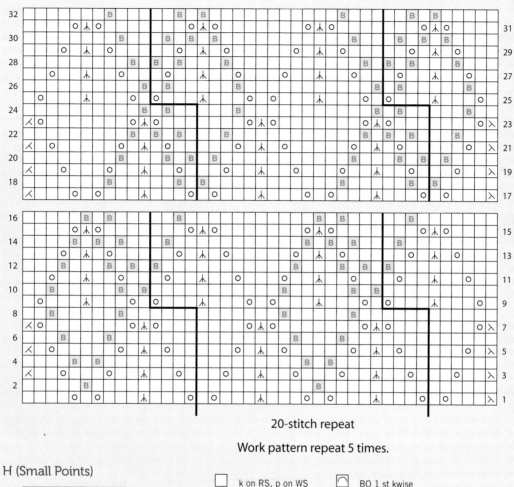

20-stitch repeat

Work pattern repeat 5 times.

H (Small Points)

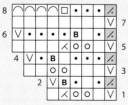

☐	k on RS, p on WS	◠ BO 1 st kwise
•	p on RS, k on WS	☐ st on right needle after last BO
○	yo	**B** place bead (see Pattern Essentials)
⟋	k2tog on RS	**B** place bead (optional), or p on WS if not beaded
⟍	ssk	⟋ knit last edging st with next shawl st
⅄	s2kp	
V	slip 1 pwise wyib on RS, wyif on WS	

Magenta Mohair Lace Stole

DESIGNED BY LIZ NIELDS

Light and airy yet warm, mohair is a wonderful fiber for shawls and stoles.
This one is worked on large needles, making a fine translucent fabric.

Finished Measurements
49"/124 cm wide and 17"/43 cm deep

Yarn
Bashful Bags and Fibers Laceweight,
70% superfine kid mohair/30% silk,
546 yds (499 m)/1.75 oz (50 g), Magenta

Needles
US 8 (5 mm) straight needles *or size you
need to obtain correct gauge* and larger
straight needle for binding off (optional)

Gauge
18½ stitches and 20 rows = 4"/10 cm in
Lace pattern, blocked

Other Supplies
Stitch markers (optional), yarn needle

Knitting the Stole

- Cast on 79 stitches loosely. Knit
  5 rows, beginning and ending with a
  WS row. Work Rows 1–12 of Lace chart
  20 times, working edge stitches as
  indicated and five repeats of marked
  section in each row. You may find
  it helpful to place markers between
  each repeat to help keep track of the
  pattern. Knit 5 rows, beginning and
  ending with a RS row.

Finishing

- Bind off on next WS row, using a
  larger needle if necessary. Weave in
  ends. Block.

Lace

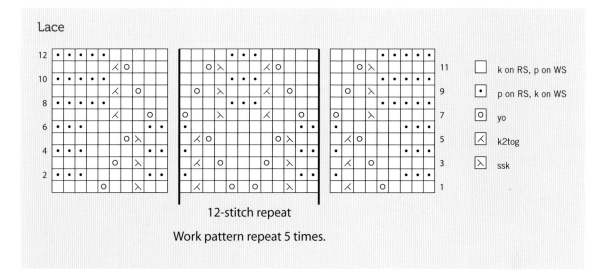

12-stitch repeat

Work pattern repeat 5 times.

☐	k on RS, p on WS
•	p on RS, k on WS
o	yo
⟋	k2tog
⟍	ssk

{ Casting On and Binding Off }

Because your lace piece will "grow" when it is blocked, it's important that the beginning and ending edges can grow with it. Use a flexible cast on such as the long-tail (see page 294) or the tubular method (see page 299). To bind off, use a needle at least two sizes larger than the one you've used for the project, or try the sewn bind off (see page 298).

Red Sky at Night Capelet

DESIGNED BY MARY C. GILDERSLEEVE

This cozy capelet is knit from the top down and uses hidden decreases that allow for extra lace patterns and flare. The coordinating border is knitted on while you bind off the bottom edge.

Finished Measurements
22"/56 cm circumference at top, 54"/37 cm circumference at bottom, and 14"/35.5 cm deep

Yarn
Cascade Heritage Hand Painted Sock Yarn, 75% superwash merino wool/25% nylon, 437 yds (400 m)/3.5 oz (100 g), Color 9883

Needles
US 6 (4 mm) circular needle 16"/40 cm long and one US 6 (4 mm) double-point needle *or size you need to obtain correct gauge*

Gauge
24 stitches and 32 rounds = 4"/10 cm in stockinette stitch; 20 stitches and 23 rounds = 4"/10 cm in Red Sky Lace pattern, blocked

Other Supplies
Eight stitch markers (one in a unique color), yarn needle, blocking wires and/or pins

Knitting the Capelet

- Cast on 112 stitches. Place the unique-colored marker and join into a round, being careful not to twist the stitches.

- ROUNDS 1, 3, AND 5: Knit.

- ROUNDS 2 AND 4: Purl.

- ROUND 6: Purl, placing markers every 14 stitches.

- Work Rounds 1–65 of Red Sky Lace chart, increasing beginning on Round 23 as shown. *You now have* 224 stitches.

242

Red Sky Lace

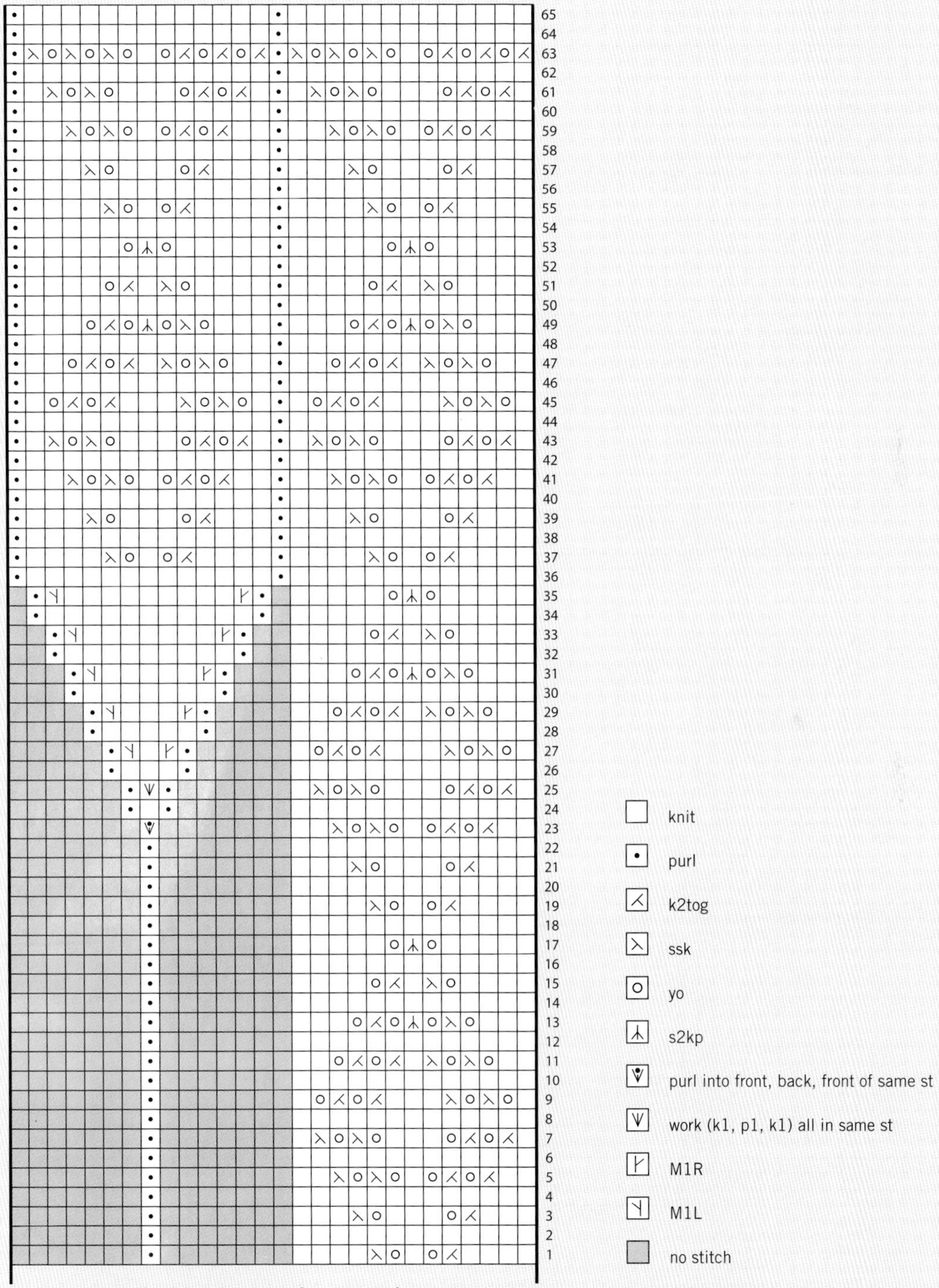
knit
purl
k2tog
ssk
yo
s2kp
purl into front, back, front of same st
work (k1, p1, k1) all in same st
M1R
M1L
no stitch

14-stitch repeat increased to 28-stitch repeat

Work pattern repeat 8 times.

Knitting the Border

- With RS facing and yarn still attached, use the backward loop method (see page 290) to cast on 8 stitches onto the left-hand needle tip. Turn work so WS is facing, and use a double-point needle to work new cast-on stitches as p7 (for border stitches), then purl the last cast-on stitch together with 1 capelet stitch, turn work. *You now have* 8 border stitches and 223 capelet stitches.

- Work Rows 1–28 of Border chart back and forth 15 times, then work Rows 1–27 once more, purling the last border stitch together with the next stitch of the capelet at the end of every WS chart row (shown shaded in gold). *You now have* 8 border stitches, and all capelet stitches have been joined.

Finishing

- Sew live border stitches to the base of the cast-on border stitches. Weave in ends. Block.

Border

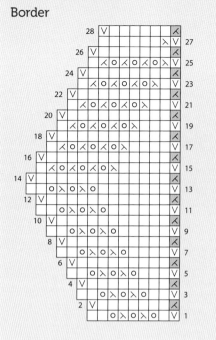

☐	knit on RS, purl on WS
⟋	k2tog
⟍	ssk
○	yo
⟋	purl last border st tog with next capelet st
V	slip 1 pwise with wyib on RS, slip 1 pwise wyif on WS

lacy accessories

Drooping Elm Headband

DESIGNED BY BARBARA BENSON

A light and lacy cotton headband can be the perfect accessory on a warm summer day. Knitted in cotton, this one tapers to a narrow strip at the back and joins end to end with a button closure, making it comfortable as well as practical.

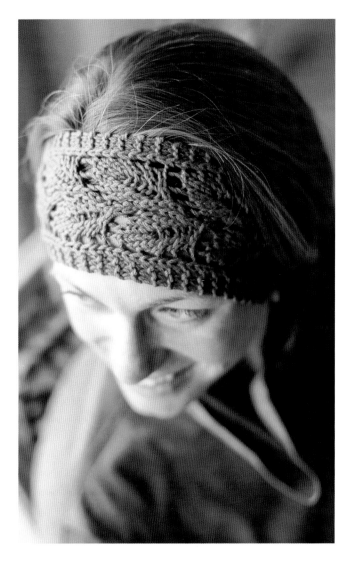

Finished Measurements

4"/10 cm wide and 20"/51 cm long

Yarn

Berroco Pure Pima, 100% pima cotton, 115 yds (106 m)/1.75 oz (50 g), Color 2267 Teal

Needles

US 7 (4.5 mm) straight needles *or size you need to obtain correct gauge*

Gauge

22 stitches and 22 rows = 4"/10 cm in pattern

Other Supplies

Button with shank, yarn needle

Special Abbreviations

sssk   slip 3 stitches individually knit-wise, place left-hand needle into front of slipped stitches and knit them together — 2 stitches decreased

Knitting the Headband

• Cast on 12 stitches.

• ROW 1 (WS): Knit.

• ROW 2 (RS): K6, yo, K6. **Note:** The yo forms the buttonhole. For a large button, work k6, yo twice, k6.

• ROW 3: Knit. **Note:** If you worked 2 yos for a large button in the previous row, knit 1 and drop the other. *You now have* 13 stitches.

Drooping Elm C

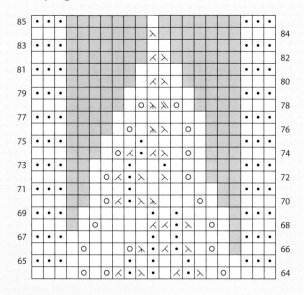

Drooping Elm B

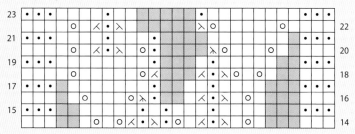

Drooping Elm A

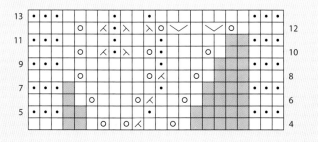

	k on RS, p on WS
•	p on RS, k on WS
o	yo
⟋	k2tog
⟍	ssk
⅄	sk2p
⅄	sssk (see Special Abbreviations)
▨	no stitch
⌄	kfb

continued on next page

- ROWS 4–13: Work in pattern from chart A. *You now have 22 stitches.*
- ROWS 14–63: Work Rows 14–23 of chart B five times.

  Note: Chart B begins with 22 stitches, decreases to 21 stitches for Rows 16 and 17, then increases back to 22 stitches for Rows 18–23.

- ROWS 64–85: Work Rows 64–85 of chart C. *You now have 7 stitches.*
- ROWS 86–110: Knit.

Finishing

- Bind off, leaving a long tail to attach the button. Attach button to the end of narrow strip. Weave in ends. Block.

Lucy Steele's Fancywork Bags

DESIGNED BY KIRSTI JOHANSON

Lucy Steele from Jane Austen's Sense and Sensibility *is the inspiration for these bags. The larger bag features I-cord handles and can be used as a small tote. The smaller bag has a satin ribbon closure and can be used as a dresser bag.*

Finished Measurements

Large bag: 4" × 4"/10 × 10 cm base and 6½"/16.5 cm tall
Small bag: 2½" × 2½"/6.5 × 6.5 cm base and 4¼"/11 cm tall

Yarn

Large bag: Madelinetosh Tosh Vintage, 100% superwash merino wool, 200 yds (183 m)/3.5 oz (100 g), French Grey
Small bag: Madelinetosh Tosh Merino Light, 100% superwash merino wool, 420 yds (384 m)/3.5 oz (100 g), French Grey

Needles

Large bag: Set of five US 7 (4.5 mm) double-point needles *or size you need to obtain correct gauge*
Small bag: Set of five US 4 (3.5 mm) double-point needles or *size you need to obtain correct gauge*

Gauge

Large bag: 16 stitches and 24 rows = 4"/10 cm in Fancywork Lace pattern
Small bag: 26 stitches and 36 rows = 4"/10 cm in Fancywork Lace pattern

Other Supplies

Large bag: Stitch marker, 160 (approximately 16 g) size 6° glass beads, small steel crochet hook that fits through the beads, size H/8 (5 mm) crochet hook, scrap yarn for holder, yarn needle, ½ yd/0.5 m lining fabric; sewing needle and coordinating thread
Small bag: Stitch marker, 160 size 8° (approximately 4 g) seed beads, small steel crochet hook that fits through beads, size D/3 (3.25 mm) crochet hook, 18"/45.5 cm thin satin ribbon, yarn needle

PATTERN ESSENTIALS

Place Bead Slide a bead onto the crochet hook, remove next stitch from left-hand needle with the crochet hook, push the bead down onto the stitch, return stitch to left-hand needle, then work the beaded stitch in pattern.

Knitting the Base

Note: Both bags are worked according to the same instructions; the different yarn and needles determine the finished size.

- Cast on 16 stitches using a provisional method (see pages 297–298).

- Knit 32 rows, but do not turn the work at the end of the last row.

- Rotate work 90 degrees and use a separate needle to pick up and knit (see page 297) 1 stitch in each garter ridge along the selvedge (16 stitches).

- Rotate work 90 degrees, undo provisional cast on, place 16 live stitches on another needle, then knit these 16 stitches.

- Rotate work 90 degrees and use another needle to pick up and knit 1 stitch in each garter ridge along the remaining selvedge (16 stitches).

You now have 64 stitches total: 16 stitches each on four needles.

- Place marker for beginning of round and knit 1 round.

Fancywork Lace

16-stitch repeat

Work pattern repeat 4 times.
See instructions for Rnd 27.

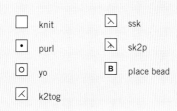

☐ knit	⟍ ssk
• purl	⟋ sk2p
○ yo	B place bead
⟋ k2tog	

Knitting the Lace

- Work Rounds 1–26 of the Fancywork Lace chart, ending 1 stitch before the beginning-of-round marker on Round 26. Temporarily slip the last stitch to the right-hand needle, remove marker, return slipped stitch to the left-hand needle, then replace the marker (repositioning the marker in this manner allows the sk2p decreases in Round 27 to align properly with the rest of the pattern). Work Rounds 27–38 of chart. Do not cut yarn.

Finishing the Large Bag

Crocheting the Top Loops

- Place the first stitch of the round on a scrap yarn holder; this stitch will later become the 4th stitch in the last group of held handle stitches.

- Using the larger (non-steel) crochet hook and yarn attached to the held stitch, insert crochet hook near the base of the stitch, yarn over hook, and draw up a loop. Single crochet the next 3 stitches together (sc3tog) by inserting the hook into the 2nd, 3rd, and 4th stitches of the round, yarn over hook, and draw a loop through these 3 stitches, then yarn over the hook and draw through both loops on hook. Continue as follows.

- (Ch 8, sc3tog) three times. *You now have 3 stitches remaining* of the 16 stitches on this side of the bag, and 1 loop on the hook.

- Place the next 4 stitches on scrap yarn (last 3 stitches on this needle and first stitch on next needle).

- *Ch 8, work 1 sc behind the held stitches, (ch 8, sc3tog) four times, place next 4 stitches on scrap yarn holder; repeat from * two more times, ending the last repeat by placing last 3 stitches of the round on the same holder as the first held stitch, then ch 8, and join with a slip stitch to first sc3tog of round. Cut yarn and fasten off last stitch.

Knitting the Handles (make 2)

- Return one set of 4 held stitches to needle, rejoin yarn, and work I-cord (see page 292) until handle is desired length (sample shown has 36 rows). Use Kitchener stitch (see page 293) to join I-cord stitches to an adjacent set of 4 held stitches. Work the other handle in the same manner. Weave in ends.

Lining the Bag

- Cut a piece of lining fabric for the base that is 4"/10 cm square plus seam allowances.

- Cut a piece of lining fabric for the bag that is 16"/41 cm × 6½"/16.5 cm plus seam allowances.

- Hem one long side of the lining rectangle for the top of the bag. Sew the two short sides of the rectangle together, making a tube. Sew the unfinished edge of the tube to the four sides of the base piece. Slip the lining into the bag with wrong sides of lining and bag touching, and use a sewing needle and thread to slipstitch the lining to the inside of the bag along the last knitted round.

Finishing the Small Bag

Crocheting the Top Loops

- Using the larger (non-steel) crochet hook, insert the crochet hook near base of the first stitch of the round, yarn over hook, and draw up a loop. Single crochet the first 2 stitches together (sc2tog) by inserting the hook into the first and second stitches of the round, yarn over hook, and draw a loop through these 2 stitches, then yarn over hook and draw through both loops on hook. *Ch 5, sc2tog; repeat from * until no stitches remain on needle, ch 5, and join with a slip stitch in first sc2tog of round. Cut yarn and fasten off last stitch. Weave in ends. Thread the ribbon through the eyelets in Round 31 of the chart; string 3 beads onto each end of the ribbon and knot the ribbon to keep them in place.

Wavelet Hair Tie

DESIGNED BY JENISE REID

Here's a great example of working with fine lace-weight yarn on large needles — the result is very light and airy. Use this tie on your ponytail, wear it tied as a headband, or wear it around your neck as a scarf. Anything goes.

251

Finished Measurements

Approximately 7"/18 cm wide and 36"/91.5 cm long

Yarn

Estelle Super Alpaca Lace, 100% super-fine alpaca, 437 yds (400 m)/1.75 oz (50 g), Color 10106 **Note:** One skein produces three or four ties.

Needles

US 7 (4.5 mm) straight needles *or size you need to obtain correct gauge*

Gauge

16½ stitches and 16½ rows = 4"/10 cm in pattern, blocked

Other Supplies

Yarn needle

Knitting the Hair Tie

• Cast on 5 stitches.

• Work Rows 1–30 of chart A once. *You now have* 29 stitches.

• Work Rows 31–54 of chart B four times.

• Work Rows 55–75 of chart C once. *You now have* 5 stitches.

• Bind off all stitches. Weave in ends. Block.

Wavelet Lace A

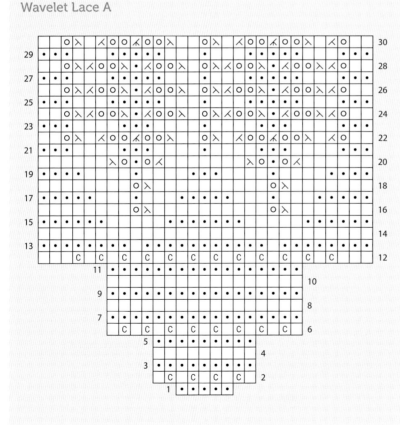

Wavelet Lace C

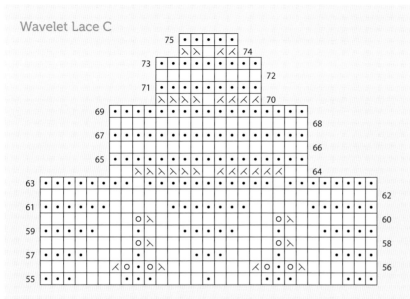

Wavelet Lace B

	k on RS, p on WS
	p on RS, k on WS
	k2tog
	ssk
	yo
	k3tog
	CO 1 st using backward loop
	yo twice

253

Linen Lace Belt

DESIGNED BY LAURA H. TURNBULL

Pair this linen belt with your favorite tank dress for a lovely summer outfit or wear it with your favorite jeans. Knit with a simple two-row repeating lace pattern, it works up quickly — you may want to knit several in different colors.

Finished Measurements

1½"/4 cm wide and 38"/96.5 cm long

Yarn

Quince & Co. Sparrow, 100% organic linen, 168 yds (154 m)/1.75 oz (50 g), Sans

Needles

US 00 (1.75 mm) straight needles *or size you need to obtain correct gauge* and US 1 (2.25 mm) short circular needle for cast on

Gauge

35 stitches and 42 rows = 4"/10 cm in Linen Lace pattern

Other Supplies

Two 1½"/4 cm D rings, yarn needle

PATTERN ESSENTIALS

Lace (worked over 13 stitches)

- **Row 1 (RS):** K1 tbl, k2, yo, k2, sk2p, k2, yo, k3.
- **Row 2 (WS):** K1 tbl, knit to end of row.
- Repeat Rows 1 and 2 for pattern.

Knitting the Belt

- Cast on 26 stitches as follows.

- Hold one size 00 straight needle next to the size 1 circular needle. Using the backward loop method (see page 290) and alternating between the needles, cast on 13 stitches onto each needle.

- Using the other size 00 needle, knit 10 rows with the stitches from the size 00 needle cast-on stitches.

- Hold the D rings together and pass the circular needle through the rings. Bring the live stitches on the size 00 needle together with the stitches on the circular needle so they surround the straight part of the D rings. Knit 1 stitch from each needle together 13 times. *You now have* 13 stitches on the size 00 needle. Knit 2 more rows.

- Work Rows 1 and 2 of Linen Lace pattern from the text or chart until belt is ½"/13 mm less than desired length, ending with Row 2.

Decreasing the End

- **ROW 1 (RS):** Ssk, k1, yo, k2, sk2p, k2, yo, k1, k2tog. *You now have* 11 stitches.

- **ROWS 2 AND 4 (WS):** K1 tbl, knit to end of row.

- **ROW 3:** Ssk, k1, yo, k1, sk2p, k1, yo, k1, k2tog. *You now have* 9 stitches.

- **ROW 5:** Ssk, k1, yo, sk2p, yo, k1, k2tog. *You now have* 7 stitches.

- **ROW 6:** K1 tbl, knit to end of row.

Finishing

- Bind off all stitches knitwise. Weave in ends.

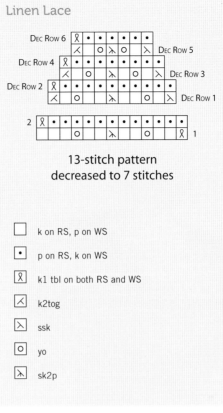

Linen Lace

13-stitch pattern
decreased to 7 stitches

k on RS, p on WS

p on RS, k on WS

k1 tbl on both RS and WS

k2tog

ssk

yo

sk2p

255

Lacy Legs!

DESIGNED BY MARINA ORRY

Around the house or around town, these lacy ribs will keep your legs nice and warm.
The simple lace rib pattern makes these a great project for beginning lace knitters.

Finished Measurements
Approximately 8½"/21.5 cm circumference, unstretched, and 14"/35.5 cm tall

Yarn
Cascade Yarns Cascade 220, 100% wool, 220 yds (201 m)/3.5 oz (100 g), Color 8339 Marine

Needles
US 8 (5 mm) 32"/80 cm circular needle for magic loop method (see page 295) or set of US 8 (5 mm) double-point needles *or size you need to obtain correct gauge*

Gauge
22½ stitches and 25 rounds = 4"/10 cm in Lacy Rib pattern

Other Supplies
Stitch marker, yarn needle

PATTERN ESSENTIALS

Lacy Rib (multiple of 6 stitches)

- **Round 1:** *K2, p1, yo, k2tog tbl, p1; repeat from * to end of round.
- **Round 2:** *K2, p1; repeat from * to end of round.
- **Round 3:** *K2, p1, k2tog, yo, p1; repeat from * to end of round.
- **Round 4:** Repeat Round 2.
- Repeat Rounds 1–4 for pattern.

Knitting the Warmers (make 2)

- Loosely cast on 48 stitches. Place marker and join into a round, being careful not to twist the stitches.
- ROUND 1: *K2, p1; repeat from * to end of round.
- Repeat Round 1 nine more times (10 rib rounds total).
- Following the written instructions or the chart, work Rounds 1–4 of Lacy Rib pattern 17 times, then work Rounds 1 and 2 once more (70 lace rounds total).
- Work 10 rounds in k2, p1 rib as at the beginning.

Finishing

- Bind off loosely in rib. Weave in ends. Block if desired.

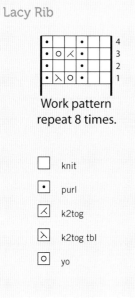

Lacy Rib

Work pattern repeat 8 times.

☐ knit

• purl

◹ k2tog

◺ k2tog tbl

○ yo

Gabriella Bracelet and Choker

DESIGNED BY NANCY MILLER

A choker that Nancy's daughter wears inspired her to knit this jewelry set, made to showcase beautiful beads and her favorite shade of green. The hemp fiber will wear in like your favorite pair of jeans.

257

Finished Measurements

Bracelet is 7"/18 cm around, including button; choker is 13"/33 cm around, including button

Yarn

B. Toucan Inc. Ultra-Fine Dyed Hemp, 100% hemp, 33 yds (30 m)/spool, Forest Green

Needles

US 2½ (3 mm) straight needles

Gauge

Not crucial to project

Other Supplies

Big-eye beading needle, two decorative flat beads of your choice with holes large enough to accommodate a double strand of hemp, six small beads to use as clasp stoppers with holes large enough to accommodate a double strand of hemp, yarn needle

Knitting the Bracelet

- Cast on 6 stitches, leaving a 10"/25.5 cm tail.
- **ALL ROWS:** Slip 1 purlwise wyib, k2, yo, k2tog, k1.
- Repeat this row until bracelet reaches the desired length when stretched (taking button size into account). Bind off, leaving a 10"/25.5 cm tail.

Knitting the Choker

- Cast on 4 stitches, leaving a 10"/25.5 cm tail.
- **ALL ROWS:** K1, yo, p2tog, k1.
- Repeat this row until choker reaches the desired length when stretched (taking button size into account). Bind off, leaving a 10"/25.5 cm tail.

Finishing the Bracelet and Choker

- Thread one tail through the big-eye beading needle, and pass it through one hole of the flat bead and back through the other hole, leaving a loop large enough to fit the 3 stopper beads through. Secure the tail to the edge of the piece and then thread it through the bead again following the same path and matching the length of the first loop. Secure the tail by weaving it into several stitches so it blends in and trim flush with surface of piece.

- On the other end, thread the tail through the big-eye beading needle, pass through the three stopper beads. Secure the tail to the edge of the piece and pass through all three beads along the same path a second time to form the end of the clasp that will slip through the loop on the flat bead. Secure the tail by weaving it into several stitches and trim flush with surface of piece.

- To close, slide the flat bead toward the bracelet/choker, put the end with three beads through the loop, and slide the flat bead back to tighten the loop.

Lace Headbands

DESIGNED BY KIM CAMERON

These three headbands are great projects for a beginner; they also make a quick and easy gift for more experienced lace knitters. One skein made all three designs shown here.

Finished Measurements

2"/5 cm wide and 20"/51 cm long

Yarn

Knit Picks CotlLin DK, 70% Tanguis cotton/ 30% linen, 123 yds (112 m)/1.75 oz (50 g), Color 23996 Moroccan Red

Needles

US 3 (3.25 mm) straight needles *or size you need to obtain correct gauge*

Gauge

11 stitches = 2"/5 cm in lace pattern

Other Supplies

Yarn needle, two ½"/13 mm buttons (for each headband), sewing needle, matching thread

PATTERN NOTES

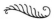

The combination of cotton-blend yarn and a lace pattern gives these headbands a tendency to stretch. Keep this in mind when you determine the length of your headband.

PATTERN ESSENTIALS

Lace A (worked over 11 stitches)

- Row 1 (RS): (K3, p1) twice, k3.
- Row 2 (WS): K1, p2, k1, p3, k1, p2, k1.
- Row 3: K1, k2tog, yo, p1, yo, k3tog, yo, p1, yo, k2tog, k1.
- Row 4: K2, p3, k1, p3, k2.
- Row 5: K1, (p1, k3) twice, p1, k1.
- Row 6: K2, p3, k1, p3, k2.
- Row 7: K1, p1, yo, k3tog, yo, p1, yo, k3tog, yo, p1, k1.
- Row 8: K1, p2, k1, p3, k1, p2, k1.
- Repeat Rows 1–8 for pattern.

Lace B (worked over 11 stitches)

- Row 1 (RS): K2, (yo, k2tog) four times, k1.
- Row 2 (WS): K1, purl to last stitch, k1.
- Row 3: K3, (yo, k2tog) three times, k2.
- Row 4: K1, purl to last stitch, k1.
- Repeat Rows 1–4 for pattern.

Lace C (worked over 11 stitches)

- Row 1 (RS): K1, p2, k5, p2, k1.
- Row 2 (WS): K3, p5, k3.
- Row 3: K1, p2, k2tog, yo, k1, yo, ssk, p2, k1.
- Row 4: K3, p5, k3.
- Repeat Rows 1–4 for pattern.

Knitting Headband A

- Cast on 11 stitches.
- Knit 10 rows.
- Work Rows 1–8 of Lace A until headband measures 19"/48.5 cm or 1"/2.5 cm less than desired length, ending with a WS row.

Knitting the Buttonholes

- ROWS 1–4: Knit.
- ROW 5 (RS, BUTTONHOLE ROW): K3, (yo, k2tog, k2) twice.
- ROWS 6–12: Knit.

Note: You can create an adjustable headband by repeating Rows 5–12 to make an extra set of buttonholes.

- Bind off all stitches. Weave in ends.

Knitting Headband B

- Cast on 11 stitches.
- Knit 10 rows.
- Work Rows 1–4 of Lace B until headband measures 19"/48.5 cm or 1"/2.5 cm less than desired length, ending with a WS row.
- Work buttonholes as for Headband A.
- Bind off all stitches. Weave in ends.

Knitting Headband C

- Cast on 11 stitches.
- Knit 10 rows.
- Work Rows 1–4 of Lace C until headband measures 19"/48.5 cm or 1"/2.5 cm less than desired length, ending with a WS row.
- Work buttonholes as for Headband A.
- Bind off all stitches. Weave in ends.

Finishing All Headbands

- Block headband to 2"/5 cm wide and required length. Overlap the ends, and sew two buttons to the RS of the garter stitch beginning section underneath the buttonholes.

Lace A

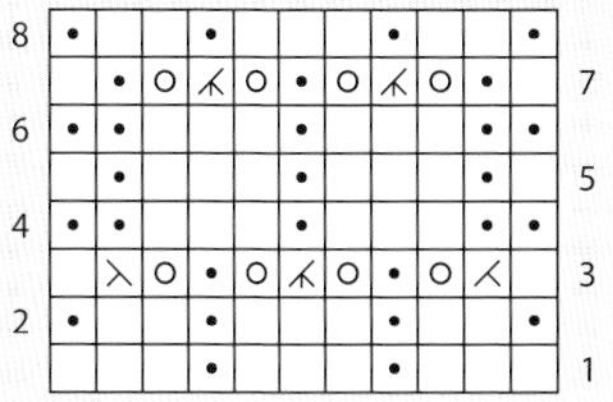

Lace B

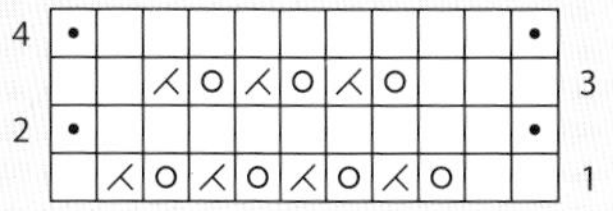

Lace C

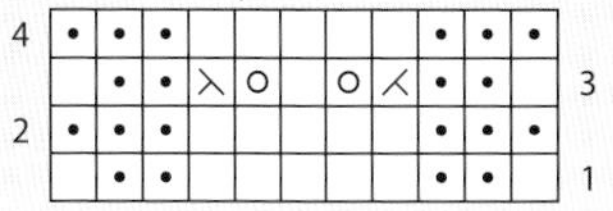

- (blank square) k on RS, p on WS
- (dot) p on RS, k on WS
- (circle) yo
- k2tog
- ssk
- k3tog

Lattice Frost Purse

Designed by Sara Delaney

Here's one for the crocheters among us. This stylish round-bottom purse has vintage appeal, and it's worked in an easy-to-remember two-row lace pattern. You can completely change the look with the lining color and button choice.

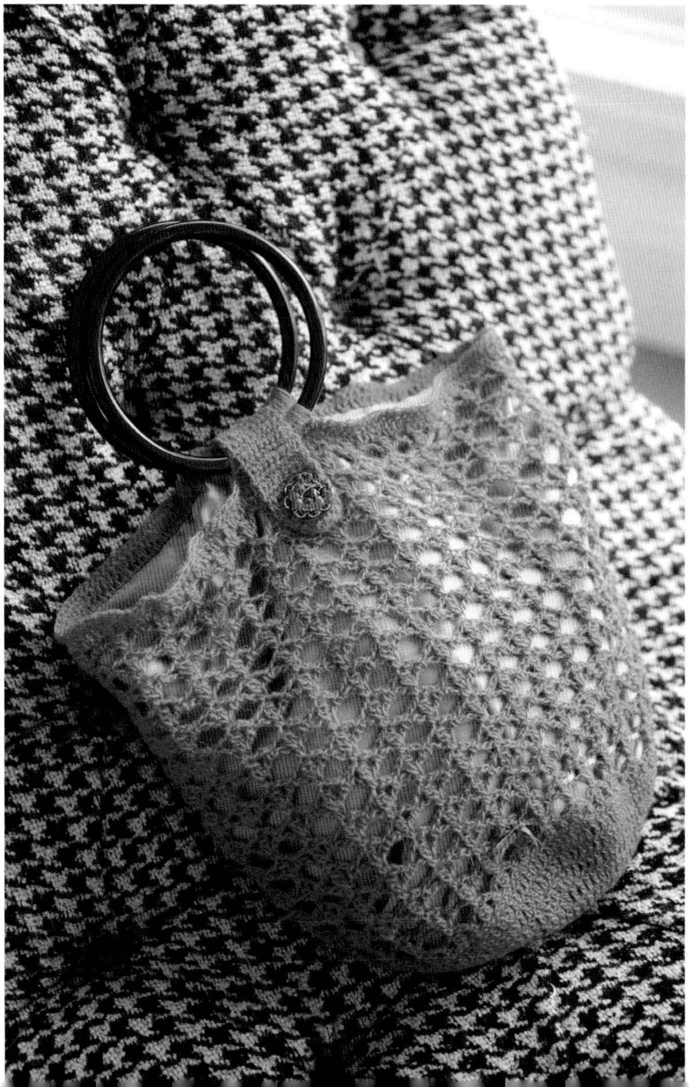

Approximately 25½"/65 cm circumference; 9½"/24 cm tall from base to upper edge, excluding handles; and 7¾"/19.5 cm diameter across base

Yarn

Lopi Einband, 100% pure new wool, 245 yds (225 m)/1.75 oz (50 g), Color 1761 Teal

Crochet Hook

US D/3 (3.25 mm) *or size you need to obtain correct gauge*

Gauge

5 repeats of Lattice Lace pattern = 4¼"/11 cm wide; 12 rounds in Lattice Lace pattern = 4"/10 cm high

Other Supplies

Two 5"/12.5 cm circular purse handles; yarn needle; large vase or rolled beach towel for blocking; ½ yd/46 cm lining fabric; circle of cardboard 7½"/19 cm in diameter for stiffening the purse bottom; sewing needle and thread that matches the lining fabric; one 1"/2.5 cm button; 1 yd/1 m satin ribbon, ⅛"/3 mm wide (optional)

Special Abbreviation

SB   slender bobble

PATTERN ESSENTIALS

Slender Bobble *Yo, insert hook into stitch, yo and draw up a loop, yo and pull through 2 loops, repeat from * once more, yo and pull through all 3 loops on hook.

Single Crochet around Handle Hold circular handle behind the work, with the top of the circle even with the stitch to be joined. Insert hook into the stitch and then into the circle; bring the yarn over the top of the circle from the front to back, yo and draw a loop through both the circle and stitch; bring the yarn over the top of the circle from back to front, yo and pull through 2 loops on hook.

Crocheting the Base

- **ROUND 1:** Ch 3, work 11 dc all in 3rd ch from hook, join with slip stitch to 3rd ch of ch-3.

- **ROUND 2:** Ch 2 (counts as 1 dc on this and all following rounds), 1 dc in same stitch, 2 dc in each stitch around, join with slip stitch to 2nd ch of ch-2. *You now have* 24 dc.

- **ROUND 3:** Ch 2, 1 dc in same stitch, 1 dc in next stitch, *2 dc in next stitch, 1 dc in next stitch; repeat from * 10 more times, join with slip stitch to 2nd ch of ch-2. *You now have* 36 dc.

- **ROUND 4:** Ch 2, 1 dc in same stitch, 1 dc in each of next 2 stitches, *2 dc in next stitch, 1 dc in each of next 2 stitches; repeat from * 10 more times, join with slip stitch to 2nd ch of ch-2. *You now have* 48 dc.

- **ROUND 5:** Ch 2, 1 dc in same stitch, 1 dc in each of next 3 stitches, *2 dc in next stitch, 1 dc in each of next 3 stitches; repeat from * 10 more times, join with slip stitch to 2nd ch of ch-2. *You now have* 60 dc.

- **ROUND 6:** Ch 2, 1 dc in same stitch, 1 dc in each of next 4 stitches, *2 dc in next stitch, 1 dc in each of next 4 stitches; repeat from * 10 more times, join with slip stitch to 2nd ch of ch-2. *You now have* 72 dc.

- **ROUND 7:** Ch 2, 1 dc in same stitch, 1 dc in each of next 5 stitches, *2 dc in next stitch, 1 dc in each of next 5 stitches; repeat from * 10 more times, join with slip stitch to 2nd ch of ch-2. *You now have* 84 dc.

- **ROUND 8:** Ch 2, 1 dc in same stitch, 1 dc in each of next 6 stitches, *2 dc in next stitch, 1 dc in each of next 6 stitches;

repeat from * 10 more times, join with slip stitch to 2nd ch of ch-2. *You now have* 96 dc.

- ROUND 9: Ch 2, 1 dc in same stitch, 1 dc in each of next 7 stitches, *2 dc in next stitch, 1 dc in each of next 7 stitches; repeat from * 10 more times, join with slip stitch to 2nd ch of ch-2. *You now have* 108 dc.

- ROUND 10: Ch 2, 1 dc in same stitch, 1 dc in each of next 8 stitches, *2 dc in next stitch, 1 dc in each of next 8 stitches; repeat from * 10 more times, join with slip stitch to 2nd ch of ch-2. *You now have* 120 dc.

- ROUND 11: Ch 1, sc in same stitch, 1 sc in each stitch around, join with slip stitch to first sc.

Crocheting the Lattice Lace

- SETUP ROUND: Ch 1, sc in same stitch, ch 2, skip 1 stitch, SB in next stitch, ch 2, skip 1 stitch, *1 sc in next stitch, ch 2, skip 1 stitch, SB in next stitch, ch 2, skip 1 stitch; repeat from * to end of round, join with slip stitch to first sc. *You now have* 30 SB stitches.

- Work Lattice Lace pattern as follows.

- ROUND 1: Ch 4, 1 sc in top of next SB, *ch 5, 1 sc in top of next SB, repeat from * to end of round, ch 2, join with slip stitch to 2nd ch of ch-4.

- ROUND 2: Ch 1, sc in same stitch, ch 2, SB in next sc, ch 2, *1 sc in next ch-5 space, ch 2, SB in next sc, ch 2; repeat from * to end of round, join with slip stitch to first sc.

- Repeat Rounds 1 and 2 thirteen more times.

Crocheting the Top Edge

- ROUND 1: Ch 2 (counts as 1 dc), 2 dc in next ch-2 space, 1 dc in top of SB, 2 dc in ch-2 space, *1 dc in sc, 2 dc in ch-2 space, 1 dc in SB, 2 dc in ch-2 space; repeat from * to end of round, join with slip stitch to 2nd ch of ch-2. *You now have* 180 dc.

- ROUND 2: Ch 1, sc in same stitch, 1 sc in each of the next 34 stitches, 1 sc around handle in next 20 stitches, 1 sc in each of next 70 stitches, 1 sc around handle in next 20 stitches, 1 sc in each of next 35 stitches, join with slip stitch to first sc.

- Fasten off.

Crocheting the Button Tab

- With RS facing and counting from right to left, rejoin yarn to 6th sc of either handle.

- SETUP ROW: Ch 1, 1 sc in next 10 sc of handle, turn.

- ROW 1: Ch 1, 1 sc in next 10 stitches, turn.

- Repeat Row 1 until piece measures 2½"/6.5 cm or desired length.

- ROW 2: Ch 2, 1 dc in each of next 3 stitches, ch 3, skip 3 stitches, 1 dc in each of next 4 stitches, turn.

- ROW 3: Ch 2, 1 sc in each of next 3 stitches, 3 sc in ch-3 space, 1 sc in each of next 4 stitches.

- Repeat Row 1 once more.

- ROW 4: Ch 2, *yo, insert hook into stitch, yo and bring up a loop, yo and pull through 2 loops; repeat from * nine more times, yo and pull through all 11 loops on hook.

- Fasten off and weave in all ends.

Finishing

- Block purse around a large vase or rolled beach towel.

Making the Lining

- Cut two circles of lining fabric 8½"/21.5 cm in diameter. With RS of lining pieces facing out, sandwich the cardboard circle for the bottom of the bag between the two pieces and baste all the way around with a ½"/13 mm seam allowance. Cut a rectangle of lining fabric about 1"/2.5 cm taller than the bag from base to upper edge, and about 26"–27"/66–68.5 cm wide. Sew short ends of the rectangle together to form a cylinder, then sew the bottom of the cylinder to the fabric-covered cardboard circle, easing it to fit. Insert lining into purse with WS of lining and purse touching so the RS of lining shows when you look into the purse. Fold the top edge of the lining ½"/13 mm to WS, and sew invisibly in place to WS of bag along the last round of the Lattice Lace pattern using small, firm stitches.

- Sew a button to the RS of the purse, centered about 1½"/4 cm below the handle without the button tab, and sewing through both layers of the purse and lining. For the optional satin ribbon, beginning and ending directly below the button, weave the ribbon around the bottom of the purse through the first Round 2 at the start of the Lattice Lace pattern. Tie ends of ribbon in a small bow as shown and trim the excess.

{ *Lining Tip* }

To make your purse even more useful, consider adding pockets to the lining. Simply cut squares or rectangles to the desired pocket sizes and sew them to the right side of the lining fabric before you join the ends to form a cylinder. You can add buttons, snaps, or Velcro to keep the pockets closed if desired.

for the home

The Iloise Lace Bath Set

DESIGNED BY MYRNA A. I. STAHMAN

This bath set is a great project for using common lace knitting maneuvers and practicing lace knitting back and forth (Cloth 1), circular flat lace knitting (Cloth 2), and circular tube lace knitting (Soap Sack). One skein of linen is just right for three bath cloths and one soap sack or two bath cloths and two soap sacks.

Finished Measurements

Cloth 1 and Cloth 2: Approximately 9"/ 23 cm square
Soap Sack: Approximately 3¼"/8.5 cm wide and 6"/15 cm high

Yarn

Louet Euroflax Sport Weight (Fine #2), 100% wet spun linen, 270 yds (250 m)/ 3.5 oz (100 g), Color 18-2474-1 Terra Cotta

Needles

Choose a size that produces the fabric you like; manufacturer's recommendation is US 2–4 (2.75–3.5 mm). A needle four or five times larger can be used for binding off (optional).
Cloth 1: Straight needles
Cloth 2 and Soap Sack: Double-point or two circular needles

Gauge

As desired, approximately 20–24 stitches = 4"/10 cm in lace patterns, blocked

Other Supplies

Stitch markers, yarn needle, crochet hook similar in size to knitting needles (for Soap Sack)

Knitting Cloth 1

This square cloth is knit back and forth in rows.

- Cast on 51 stitches: 43 stitches for the lace pattern and 4 stitches for each side border.

Knitting the Bottom Seed Stitch Border

- ROWS 1–5: Slip 1 purlwise wyif, *k1, p1; repeat from * to last 2 stitches, k2.

Knitting the Lace

- NEXT ROW (RS): Slip 1 purlwise wyif, k1, p1, k1, work Row 1 of Cloth 1 chart over center 43 stitches, k1, p1, k2.

- Keeping the first and last 4 stitches as established for side borders, work Rows 2–20 of Cloth 1 chart once, then work Rows 1–20 two more times. *Note:* Only RS rows are charted; on all even-numbered WS rows work 4 border stitches as established, purl to last 4 stitches, work 4 border stitches.

Knitting the Top Seed Stitch Border

- Work Rows 1–5 as for Bottom Seed Stitch Border.

- Bind off in pattern, using a needle four or five sizes larger than the main needles, if desired. Weave in ends. Block.

Knitting Cloth 2

This square cloth is knit flat, in the round from the center out.

Note: Begin the square on double-point needles and switch to a circular needle once there are sufficient stitches for comfortable circular knitting.

- Cast on 8 stitches using a circular cast-on method (see page 290). Knit 1 round.

Knitting the Lace

- Work Rounds 1–34 of Cloth 2 chart, working four repeats for each round. *You now have* 168 stitches total: 42 stitches in each of four sections.

Knitting the Border

- Place a marker at the end of each section if you have not already done so; take care that the markers do not slip underneath any yarnovers at the corners.

- ROUND 1: (Yo, *k1, p1; repeat from * to 2 stitches before marker, k1, yo, p1, slip marker) four times — 8 stitches increased, 2 stitches in each section.

- ROUND 2: Work in seed stitch (i.e., purl the knits and knit the purls as they appear), working new stitches into pattern.

- ROUND 3: (Yo, work in seed stitch to 1 stitch before marker, yo, work corner stitch as either k1 or p1 to maintain pattern, slip marker) four times — 8 stitches increased, 2 stitches in each section.

- ROUNDS 4–6: Repeat Rounds 2 and 3, then work Round 2 once more. *You now have* 192 stitches total: 48 stitches each in four sections.

- Bind off in seed stitch, using a needle four or five sizes larger than main needles.

Knitting the Soap Sack

The Soap Sack is knit circularly from the top down.

Note: Use two circular needles for this project, each needle holding one seed stitch column followed by one lace pattern repeat.

- Cast on 53 stitches. Place marker and join into a round, being careful not to twist the stitches.

Knitting the Top

- ROUND 1: *K1, pl; repeat from * to last st, k1.

- ROUND 2: *Pl, k1; repeat from * to last st, pl.

- ROUNDS 3–8: Repeat Rounds 1 and 2 three times.

- ROUND 9 (EYELET ROUND): *Yo, sk2p; repeat from * to last 2 stitches, yo, ssk. *You now have* 36 stitches.

- ROUND 10: Knit.

Knitting the Lace

- ROUNDS 11–48: Working each row of chart twice for each round, work Rounds 1–20 of Soap Sack chart once, then work Rounds 1–18 once more.

- ROUND 49 (ROUND 19 OF CHART): *Work 3 stitches of seed stitch column as sk2p, work next 15 chart stitches; repeat from * once more. *You now have* 32 stitches.

- ROUND 50: Knit.

Knitting the Bottom

- ROUND 51: *K1, pl; repeat from * to end of round.

- ROUND 52: *Pl, k1; repeat from * to end of round.

- ROUND 53: Repeat Round 51.

- Arrange stitches evenly on two needles if you have not already done so, and join live stitches together with Kitchener stitch (see page 293). Weave in ends. Block.

Finishing

- Crochet a chain about five times the width of the soap sack, and fasten off last stitch. Weave the cord through the Eyelet Round twice. Tie the ends of the cord together.

Soap Sack

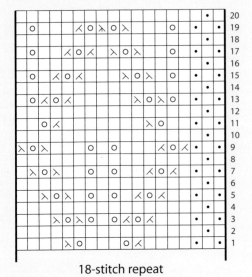

18-stitch repeat

☐	knit
•	purl
⟋	k2tog
⟍	ssk
○	yo
⅄	sk2p

Cloth 1

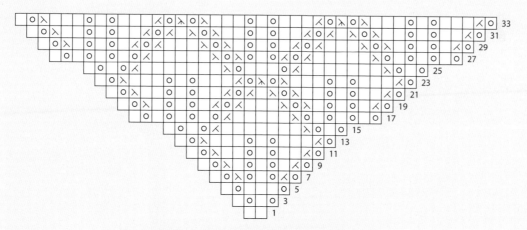

Only RS (odd-numbered) rows are charted.

See instructions for WS rows and borders.

Cloth 2

Only odd-numbered (RS) rounds are charted.

Knit all even-numbered (WS) rounds.

Lace Bottle Cozy

DESIGNED BY KENDRA NITTA

*A cozy adds a special touch
to any gift of wine or spirits.
Worked in the round in one piece
with simple shaping, this quick
project is a great introduction
to circular lace knitting for
adventurous beginners.*

Finished Measurements

To fit a standard wine bottle, approximately 9"/23 cm circumference and 12"/30.5 cm tall from base to upper edge

Yarn

Blue Sky Alpacas Alpaca Silk, 50% alpaca/ 50% silk, 146 yds (133 m)/1.75 oz (50 g), Color 128 Plum

Needles

One US 3 (3.25 mm) circular needle 9"/ 23 cm long (for circular knitting) or 32"/80 cm long (for magic loop knitting), or two US 3 (3.25 mm) circular needles 16"/40 cm long, and set of four US 3 (3.25 mm) double-point needles *or size you need to obtain correct gauge*

Gauge

26 stitches and 33 rows = 4"/10 cm in stockinette stitch; 24 stitches and 36 rounds = 4"/10 cm in Japanese Feather Lace pattern

Other Supplies

Scrap yarn for provisional cast on, stitch markers, yarn needle, cable needle, stitch holder, bottle for blocking

PATTERN ESSENTIALS

Conch Bind Off (worked over a multiple of 5 stitches)

*(K3, slip same 3 stitches back to left-hand needle) twice, bind off 5 stitches in pattern; repeat from * until all stitches are bound off.

Cabled Cord (worked over 6 stitches with RS always facing)

- **Row 1:** K1, slip 2 stitches to cable needle and hold in front, k2, k2 from cable needle, k1; slide all stitches back to tip of needle, bring yarn across WS into position to work another RS row.
- **Rows 2–6:** K6; slide all stitches back to tip of needle, bring yarn across WS into position to work another RS row.
- Repeat Rows 1–6 for pattern.

Knitting the Cozy

Note: The cozy may be knit using the magic loop method (see page 295) with one long circular needle, or with stitches divided onto two circulars, or with all stitches on one short circular needle. Knitting the whole project on double-point needles requires shifting stitches between needles and is recommended for experienced lace knitters only.

- Using a provisional method (see pages 297–298), cast on 55 stitches. Place marker and join into a round, being careful not to twist the stitches.
- **SETUP ROUND:** *K10, p1, place marker; repeat from * to end of round.
- Work Rounds 1–26 of Japanese Feather Lace chart three times, then work Rounds 1–10 once more.

Knitting the Top of the Cozy

Note: Rows 1–11 are worked back and forth to create an opening for the cord, then the piece is joined again for circular knitting.

- Work Rows 1–11 of Cozy Top chart, then rejoin for working in the round and work Rounds 12–26 of chart. *You now have 50 stitches.*
- Bind off using the Conch Bind Off.

Knitting the Base of the Cozy

- Carefully remove the provisional cast on and place 55 stitches onto double-point needles. Work Rounds 1–14 of Cozy Base chart. *You now have 5 stitches.*
- Cut yarn, leaving an 8"/20.5 cm tail. Thread tail onto yarn needle and draw through remaining stitches; pull up snugly and secure. Weave in end.

Knitting the Cord and Leaves

- Using double-point needles, with RS facing and body of cozy to the right, pick up and knit (see page 297) 8 stitches along the lower edge of the neck opening where piece was worked back and forth.

Knitting the Cord

- **SETUP ROW (WS):** P2tog, p4, p2tog tbl. *You now have 6 stitches.*
- Work 4 rows in stockinette stitch, ending with a WS row.
- Work Rows 1–6 of Cabled Cord pattern seven or eight times, until cord is about 6½"–7"/16.5–18 cm from beginning, ending with Row 2. Do not cut yarn.

Knitting the Leaves

- Slide stitches to needle tip in order to begin with a RS row. Work Row 1 of Leaf chart over the first 3 stitches, then place the remaining 3 stitches on holder. Work Rows 2–17 of Leaf chart, then fasten off the last stitch. Return 3 held cord stitches to needle and work 2 rows as follows: *K3; slide all stitches back to tip of needle, bring yarn across WS in position to work a RS row; repeat from * once more. Work Rows 1–17 of Leaf chart, then fasten off the last stitch.

Finishing

- Weave in ends. Block the bag using a bottle of about the same size and shape as the bottle you intend to gift. If the bottle still has a label on it, cover the bottle with plastic wrap first to avoid damaging the yarn. Block the leaves flat.

Cozy Base

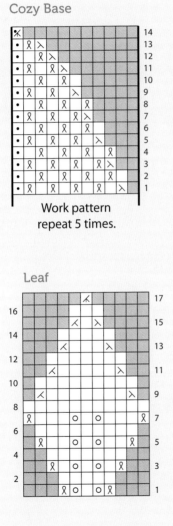

Work pattern repeat 5 times.

Leaf

Cozy Top

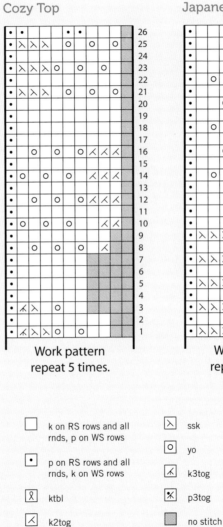

Work pattern repeat 5 times.

Japanese Feather Lace

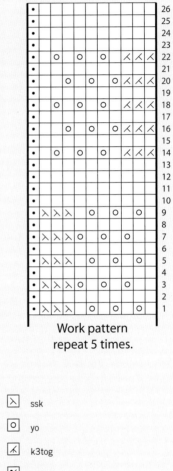

Work pattern repeat 5 times.

☐ k on RS rows and all rnds, p on WS rows	⟍ ssk
• p on RS rows and all rnds, k on WS rows	○ yo
႙ ktbl	⟋ k3tog
⟋ k2tog	⚹ p3tog
	▨ no stitch

The Alka Dishcloth Set

DESIGNED BY MYRNA A. I. STAHMAN

These 100 percent cotton, diamond-shaped dishcloths in three sizes, using the Alka lace pattern stitch, are a great addition to any kitchen. Pick and choose what size cloths you wish to make from the four-ounce ball.

Finished Measurements

Small cloth:
Approximately 5"/12.5 cm square
Medium cloth:
Approximately 7¼"/18.5 cm square
Large cloth:
Approximately 9¼"/23.5 cm square

Yarn

Lily Sugar'n Cream New Super Size, 100% cotton, 200 yds (184 m)/4 oz (113 g), Color 18010 Yellow

Needles

US 7 (4.5 mm) straight needles *or size you need to obtain correct gauge*

Gauge

14 stitches and 19 rows = 4"/10 cm in Alka pattern

Other Supplies

Yarn needle

PATTERN NOTES

The large cloth used 36 grams of yarn, the medium cloth took 22 grams, and the small cloth used 12 grams. One supersize Sugar'n Cream ball made one large, three medium, and one small cloth, which all together weighed 114 grams even though the skein is marked 113 g.

273

Alka

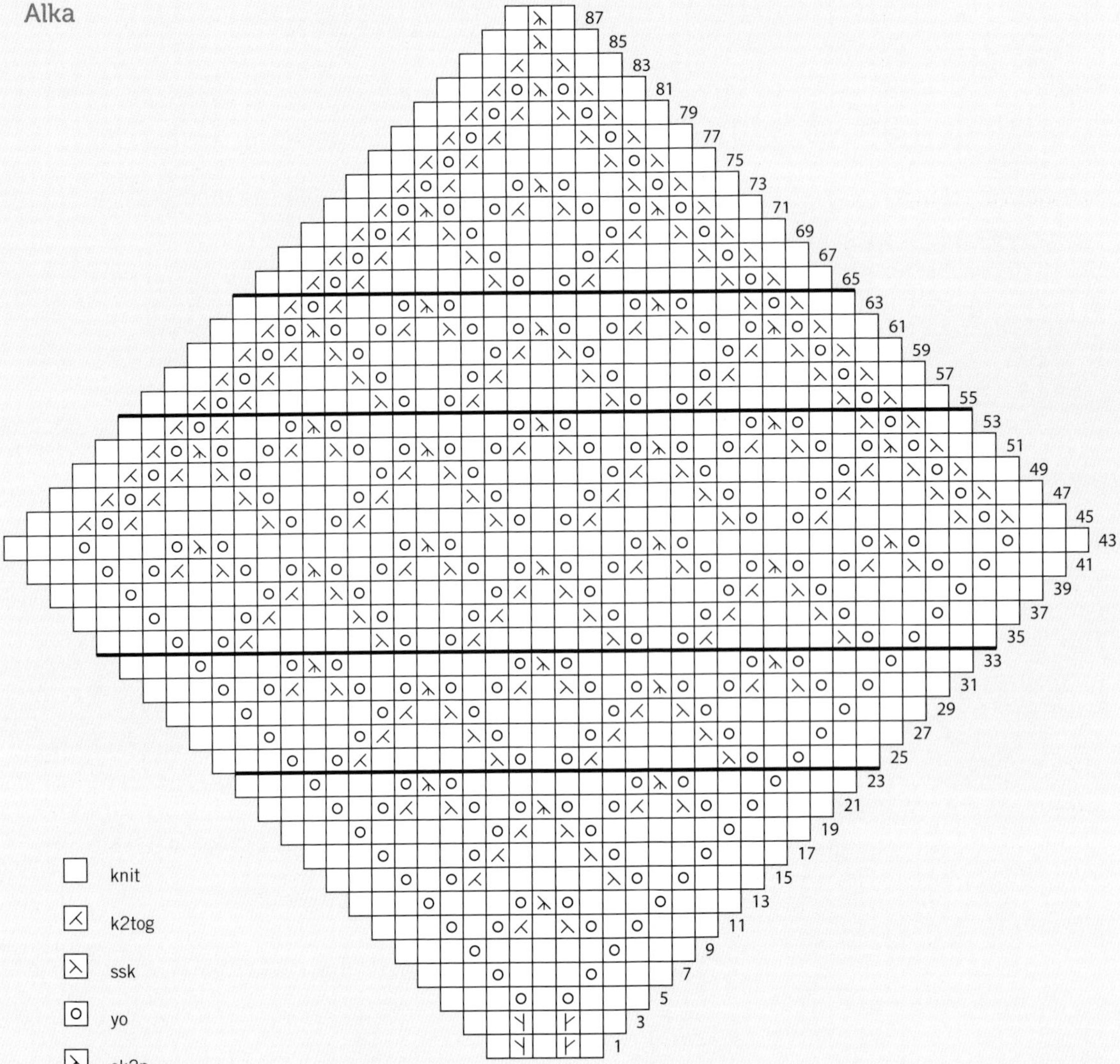

knit
k2tog
ssk
yo
sk2p
M1R
M1L

Only odd-numbered (RS) rows are charted.

Knit all even-numbered (WS) rows.

Knitting the Cloths

- Using your favorite method, cast on 3 stitches. Knit 1 (WS) row.

  Note: Only RS rows are charted; knit all even-numbered WS rows.

- Follow the Alka chart to work each size cloth as follows.

- *For the small cloth:* Work Rows 1–24. *You now have* 27 stitches.

- Skip Rows 25–64, and then work Rows 65–88. *You now have* 3 stitches.

- *For the medium cloth:* Work Rows 1–34. *You now have* 37 stitches.

- Skip Rows 35–54, and then work Rows 55–88. *You now have* 3 stitches.

- *For the large cloth:* Work Rows 1–88 as they appear, increasing and decreasing as shown on chart. *You now have* 3 stitches.

Finishing for All Sizes

- Bind off the remaining 3 stitches. Secure the end by making three knots along the side of the cloth, then cut off the remaining yarn.

Firefly Table Mat

DESIGNED BY MEG MYERS

This round mat is worked from the center out in eight sections, each containing a two-diamond lace motif emerging from a stockinette center column on a garter stitch ground, and separated by a single stockinette stitch.

Finished Measurements

Approximately 14"/35.5 cm diameter

Yarn

Classic Elite Yarns Firefly, 75% viscose/
25% linen, 155 yds (142 m)/1.75 oz (50 g),
Color 7795 Thistle

Needles

US 5 (3.75 mm) circular needle 16"/40 cm,
US 5 (3.75 mm) circular needle 24"/60 cm
long, and set of four US 5 (3.75 mm)
double-point needles *or size you need
to obtain correct gauge*

Gauge

21 stitches and 31 rounds = 4"/10 cm in
garter stitch, blocked

Other Supplies

Locking stitch marker, yarn needle

	knit
•	purl
o	yo
⟋	k2tog
⟍	ssk
⟝	sk2p
	no stitch

Firefly Lace

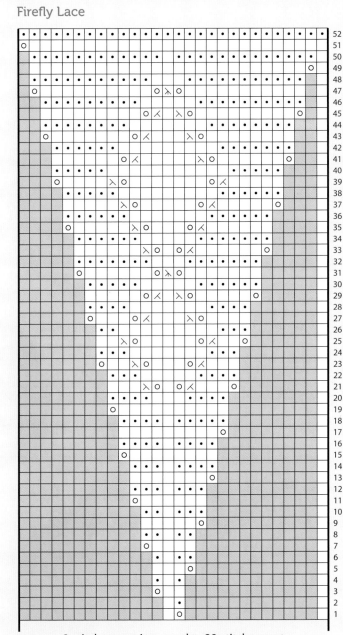

2-stitch repeat increased to 28-stitch repeat

Work pattern repeat 8 times.

Knitting the Mat

- With double-point needle, cast on 8 stitches. Divide stitches onto three double-point needles and join into a round, being careful not to twist the stitches. Place a locking stitch marker in the first stitch for beginning of round; move the stitch marker up as you work.

- Knit 1 round.

- **INCREASE ROUND:** *K1, yo; repeat from * to end of round. *You now have* 16 stitches.

- Work Rounds 1–52 of Firefly Lace chart, working eight repeats in each round, switching to 16"/ 40 cm and then 24"/60 cm circular needles when you have enough stitches, and transferring the marker to the needle when you begin on circulars. *You now have* 224 stitches.

- Bind off all stitches knitwise.

Finishing

- Block, taking care not to over-stretch or flatten the garter stitch. Weave in ends.

New Wave Sachets

DESIGNED BY CYNTHIA ALLEN

Insert a bag of your favorite potpourri into these sachets and store them in your drawers to freshen your wardrobe. One skein will make three sachets, which make a wonderful gift.

277

Finished Measurements

3¼"/8.5 cm wide and 5"/12.5 cm tall

Yarn

Knit Picks Shine Sport, 60% cotton/
40% modal, 110 yds (100 m)/1.75 oz
(50 g), Sky

Needles

US 3 (3.25 mm) straight needles *or size
you need to obtain correct gauge*

Gauge

24 stitches and 34 rows = 4"/10 cm in
stockinette stitch and lace pattern

Other Supplies

2 yds/1.8 m satin ribbon, ¼"/6 mm wide
(24"/61 cm for each sachet), yarn needle

Knitting the Sachet

Note: The sachet begins at the top of the
lace-patterned front, is worked down to
the bottom turning ridge, then upward
to end at the top of the stockinette back.

- Cast on 21 stitches.
- ROWS 1–3: Knit.
- ROW 4 (WS): Purl.
- ROWS 5, 7, AND 9: Knit.
- ROWS 6, 8, AND 10: Purl.
- ROW 11 (RS, EYELET ROW): K3, *yo, k2tog;
  repeat from * to last 2 stitches, k2.
- ROWS 12, 14, AND 16: Purl.
- ROWS 13 AND 15: Knit.

Beginning the Lace Pattern

- ROW 1 (RS): K4, ssk, yo, k4, yo, k2tog, k2,
  ssk, yo, k5.
- ROW 2 AND ALL EVEN-NUMBERED ROWS
  THROUGH ROW 12 (WS): Purl.

- ROW 3: K5, yo, k2tog, k1, k2tog, yo, k1, yo, ssk, k2, yo,
  k2tog, k4.
- ROW 5: K7, k2tog, yo, k3, yo, ssk, k7.
- ROW 7: K6, k2tog, yo, k5, yo, ssk, k6.
- ROW 9: K4, yo, sk2p, yo, k3, yo, k2tog, k2, yo, sk2p, yo, k4.
- ROW 11: K5, yo, ssk, k2, ssk, yo, k4, yo, ssk, k4.
- Repeat Rows 1–12 once more.
- Knit 1 row, purl 1 row, then knit 2 rows. **Note:** This last knit
  row forms a turning ridge on the outside of the sachet bot-
  tom. Do not cut the yarn.

Knitting the Back of the Sachet

- Work 32 rows in stockinette stitch, ending with a WS row.
- Repeat RS Row 11 (Eyelet Row) from beginning.
- Work 6 rows in stockinette stitch. **Note:** The purl row fol-
  lowing the Eyelet Row counts as the first of these 6 rows.
- Knit 3 rows. Bind off.

Finishing

- Block, pinning out the sides so they don't roll. When dry,
  fold the bag in half along the turning ridge at the bottom
  and use mattress stitch (see page 296) to join the sides. Cut
  ribbon into three 24"/61 cm lengths and trim the ends on
  the diagonal. Thread ribbon through the eyelets beginning
  and ending at center front and tie in a bow.

Tilting Blocks Pillow

DESIGNED BY GWEN STEEGE

From Barbara Walker's Craft of Lace Knitting *(Scribner's, 1971), the lace center panel conveys a sense of motion, a bit like op art. The linen yarn may at first seem stiff, but after washing (and use), like any linen, it softens considerably. It also holds its shape beautifully, an important characteristic for home decor items.*

Finished Measurements

10" × 10"/25.5 × 25.5 cm

Yarn

Louet Euroflax Sport Weight (Fine #2), 100% wet spun linen, 270 yds (247 m)/ 3.5 oz (100 g), Color 55 Willow

Needles

US 4 (3.5 mm) straight needles and US 4 (3.5 mm) circular needle 16"/40 cm long *or size you need to obtain correct gauge*

Gauge

20 stitches and 36 rows = 4"/10 cm in Tilting Blocks pattern

Other Supplies

Stitch markers (one in a unique color), yarn needle, ½ yd/0.5 m linen or cotton fabric, 10"/25.5 cm knife-edge pillow form, embroidery needle, US E/4 (3.5 mm) crochet hook

Special Abbreviations

Kfbf Knit into the front of the stitch and leave it on the needle, knit into the back of the stitch and leave it on the needle, knit into the front of the stitch and drop it from the needle — 3 stitches made from 1 stitch

279

PATTERN ESSENTIALS

Tilting Blocks
(Multiple of 16 stitches plus 1)

- **Rows 1, 3, 5, and 7 (RS):** *(Ssk, yo) four times, k8; repeat from * to last stitch, k1.
- **Rows 2, 4, 6, and 8:** *K9, p7; repeat from * to last stitch, k1.
- **Rows 9, 11, 13, and 15:** K1, *k8, (yo, k2tog) four times; repeat from * to end of row.
- **Rows 10, 12, 14, and 16:** K1, *p7, k9; repeat from * to end of row.
- Repeat Rows 1–16 for pattern.

Knitting the Pillow Front

- Cast on 33 stitches.
- Work Rows 1–16 of Tilting Blocks pattern four times (64 rows total). Do not bind off.
- Turn work so RS is facing you. From here on, you will be knitting in the round, so place the 33 stitches on a circular needle.
- **ROUND 1:** Kfbf, placing the unique-colored stitch marker before the center stitch of this triple increase, k32; *pick up 1 stitch in the corner and work it as kfbf, again placing a marker before the center stitch, pick up and knit 32 stitches along the selvedge**; repeat from * to ** once more, picking up stitches along the cast-on edge, then repeat from * to ** once more, picking up stitches along the remaining selvedge. You now have 140 stitches: 35 on each side. Knit the first stitch of the first kfbf again to

end at the different-colored marker. This is the beginning of the round.

- **ROUND 2 AND ALL EVEN-NUMBERED ROUNDS:** Knit.
- **ROUND 3 AND ALL ODD-NUMBERED ROUNDS:** *K1, yo, ssk, yo, knit to 2 stitches before marker, yo, k2tog, yo, slip marker; repeat from * to end of round — 8 stitches increased: 2 stitches on each side.
- Repeat Rounds 2 and 3 five more times until you have 47 stitches on each side, or until border is the desired width; in the sample shown, the border is 1½"/4 cm wide. Bind off very loosely. *Note:* You will be crocheting into these bound-off stitches, and because the linen has little or no elasticity, it's important to bind off loosely or you will have difficulty getting your crochet hook into the stitches.

Assembling the Pillow

- Wash and block the completed piece to 10"/25.5 cm square. Weave in ends.
- Make fabric pillow cover to fit 10"/25.5 cm square pillow form, leaving a large opening for inserting pillow form, and turn it right side out.
- Using the linen yarn, work embroidered chain stitch (see page 291), at 5 chain stitches to an inch, near the seam line around all four sides of fabric pillow cover (about 47 stitches on each side). As with the bind off, take care to keep these embroidery stitches quite loose.
- Attach the knit panel to the pillow cover with single crochet, as follows: Beginning at the bottom center of the knit panel with RS facing you, ch 1, *work 1 sc through 1 bound-off stitch and 1 embroidered chain stitch to join them, and continue to join along the entire edge to the corner in this manner; at the corner, work 3 sc in same pair of joined stitches; repeat from * until you reach the starting point, then join with slip stitch to top of ch-1. Fasten off last stitch. Insert pillow form into fabric cover and close the opening.

Circular Magic Trivet Set

DESIGNED BY MYRNA A. I. STAHMAN

When knitting a flat, circular design, such as a doily or tablecloth, you usually increase eight stitches every other round. Break that rule and change the number of increases and the circle becomes a square, pentagon, hexagon, heptagon, or octagon. Magic!

Finished Measurements
Varies from approximately 4"/10 cm square to approximately 8"/20.5 cm in diameter for an octagon

Yarn
Louet Euroflax Bulky/Chunky Weight, 100% linen, 150 yds (137 m)/3.5 oz (100 g), Chamomile

Needles
US 8–10 (5–6 mm) *or size you need to obtain a loose gauge that you like* and a needle three or four sizes larger for binding off

Gauge
Approximately 14–16 stitches = 4"/10 cm. **Note:** Exact gauge is not critical for this project, but it is important to achieve a fairly relaxed gauge (especially with the larger trivets) so the pieces can be blocked flat.

Other Supplies
Yarn needle

Knitting the Trivets

- Using a circular cast on (see page 290), cast on the following number of stitches:
  - For the square, 4 stitches
  - For the pentagon, 5 stitches
  - For the hexagon, 6 stitches
  - For the heptagon, 7 stitches
  - For the octagon, 8 stitches

- Using either the chart or the written instructions, work Rounds 1–15, working the repeat as many times in each round as the number of stitches cast on. In other words, for the square work the chart four times in each round, for the pentagon work the chart five times in each round, and so on.

- **ROUNDS 1 AND 2:** Knit.

- **ROUND 3:** *Yo twice, k1; repeat from * to end of round. *You now have* 3 stitches in each repeat.

- **ROUND 4:** *Work (k1, p1, k1) into the double yo of previous round, k1; repeat from * to end of round. *You now have* 4 stitches in each repeat.

- **ROUND 5 AND ALL ODD-NUMBERED ROUNDS TO ROUND 13:** Knit.

- **ROUND 6:** *Yo, k3, yo, k1; repeat from * to end of round. *You now have* 6 stitches in each repeat.

- **ROUND 8:** *Yo, k5, yo, k1; repeat from * to end of round. *You now have* 8 stitches in each repeat.

- **ROUND 10:** *Yo, ssk, k3, k2tog, yo, k1; repeat from * to end of round.

- **ROUND 12:** *Yo, k1, yo, ssk, k1, k2tog, (yo, k1) twice; repeat from * to end of round. *You now have* 10 stitches in each repeat.

- **ROUND 14:** *Yo, k3, yo, sk2p, yo, k3, yo, k1; repeat from * to end of round. *You now have* 12 stitches in each repeat.

- **ROUND 15:** Knit.

Finishing

- Bind off loosely knitwise using your favorite method and the larger needle. Block. Weave in ends.

Trivet Lace

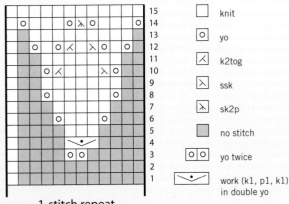

1-stitch repeat
increased to 12-stitch repeat

Work pattern repeat according to directions.

appendix

About the Designers

Cynthia Allen

Knitting has been a big part of Cynthia's life for nearly 20 years, and she's also an avid crocheter. Her next big life adventure will be relocating in 2013 from the snowy Northeast to the sunny Southwest. She's known as Missallen on Ravelry, and is usually hanging out with Dr. Who, Nerdy Knitters, or another arcane group.

Julie L. Anderson

Julie is a designer of knit toys and a knitting instructor. She strives to design toys with a whimsical feel that children will love. She likes to incorporate different textures into her designs as well as fun colors. You can find Julie's work at *www.the-byrds-nest.com*.

Sharon Ballsmith

Sharon is an indie crochet designer. Her designs have appeared in magazines such as *Interweave Crochet*, *Crochet!*, and *Tangled*. She also has designs in *Oh Baby! Crochet* (DRG) and *Crochet One-Skein Wonders*, as well as upcoming books by Cooperative Press. Find Sharon on Ravelry as stitchesandstones.

Tonia Barry

Tonia lives in New Hampshire with her husband, daughters, and a beagle. She is a designer at Classic Elite Yarns and also designs independently for various knitting publications. To see more of her designs visit *www.toniabarrydesigns.com* or check her out on Ravelry.

Barbara Benson

Despite the fact that Atlanta doesn't have ideal knitwear weather, Barbara loves living and knitting in the South. Self-proclaimed as "a bit of silly and a bit nerdy," this often translates into her designs. When not knitting she can be found elbow deep in the kitchen, garden, or Play-Doh. You can also find her blogging around as Tumped Duck at *http://tumpedduck.wordpress.com*.

Rae Blackledge

Rae lives in Charlotte, North Carolina, where she works in the design department at Universal Yarn. She also owned and operated Rae's Yarn Boutique in Lansing, Michigan, for nine years. Her designs can be found online under the name Extravayarnza.

Julie Blagojevich

Julie's been crocheting since she was eight years old. She works with a community of knitters at Haus of Yarn in Nashville, Tennessee, and is continually inspired by their talent and creativity. Accessories are her favorite projects, especially shawlettes, necklaces, and purses.

Heather Broadhurst

When not playing with her computer network or techwriting/editing, Heather, a.k.a. walkaboutknitter, can be seen walking and knitting in San Diego, California. She loves knitting just about anything but loves it all a bit more if math and lace are involved.

Christiane Burkhard

The love for knitting, crocheting, and fashion has a long tradition in Christiane's family. Since moving to the United States from Switzerland, she's spent a lot of time designing and teaching knitting and crochet. She is Lismi on Ravelry and blogs at *http://lismiknits.blogspot.com*.

Sarah Burton

Sarah blogs about knitting and environmental issues at *www.verdigrisknits.com*. She shares her Indianapolis, Indiana, home with a husband, dogs, and two horses. Look for her knitting in the crowd at the Indianapolis 500.

Kim Cameron

Kim has been knitting for almost 40 years, but it wasn't until she started working at Knit Picks, surrounded by all its creativity, that she started to design. She's inspired by family and friends, and loves to create lots of texture in her designs.

Amanda Carrigan

Due to heredity and the Canadian climate, Amanda has never met a fiber art she disliked. A biochemistry graduate and horticulture student, she indulges her creative side by writing patterns (found on Ravelry as KnitPicks) and dyeing yarn for her Etsy shop, Wayside Weeds and Wool.

Jean M. Clement

Designing professionally since 2005, Jean's favorite designs are classic in style yet unique in construction. Living on the high plains of Colorado, she finds inspiration all around her. Jean's designs can be found in knit.wear, Knitscene, Twist Collective, and other knitting publications. She showcases her self-published designs at www.drdesigns.net.

Terry Collard

Terry works as a manager for Harrisville Designs and at Painted Shadow Farms, owned by her daughter, Bonny. She fills a lot of her time helping out with her flock of more than 100 colored Angora and Pygroa goats. Having a never-ending supply of fiber available helps inspire new projects every day and leads to hours of playing with the "kids!"

Tamara Del Sonno

Tamara's been knitting and crocheting since she was eight years old. These endeavors are a great joy, second only to her grandchildren. She has been a pattern contributor for several publications, and her Clickity Sticks patterns can be found on Ravelry and Craftsy.

Sara Delaney

A crocheter and knitter for 30 years, Sara is a teacher at WEBS, where she helped to develop the crochet curriculum. She's been publishing patterns with WEBS's own Valley Yarns and self-publishing since 2009. She also raises chickens and makes maple syrup. You can follow Sara on Facebook at ChickenBettyDesigns or on Twitter @ChickenBetty.

Kerin Dimeler-Laurence

A knitter for more than 25 years, Kerin's fine art and graphic design background influences the aesthetics of her work. Counted among her inspirations are the natural wonders of the plants, animals, and geology of the Pacific Northwest, and the math and science that gives them depth. Kerin is a pattern writer for Knit Picks.

Judith Durant

Judith is the editor of the best-selling One-Skein Wonders series, as well as author and/or coauthor of a half dozen other books including Knitting Know-How. She loves to teach knitting and does so where and when she can. She lives in Lowell, Massachusetts, and can be found at http://judithdurant.com.

Laura Hein Eckel

Laura is a fiber artist whose design expertise spans several fields including knitting, weaving, sewing, and gardening. She has designs published for Storey Publishing and Tahki Yarns. She is owner of Fibers Entwined, is a knitting and weaving instructor, and works in her LYS.

J. M. Ellis

Taught by her grandmothers, J. M. is a lifelong knitter, crocheter, and spinner, as well as a designer and test knitter for many renowned designers and companies. She is a patient teacher, encourager, and friend.

Diana Foster

Diana is owner and designer for Lowellmountain Wools, LLC, a farm shop with sheep in the Northeast Kingdom of Vermont that offers knitting classes. She is a member of the Knitting Guild Association and knitting instructor at The Old Stone House Museum in Brownington, Vermont.

Mary C. Gildersleeve

Mary began designing shortly after teaching herself to knit at age eight. An avid hand-knitter and designer for more than 40 years, she runs By Hand, With Heart, works at her LYS, designs for a cashmere goat breeder, and sells patterns on Ravelry and Craftsy. Visit her at www.marygildersleeve.com.

Ellen Harvey

A lifelong knitter, Ellen's designs have appeared in Knit It! magazine, Simple Knits for Sophisticated Living, and in many knitting pattern calendars. A CYCA certified knitting instructor, Ellen teaches in various settings in Connecticut and New York. When not knitting, she can be found in the library, working as a reference librarian.

Debbie Haymark

Debbie and husband, Joe, happily reside in the greater Houston area. In July of 2012 they opened their yarn shop, iPurl, in The Woodlands, Texas. An avid, possibly obsessed knitter, Debbie's days are spent in the shop with lots of yarn and visiting with friends, old and new.

Naomi Herzfeld

Naomi has always loved interacting with great fibers, believing that the history of fiber is the history of humankind. Most recently, she learned to knit and weave, and now co-owns Bella Yarns in Warren, Rhode Island (www.bellayarns.com) where she gets to buy and try an amazing variety of useful, lovely, and inspirational yarns.

Marianne Hobart

Marianne lives with her family, dog, and two cats in the suburbs of Washington, D.C. Her day job as an accountant leaves little room for creativity. Thankfully, she has knitting and designing as an outlet for fun and artistic expression, and plenty of great knitwear as a result of her efforts.

Sarah Jean Hood

Sarah Jean is an avid knitter and lifelong student of color, Fair Isle, and lace. She's happiest teaching, designing, and writing patterns for her LYS in Kent, Connecticut, and pleased with her designated title "Friend of Store." On a good day she's outfitted in a cashmere tee, Fair Isle cardigan, lace scarf, and felted bag, dreaming of lace skirts, Fair Isle leggings, and assorted hats and mitts.

Gina House

Gina, author of *Dreamscape and Wonderlace* (soon to be published), loves to design luxurious and unique knitwear accessories. Her SleepyEyes app is free on iTunes, includes free patterns to download, patterns to purchase, and other knitting tools. You can visit Gina on her Facebook page (sleepyeyesknits) and website, *www.ginahouse.net*.

Kirsti Johanson

Kirsti spends her days teaching musical theater at MadCAP School of the Arts where she is Artistic Director. When not directing or knitting, she enjoys adventures with her husband, Steve. Kirsti has been published in *Spin Off* and *Jane Austen Knits*. Kirsti lives in Madison, Wisconsin, and can be found at *http://travellingstitchsisters.com* and @kjerstie (Twitter).

Molly Kent

Molly is a dyed-in-the-wool Northwesterner, currently stuck in the Midwest where she knits non-stop to keep warm. She draws inspiration from science, history, and nature. And she likes to make stuff, the more challenging the better. Molly can be found online at *www.octopuspaper.com* or on Ravelry as beadskater.

Knit Picks Design Team

Knit Picks proudly gives in to the siren song of the handmade. Never accepting that the end result is the only exciting part of the process, they strive for designs that feel decidedly unexpected, but always joyous to make.

Brigitte Lang

Brigitte learned to knit as a child and got really hooked while in college. She still knits daily, rarely using a pattern. Most of what she knits she makes up as she goes. Brigitte owns a yarn shop in Germantown, Tennessee.

Lindsay Lewchuk

A gift received became a passion embraced as Lindsay sought distraction from a medically mandated isolated life. One sweater accelerated into "Eco ChicKnits," in which three key philosophies reign: knits that fit curves; unique, intricate patterns; and eco materials. Concurrently, Lindsay is pursing an MA in philosophy and authored *Cheeky's Tales*.

Henna Markkanen

Henna is a budding knitwear designer from Finland. She loves lace, especially shawls, and gets bored easily with too simple patterns. You can find her on Ravelry as henna-markkanen.

Ann McClure

Ann is a professional writer and editor who has been crocheting since she was a child and knitting since 2001. When she isn't playing with yarn she enjoys spending time with her husband, Brian, and their two golden retrievers. Her patterns have also appeared in *Luxury Yarn One-Skein Wonders*, *Sock Club: Join the Knitting Adventure*, and *Sock Yarn One-Skein Wonders*. She blogs about her crafts and her dogs at *http://travelingann.blogspot.com*.

Marin Melchior

Marin's mom, Lois, taught her to knit when she was seven years old. She designed her first garment while in junior high school with the aid of Barbara Walker's *Treasury of Knitting Patterns*; it was a cabled vest. She enjoys making one-of-a-kind items, preferring to knit something only once.

Rebecca Mercier

Rebecca began knitting for what may seem an unusual reason. Living with severe pain, Rebecca hoped and prayed for something that she could do that would both occupy her time and take her mind off the pain. She discovered knitting and designing in 2004 and happily reports it helps with her pain. You can find her at *http://whimsicalknitting.blogspot.com* (personal) or *http://whimsicalknittingdesigns.blogspot.com* (design).

Nancy Miller

Nancy has been knitting for more than 20 years. She is a fiber addict who also loves to felt, spin yarn, and hook rugs. She teaches workshops on a variety of fiber topics and has had several of her designs and patterns appear in recent publications. Nancy lives in Maine, along with her husband and three daughters (who have already gotten hooked on felting), in a big old house by the sea that is busting with fiber.

Lorna Miser

Lorna has always loved all things girly: lace, lavender, makeup. Now she is lucky to have granddaughters to knit for also.

Michaela Moores

Michaela is a British designer from London. Her designs focus on playing with shape and scale and often feature original stitch patterns. She can be contacted via *www.michaelaknits.com*.

Jillian Moreno

Jillian Moreno spends her days and nights spinning yarn then knitting it; any extra time is spent talking and writing about the process. She is the editor of *Knittyspin*, Knitty.com's spinning little sister, and is on the editorial advisory board for *PLY Magazine*. She lives in a house packed with fiber and books in Ann Arbor, Michigan.

Melissa Morgan-Oakes

Melissa, author of *2-at-a-Time Socks*, *Toe-Up 2-at-a-Time Socks*, and *Teach Yourself Visually Circular Knitting* was taught to crochet, tat, and sew at an early age by women who encouraged her to create without patterns. Knitting she learned on her own, and she hasn't looked back since.

Angela Myers

Angela currently lives in northern California. She has been knitting since she was 10. She spends her days chasing her family and two dogs while attempting to knit, spin, and design fun patterns.

Meg Myers

Facing the long commute between her hometown in southern Colorado and college in Boston, Meg learned to knit as a practical way to pass the time. She got to work at her LYS while in school and joined Classic Elite Yarns after graduating. Learning to knit might have been her best idea, ever. Visit her at *www.my-meg.com*.

Liz Nields

Liz is an independent designer from Carlisle, Massachusetts. She has had her designs published by *Interweave Knits*, *Knit Simple*, *Vogue on the Go*, *Sock Yarn One-Skein Wonders*, Nashua Handknits, and Manos del Uruguay. When not knitting she's out in the gardens, New England weather permitting.

Christine Nissley

Christine started knitting about nine years ago thanks to a very good friend who introduced her to novelty yarn. Henceforth, Chrissie's Creations evolved. She has been knitting and designing for Laura Bryant of Prism Yarns for about seven years. Christine would like to further the adventure and try her hand at dyeing yarn.

Kendra Nitta

Kendra knits and designs primarily with silk and plant-based fibers. Her patterns have been featured in numerous books and magazines. Follow along at *www.missknitta.com*.

Cheryl Oberle

Cheryl is the author of three knitting books, including *Folk Shawls*, which contains knitted lace from around the world. At her studio in Denver, Colorado, Cheryl teaches lace and shawl knitting in classes and in her popular studio retreats. Cheryl enjoys sharing her lace knitting passion with other knitters. You can find her at *www.cheryloberle.com*.

Ohmay Designs

May, of Ohmay Designs, is a native of the San Francisco Bay area and owner and designer of the online hobby business *www.etsy.com/shop/ohmay*. Knitting has been a passion of hers for decades, and she has designed and created many patterns, with many more to come.

Marina Orry

Marina is a French designer living in Italy with her husband, baby boy, and two cats. She's the author of the book *Tricot: Premières Leçons* (France). She translates patterns for yarn companies and dreams about creating her own hand-dyed yarns. She blogs at *www.melusinetricote.com*.

Izumi Ouchi

Born in Tokyo, Izumi designs for books and magazines while teaching Ipponbari knitting in Japan. You can find more information on her knitting blog, Izumi's Knitting Notes, at *http://something.exblog.jp*.

Paula Papoojian

Paula learned to knit at the age of 10. Her passion for knitting continued through experiments with structure and design elements. Today she works at Harrisville Designs and has found a comfort zone in weaving fabric as well.

Sarah-Hope Parmeter

Sarah-Hope teaches writing and knits and writes about knitting at *www.whatifknits.com*. Nothing pleases her more than finding a new stitch in an obscure stitch dictionary. She and her wife share their lives with six very fine cats, indeed.

Brenda Patipa

Brenda has designed patterns for Knitty, *Knitter's Magazine*, *Knitscene*, and *Twist Collective*. Her pattern line, Brenda Patipa Knits, debuted in 2006 with Lisa Souza Knitwear and Dyeworks. Brenda teaches and lives in the San Francisco Bay area. You can find her designs on Ravelry as Beeeepatipaknits.

Jenise Reid

Between baking, sewing, and playing with her nieces and nephews, Jenise madly knits and publishes her patterns on Ravelry and with Knit Picks. She likes to have a long, complex project on her needles at all times and takes periodic breaks by knitting toques, gloves, and lace scarves.

Karlie Robinson

Sometimes it's hard to tell if Karlie is a high-tech entrepreneur or a housewife from a different time. See more of her patterns at *http://karlierobinson.com*.

Hélène Rush

Hélène is the owner of the yarn company Knit One, Crochet Too. She sold her first design in 1979 and has added more than 1,000 to her list since then. She loves to knit!

Yumiko Sakurai

Yumiko has been designing for Knitty, Petite Purls, and *Interweave Knits* since 2009. She lives in Atlanta, Georgia, with her husband, two children, and a dog. She loves photography and playing music in her free time. Please see more of her work at *www.harumidoridesigns.com*.

Vera Sanon

Vera is a knit and crochet designer who learned the craft as a young child and started designing as a teenager. Her designs can be found in various well-known publications, as well as on Ravelry.

Kerri Shank

Kerri owns The Dragonfly Yarn Shop. Open since 2004, the shop offers a variety of wool and luxury yarns and is the only yarn shop in Jonesville, Wisconsin. Monthly classes in addition to lessons by the hour are offered. Stop in for Open Knitting on Thursday afternoons.

Carol J. Sorsdahl

After losing her son in 2004 to brain cancer, Carol has knitted close to 1,000 hats and baby sweaters for charity in his name. Her patterns have appeared in machine and hand-knitting magazines and books. She lives in Gig Harbor, Washington, where she plays keyboard for her church.

Myrna A. I. Stahman

Myrna, author, designer, and publisher of *Stahman's Shawls and Scarves – Faroese-Shaped Shawls from the Neck Down and Seamen's Scarves*, enjoys exploring the many facets of lace knitting and introducing others to those explorations through her teaching and publishing endeavors. She currently has two books on lace knitting in the works.

Gwen Steege

A confirmed fiber fanatic since childhood, Gwen has edited more than two dozen books on crochet, knitting, spinning, weaving, and dyeing, and has contributed designs to several of them. She shares her passion for fiber in her book, *The Knitter's Life List*. She lives in Williamstown, Massachusetts, and blogs at *http://theknitterslifelist.wordpress.com*.

Meg Strong

Meg is a Nashville-based self-taught knitter who works at her LYS, Haus of Yarn. In other words, she's living the dream. She loves trying to convince friends to take up the craft, but doesn't hold it against them if they don't. She is also the founder and creative director of *knitknotes.com*, which produces clever knitting-based gift enclosures.

Lisa Swanson

Lisa is a novice designer, urged on by the wonderful group of women she knits with regularly, the Nokomis Beach Knitters. She never leaves the house without a project bag because, "You just never know where or when you'll find some knitting time!"

Laura H. Turnbull

Laura is a busy wife, mom, and social worker, who never leaves the house without a knitting project. She remembers asking her mom to teach her to knit when she was a little girl, never knowing it would become a lifelong passion.

Mindy Vasil

Mindy was born and raised in south Florida and still lives within 30 minutes of the beautiful Florida beaches with her husband and daughter. For the most up-to-date information, be sure to check out her website at *www.minknit.com*.

Katherine Vaughan

Katherine has been knitting for 25+ years and designing for more than five. She primarily designs children's clothing and accessories for adults and the home. She daylights as a medical librarian in North Carolina, where it is (almost) never too hot to knit. Visit her website at *www.ktlvdesigns.com*. Her Ravelry ID is KTLV.

Kim Whelan

Kim lives in Berkley, Michigan, where she is married and the mother of three adult children. When she is not at work, she spends her time designing knitwear, planning knitting projects, talking about knitting, hanging out on Ravelry, and actually, maybe, knitting.

Lynn M. Wilson

Lynn is a designer, knitting instructor, and dedicated knitter. Her designs have been featured in various knitting books and magazines. She has designed for Tahki Stacy Charles and Be Sweet and has her own collection of Lynn Wilson Designs knitting patterns. For more information, visit her website: *www.lwilsondesigns.com*.

Jill Wright

Jill learned to crochet at age eight in Newcastle, England. Jill has had designs published in *Interweave Crochet, Crochet!*, and *Love of Crochet*. Jill also designs for yarn companies such as Classic Elite, Universal, and Bison Basin Ranch. Jill's website is *www.woolcrafting.com*.

Abbreviations

CH	chain crochet
DC	double crochet
K	knit
K2TOG	knit 2 stitches together (1 stitch decreased)
K3TOG	knit 3 stitches together (2 stitches decreased)
KFB	knit into the front and back of stitch (1 stitch increased)
M1	make 1 stitch (see page 295)
M1L	make 1 stitch, left leaning (see page 295)
M1LP	make 1 purl stitch, left leaning (see page 295)
M1R	make 1 stitch, right leaning (see page 295)
M1RP	make 1 purl stitch, right leaning (see page 295)
P	purl
P2TOG	purl 2 stitches together (1 stitch decreased)
P3TOG	purl 3 stitches together (2 stitches decreased)
PFB	purl into the front and back of stitch (1 stitch increased)
PSSO	pass slipped stitch over last stitch on needle
RS	right side
S2KP	slip 2 stitches together knitwise, knit 1, pass 2 slipped stitches over (2 stitches decreased)
SC	single crochet
SKP	slip 1, knit 1, pass slipped stitch over knit stitch (1 stitch decreased)
SK2P	slip 1, k2tog, pass slipped stitch over knit together stitches (2 stitches decreased)
SSK	slip 1, slip 1, place left needle into front of slipped stitches and knit them together (1 stitch decreased)
SSP	slip 1, slip 1, place left-hand needle into back of slipped stitches and purl them together (1 stitch decreased)
TBL	through back loop
TR	treble crochet
WS	wrong side
WYIB	with yarn in back
WYIF	with yarn in front
YO	yarn over needle

Glossary

BACKWARD LOOP CAST ON. Hold the end of the yarn and a knitting needle in your right hand. Hold the working yarn in your left hand. Bring your left thumb over the top, down behind, and up in front of the yarn, creating a loop. Insert needle into loop on thumb as if to knit and slide loop onto needle. You may also use the backward loop cast on to add stitches to the end of a row of knitting or to increase stitches mid-row.

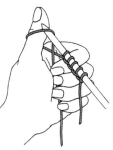

CABLE CAST ON. Make a slip knot and place it on your left-hand needle. Follow steps 1 and 2 for knitted-on cast on (see page 294) and then proceed as follows.

1. Place the second needle between the 2 stitches on the first needle (see figure 1).

2. Knit a new stitch between the 2 stitches, pull it long, and place in on the left-hand needle (see figure 2).

Continue in this manner, knitting between the last 2 stitches on the left-hand needle until you have the required number of stitches.

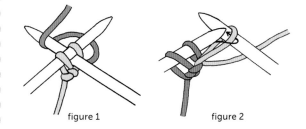

figure 1   figure 2

CHAIN (CROCHET). Begin with a slip knot on the hook. Wrap yarn over the hook and pull the loop through the slip knot. Yarn over hook, and pull loop through loop on hook to make second chain. Repeat for the required number of chain stitches.

CIRCULAR CAST ON (CAST ON AND DIVIDE). Using double-point needles, cast on the desired number of stitches and slip half of the stitches to a second needle. Join into a round and knit the stitches evenly onto three or four needles.

CIRCULAR CAST ON (CROCHET).

1. Leaving a 4"/10 cm tail, wrap the ball of yarn loosely around your thumb. Remove the loop from your thumb and work a single crochet into the loop for the desired number of stitches.

2. Distribute the stitches evenly onto three or four double-point needles.

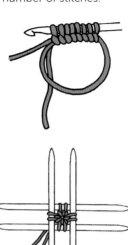

3. Pull up on the tail to snug the stitches into a tight ring.

CIRCULAR KNITTING ON TWO CIRCULAR NEEDLES.

Using two circular needles of the same size and length (16"/40 cm for small projects), cast on the required number of stitches onto one needle, then divide them evenly between the two needles, keeping the stitches on the needle tips. Holding the needle tips parallel, slide the stitches from both needles down along the cables and up onto the needle tips at the opposite ends. The working yarn should be at the right-hand side of the back needle (figure 1). Still holding the tips parallel, pick up the empty needle tip of the front needle and use it to knit the first stitch on the front needle, joining the stitches into a round (figure 2). Knit the remaining stitches from the front needle and drop the empty needle tip.

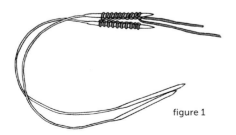

figure 1

Turn the work and slide the stitches that are now on the front needle down along the cable to the other needle tip. Pick up the empty needle tip of the front needle and work the stitches from this same needle. Continue in this manner, sliding stitches and knitting half the stitches with one needle and half the stitches with the other needle (figure 3).

figure 2

figure 3

DOUBLE CROCHET. Yarn over hook. Insert hook through both loops of the next stitch. Draw a loop through the stitch. Yarn over hook. Draw loop through the first 2 loops on the hook. Yarn over hook. Draw loop through 2 loops on hook.

EMBROIDERED CHAIN STITCH. Bring the needle from the back to the front through the fabric at the starting point and pull all but a short tail through the fabric. Bring the needle from front to back one or two threads away from the starting point and pull the thread through, leaving a small loop of thread on the front. Bring the thread to the front and through the loop at the desired length of your chain stitch. Bring the thread to the back one or two threads away from the last point, catching the loop; pull the thread through to the back, leaving a loop for the next stitch.

FIGURE-8 CAST ON.

1. Hold two double-point needles parallel. Leaving about a 4"/10 cm tail, and holding the tail against the needles with your left hand, *bring the yarn over the top needle from front to back, then bring the yarn between the needles and under the bottom needle from front to back (figure 1). Repeat from * until you have the desired number of stitches, with the same number on each needle.

2. With a third needle, knit the stitches from the top needle (figure 2). Turn the work 180 degrees and, with another needle, knit the stitches from the bottom needle.

figure 1

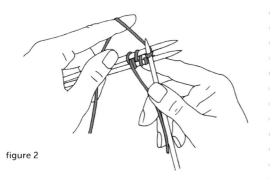

figure 2

GARTER STITCH. When knitting back and forth in rows, knit all rows. When knitting circularly, knit 1 row, purl 1 row.

I-CORD. Use two double-point needles to make I-cord. Cast on the required number of stitches. *Knit all stitches. Without turning work, slide the stitches to the other end of the needle. Pull the working yarn across the back. Repeat from * until cord is desired length. Bind off.

I-CORD BIND OFF. At the beginning of the bind-off row, cast on 3 stitches using the cable cast on (see page 290). *K2, ssk. Slip the 3 worked stitches back onto the left-hand needle. Pull the working yarn across the back of those 3 stitches and repeat from *. When 3 stitches remain, k3tog tbl.

To work the bind off with 2 stitches, work k1, ssk instead of k2, ssk; to work the bind off with 4 stitches, work k3, ssk instead of k2, ssk, and so on.

JUDY'S MAGIC CAST ON. This invisible cast on for sock toes, mitten and hat tops, and bag bottoms comes to the knitting world from Judy Becker. To see Judy's original instructions, go to *www.persistentillusion.com/blogblog/techniques/magic-cast-on*.

1. Hold two double-point needles together with your right hand, tips pointing left.

2. Loop the yarn around the top needle, with the tail sandwiched between the top needle and the bottom needle and coming out the back. The tail should measure approximately ¾"/2 cm for each stitch you are casting on. The working yarn goes over the top needle.

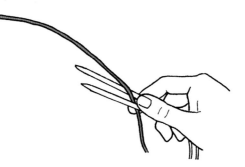

3. Pick up the yarns with your left hand in the sling-shot position, with the tail over your index finger and the working yarn over your thumb. This twists the yarns and creates a loop on the top needle that counts as the first stitch.

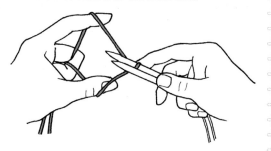

4. While holding the stitch in place with a finger on your right hand, rotate the pair of needles up and wrap the yarn on your finger around the bottom needle, as if making a yarnover. Gently tighten the loop.

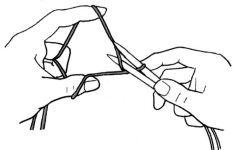

5. Rotate the pair of needles downward and wrap the thumb yarn around the top needle as if making a yarnover. Gently tighten the loop.

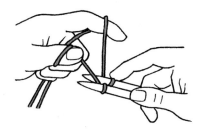

6. Repeat steps 4 and 5 to cast on the desired number of stitches. Alternate between top and bottom needles, with thumb yarn wrapping around the top needle and finger yarn wrapping around the bottom needle. End with step 4.

7. Turn the needles so that the bottom one is on top and the yarn ends on the right. Drop the tail and bring the working yarn up behind the top needle. Make sure the tail lies under the working yarn, between it and the needle. This twists the yarns so you can knit the first stitch. Knit the first row. The first stitch may become a little loose; just pull on the tail to tighten it.

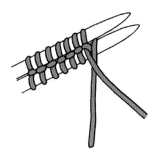

8. Turn needles at end of the first row and knit the next row (the second half of the first round).

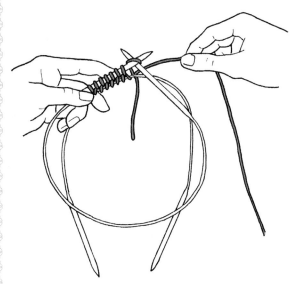

KITCHENER STITCH. This grafting technique is used to join two sets of live stitches invisibly. It is most often used for sock toes but can be used to join shoulder seams or two halves of a scarf.

1. Place the two sets of live stitches to be bound off on separate needles. Hold the needles parallel in your left hand with right sides of the knitted fabric together.

2. Thread the yarn tail on a yarn needle, insert the yarn needle into the first stitch on the front needle as if to knit, and slip the stitch off the needle. Then insert the yarn needle into the next stitch on the front needle as if to purl, and leave the stitch on the needle (figure 1).

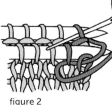

figure 1

3. Insert the yarn needle into the first stitch on the back needle as if to purl, and slip the stitch off the needle (figure 2).

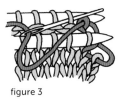

figure 2

4. Insert the yarn needle into the next stitch on the back needle as if to knit, and leave the stitch on the needle (figure 3).

figure 3

Repeat steps 2–4 until all stitches have been joined.

KNITTED-ON CAST ON. Make a slip knot and place it on your left-hand needle.

1. Knit a stitch into the slip knot, leaving the slip knot on the needle (figure 1).

2. Place the new stitch onto the left-hand needle by inserting the left-hand needle into the front of the new stitch (figure 2).

figure 1

3. Tighten the stitch and continue until you have the required number of stitches (figure 3).

figure 2

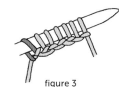

figure 3

KNITWISE. When a pattern says "slip the next stitch knitwise," insert your needle into the next stitch on the left-hand needle from front to back as if you were going to knit it, then slip it to the right-hand needle without knitting it.

LONG-TAIL CAST ON. Leaving a tail long enough to cast on the desired number of stitches (a generous guess would be 1"/2.5 cm per stitch), make a slip knot and place it on the needle.

1. Wrap one of the tails around your thumb and the other around your index finger. Hold the tails with your other three fingers (figure 1).

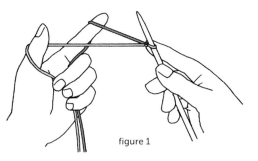

figure 1

2. Insert the needle into the loop around your thumb from front to back and over the yarn around your index finger (figure 2).

3. With the needle, bring the yarn from in front of your index finger down through the loop around your thumb (figure 3).

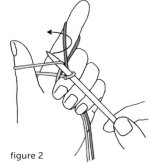

figure 2

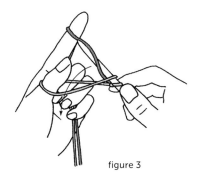

figure 3

4. Drop the loop off your thumb, tighten the stitch, and form a new loop around your thumb (figure 4).

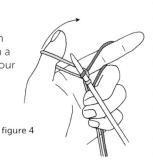

figure 4

M1 (MAKE 1) INCREASE. This increase is worked into the strand between the current stitch and the next one. Work in pattern to where you want to increase, lift the strand between the two needles, place the lifted strand on the left-hand needle as shown below, then knit or purl the stitch.

M1L (LEFT SLANT, KNIT). Insert the left-hand needle from front to back, knit through the back.

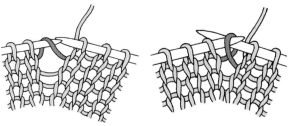

M1R (RIGHT SLANT, KNIT). Insert the left-hand needle from back to front, knit through the front.

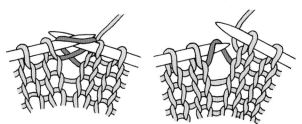

M1LP (LEFT SLANT, PURL). Insert the left-hand needle from front to back, purl through the back.

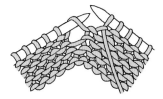

M1RP (RIGHT SLANT, PURL). Insert the left-hand needle from back to front, purl through the front.

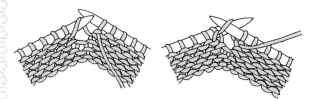

MAGIC LOOP. Using a circular needle at least 32"/ 80 cm long, cast on the required number of stitches and slide them onto the cable. Pull a loop of cable out between the two center cast-on stitches. Keep pulling the cable out between the stitches until the stitches are moved onto the needle tips, half the stitches on each tip (figure 1).

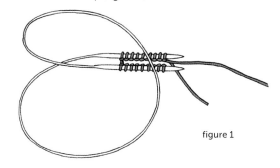

figure 1

Hold the needle tips parallel and make sure the working yarn is on the back needle tip — if it's not on the back needle, slide the stitches back to the cable and start again, making sure the yarn ends up on the back needle tip. Now slide the stitches on the back needle tip down onto the cable and use the back needle tip as your working (right-hand) needle to knit the stitches from the other (left-hand) needle tip (figure 2). You've just knit half the round.

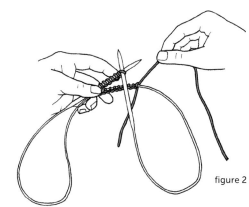

figure 2

295

Turn the work and hold the needles with both tips facing to the right and slide the unknit stitches onto the free needle tip and then slide the stitches that you just knit onto the cable. Now use the free needle tip as your right-hand needle to knit the second half of the round (figure 3). Continue in this manner, rearranging the stitches after completing each half-row.

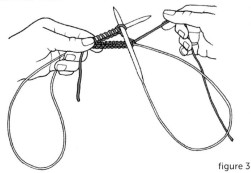

figure 3

MATTRESS STITCH. For a half-stitch seam allowance, work through the horizontal bar at the base of the stitches in every other row (figure 1).

For a full-stitch seam allowance, work through two horizontal bars on either side of the stitches (figure 2).

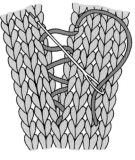

figure 1   figure 2

MÖBIUS CAST ON. This clever cast on was made popular by Cat Bordhi in *A Treasury of Magical Knitting*. It requires a 40"/100 cm circular needle. For more information visit *http://catbordhi.com*.

1. Holding the needle in a circle with the tips at the top, make a slip knot with a short tail, place it on the left-hand needle, and slide it into the middle of the cable; let the left-hand needle tip dangle.

2. Hold the yarn attached to the ball from behind the needle with your left hand and pinch the left side of the cable with the thumb and middle finger of your left hand. The yarn, your hand, and the cable of the circular needle make a kind of triangle. Your right hand holds the right-hand needle tip, while pinching the slip knot with the thumb and middle finger of the right hand. This is the "home" position.

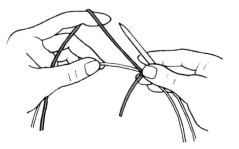

3. Reach the right-hand needle tip in front of the cable, then underneath the cable and up between the cable and yarn.

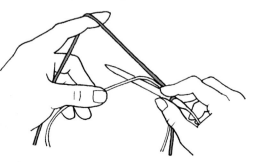

4. Reach the needle over the top of the yarn and scoop it forward and under the cable, then back up top to the home position.

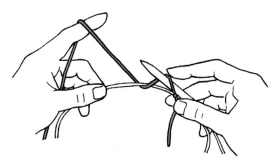

5. Reach the needle up, over, and behind the yarn and scoop a loop forward. (This looks like a yarnover). Both stitches will be slanting the same way.

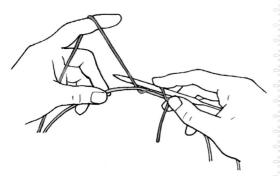

6. Repeat steps 3–5 for the desired number of stitches. Count each stitch made by the right-hand needle as 1 stitch. Do not count the stitches that appear on the cable beneath the needle.

7. To keep the stitches from twisting, make sure the cable and needles cross only once (making that Möbius twist). To do this, push/pull the cable, needles, and stitches so that the cable is flat and the sides are parallel to each other. With both needles at the top ready to knit, let the right-hand needle cross the cable at the top. The cable and left-hand needle are parallel to each other all the way around. You may have to rotate the left-hand needle around the cable to make this happen.

8. Place a marker on your right-hand needle and knit the slip knot.

9. The stitches on the first half of the round often tend to slide out of order and over each other, so make sure you spread them out as you move them up onto the left-hand needle. Notice, too, that the stitches are mounted alternately. Your job is simply to knit through whatever open triangle presents itself. This means you knit 1 stitch through the back and the next stitch through the front.

10. When you have knit to the point where the stitch marker is hanging on the cable beneath your needle (it cannot be removed at this point), you are halfway around. You'll see your original slip knot again, too. Tug down on it, and knit into the stitch formed by the side of the slip knot.

11. Continue knitting (all stitches are now mounted correctly, although they now look as though you've purled them) until the stitch marker reaches the left-hand needle tip. You have completed the first round. From this point on, knit each round as desired.

PICK UP AND KNIT. With right side facing, insert the needle under both strands of the edge stitch, then wrap the yarn around the needle and knit the picked-up stitch.

PICK UP AND PURL. Insert the needle under both strands of the edge stitch from back to front, then wrap the yarn around the needle and purl the picked-up stitch.

PROVISIONAL CAST ON (CROCHET CHAIN).
1. Make a crochet chain with scrap yarn that is at least 6 chains longer than the number of stitches to be cast on.

2. Cast on by knitting with the project yarn into the back loops of the chain.

3. To remove the scrap yarn when you've finished the knitting, pull out the crocheted chain and carefully place the live stitches on a needle.

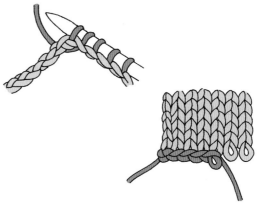

PROVISIONAL CAST ON (CROCHET OVER NEEDLE).

1. Make a slip knot and place it on a crochet hook. Hold your knitting needle on top of a long strand of yarn (figure 1).

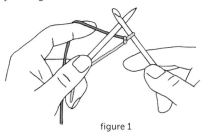

figure 1

2. *With the crochet hook, draw the yarn over the needle and through the loop on the hook. To cast on another stitch, bring yarn behind knitting needle into position as for step 1, and repeat from * (figures 2 and 3). *Note: If you find it awkward to cast on the first couple of stitches, work a few crochet chain stitches before casting onto the needle so you have something to hold on to.*

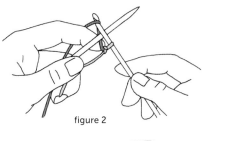

figure 2

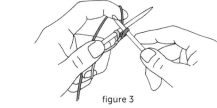

figure 3

3. When the last stitch has been cast on, work 2 or 3 extra crochet chain stitches without taking the yarn around the knitting needle, then cut the yarn, leaving a 10"/25.5 cm tail, draw the tail through the last loop on the hook, and pull the tail to close the loop loosely — just enough so the tail can't escape. To remove the scrap yarn when you've finished the knitting, pull the tail out of the last loop and gently tug on it to "unzip" the chain and carefully place the live stitches

on a needle, holder, or separate length of scrap yarn as they are released (figure 4).

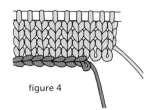

figure 4

PURLWISE. When a pattern says "slip the next stitch purlwise," insert your right-hand needle into the next stitch from back to front as if you were going to purl it, then slip it to the right-hand needle without purling it.

SEWN BIND OFF. Cut yarn three times the width of knitting to be bound off, and thread it onto a yarn needle. Working from right to left, *insert the yarn needle purlwise (from right to left) through the first 2 stitches (figure 1) and pull yarn through.

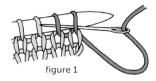

figure 1

Bring the yarn needle knitwise (from left to right) through the first stitch (figure 2), pull yarn through, and slip this stitch off the knitting needle. Repeat from *.

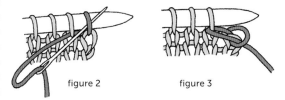

figure 2   figure 3

SINGLE CROCHET. Insert hook into next stitch, wrap yarn over hook, and draw the loop through the stitch. You now have 2 loops on the hook. Yarn over hook and draw loop through both loops on hook.

SLIP STITCH CROCHET. Insert hook into the next stitch, wrap yarn over hook, and draw the loop through the stitch and the loop on the hook.

STOCKINETTE STITCH. When knitting back and forth in rows, knit the right-side rows, purl the wrong-side rows. When knitting circularly, knit all rounds.

THREE-NEEDLE BIND OFF. This technique is used to join two sets of live stitches.

1. Place the two sets of stitches to be bound off on separate needles. Hold the needles parallel in your left hand with right sides of the knitted fabric touching.

2. Insert the tip of a third needle into the first stitch on both needles and knit these 2 stitches together.

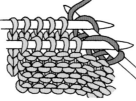

3. Repeat step 2. *You now have* 2 stitches on the right-hand needle. With one of the needles in your left hand, lift the first stitch on the right-hand needle over the second and off the needle as for a regular bind off. Repeat until all stitches are bound off.

TUBULAR CAST ON. Using scrap yarn and your method of choice, cast on half the number of stitches needed. Divide the stitches onto four double-point needles, join for working in the round, and knit 1 round with a smooth cotton cord. Join the main yarn and proceed as follows.

ROUND 1: *K1, yo; repeat from * to end of round.

ROUND 2: *K1, yarn forward, slip 1 purlwise, yarn back; repeat from * to end of round.

ROUND 3: *Yarn back, slip 1 purlwise, yarn forward, p1; repeat from * to end of round.

ROUND 4: *K1, p1; repeat from * to end of round.

When you've completed the rib, pull the cotton cord gently to remove it and the scrap yarn from the work.

GUIDE TO YARN WEIGHTS		
TYPES OF YARN	**STITCHES IN 4"/10 CM STOCKINETTE STITCH**	**RECOMMENDED NEEDLE SIZE**
0 LACE (10-count crochet thread, lace, fingering)	33–40	000–1 (1.5–2.25 mm)
1 SUPER FINE (sock, fingering, baby)	27–32	1–3 (2.25–3.25 mm)
2 FINE (sport, baby)	23–26	3–5 (3.25–3.75 mm)
3 LIGHT (DK, light worsted)	21–24	5–7 (3.75–4.5 mm)
4 MEDIUM (worsted)	16–20	7–9 (4.5–5.5 mm)
5 BULKY (chunky, craft)	12–15	9–11 (5.5–8 mm)

This system of categorizing yarn, gauge ranges, and recommended needle and hook sizes was developed by the Craft Yarn Council of America and was used to classify the projects in this book.

Index

Italics indicate illustrations; **bold** indicates charts.

A

Absolu Lace Cowl, 187–88

Alexandra Hat, 23–24, **24**

Alka Dishcloth Set, 273–75, **274**

Allen, Cynthia, 277, 284

Anderson, Julie L., 124, 284

April Showers Cowl, 173–74

B

baby blankets

    Granny's Little Diamond Lace Blankie, 122–23, **123**

    Lacy Pig Buddy, 124–26

    Welcome Home Baby Blanket, 120–21, **121**

Baby Twist Pullover, 103–5

baby and toddler wear

    Baby Twist Pullover, 103–5

    Bunny Check Baby Hat, 90–91, **91**

    Coral Reef Hat, 86–87, **87**

    Hana, 109–11

    Haru, 112–14, **114**

    I Heart You Dress, 115–19, **117**

    Kaya Baby Sweater, 95–99, **96, 99**

    Lace Baby Top, 100–2

    Little Leg Warmers, 92–94, **94**

    Sea Mist Baby Hat, 88–89

    Three-Button Baby Sweater, 105–8

backward loop cast on, 290, *290*

bags

    Lattice Frost Purse, 261–64

    Lucy Steele's Fancywork Bags, 248–51, **250**

Ballsmith, Sharon, 8, 224, 284

Barry, Tonia, 86, 284

beads, knitting with
  Beaded Lace Scarf, 134–36, **136**
  Gabriella Bracelet and Choker, 257–58
  Julep's Beaded Shawl, 207–10, **208–9**
  Lake Effect Scarf, 148–49
  Lucy Steele's Fancywork Bags, 248–51, **250**
  Moss & Leaves Stole, 233–39, **235–37, 239**
  PB (place bead), 134, 149, 207, 233, 249
Belt, Linen Lace, 254–55, **255**
Benson, Barbara, 246, 284
bind off
  conch, 271
  I-cord, 292
  picot, 86, 140, 168
  sewn, 241, 298, *298*
  three-needle, 299, *299*
  with larger needle, 241
Blackledge, Rae, 8, 143, 188, 193, 284
Blagojevich, Julie, 8, 211, 284
blankets. *See* baby blankets
bobble, 183
bobble, slender (crochet), 262
Bracelet and Choker, Gabriella, 257–58
brk (brioche knit, or "bark"), 149
Broadhurst, Heather, 218, 284
Broomstick Lace Scarf, 157–58
Buckhorn Socks, 71–73, **72**
Bunny Check Baby Hat, 90–91, **91**
Burkhard, Christiane, 82, 284
Burton, Sarah, 148, 284
Butterflies Are Free, 145–47, **147**

C
cable cast on, 290, *290*
cables
  C4B and C4F, 33
  C8B, 74

½ left and ½ right, 22
Cameron, Kim, 259, 284
caps. *See* hats and caps
Carrigan, Amanda, 8, 214, 226, 285
cast on
  backward loop, 290, *290*
  cable, 290, *290*
  circular, 290, 291, *291*
  figure-8, 292, *292*
  Judy's magic, 292–93, *292–93*
  knitted-on, 294, *294*
  long-tail, 294–95, *294–95*
  möbius, 296–97, *296–97*
  provisional (crochet chain), 297, *297*
  provisional (crochet over needle), 298, *298*
  tubular, 299
centered double decrease, 188
chain stitch, embroidered, 291–92, *292*
chain, making a (crochet), 290
Chantilly Lace Scarf, 155–56, **156**
Choose Your Look Scarf, 167–68
Christine's Alpaca Lace Scarf, 132–34, **133**
circular cast on, 290, 291, *291*
circular knitting on two circular needles, 291, *291*
Circular Magic Trivet Set, 281–82, **282**
Clement, Jean M., 150, 285
Cleopatra Scarf, 158–63, **160–62**
cluster, stitch, 116, 194
Collard, Terry, 88, 180, 285
Coral Reef Hat, 86–87, **87**
Cortona Kerchief, 211–13
cowls
  Absolu Lace Cowl, 187–88
  April Showers Cowl, 173–74
  Flying Gulls Cowl, 180–81
  Islandwood Cowl, 183–85, **185**
  Jade Sapphire Cowl, 177–79, **179**

Mari Lace Cowl, 174–75
  Pitched Cowl, 186–87, **187**
  Silver Lamé Cowl, 176–77, **177**
  Violeta Cowl, 181–82, **182**
Crashing Waves Shawl, 200–203, **202–3**
crochet projects
  Cortona Kerchief, 211–13
  Lattice Frost Purse, 261–64
  Simply Sweet Shawl, 224–26
crochet techniques
  chain, 290
  circular cast on, 291, *291*
  double crochet, 291
  extended double crochet, 225
  picot, 211, 225
  point shell, 225
  single crochet, 298
  single crochet around handle, 262
  slender bobble, 262
  slip stitch, 298
  treble cluster, beginning and ending, 225
  V-stitch, 225
cuffs. *See* mitts, gloves & cuffs

D
Damask Lace Gloves, **56**, 56–59
Del Sonno, Tamara, 39, 285
Delaney, Sara, 8, 261, 285
decrease
  centered double, 188
  5 to 1, 116
decreasing twist (left and right), 22
Dimeler-Laurence, Kerin, 21, 285
Doll Ensemble, Meg's, 126–28
double crochet, 291
double crochet, extended, 225
Downy Buffalo Socks, 62–64, **63**
Drooping Elm Headband, 246–248, **247**
Durant, Judith, 8, 29, 115, 145, 230, 285

E

Eckel, Laura Hein, 152, 285
Ellie's Orange Tam, 29–30, **30**
embroidered chain stitch, 291–92, *292*
Emerald Lace Scarf, 141–42, **142**
Ellis, J. M., 181, 285
Etta Hat, 10–11
extended double crochet, 225

F

figure-8 cast on, 292, *292*
Firefly Table Mat, 275–77, **276**
Flemish Lace Socks, 79–81, **81**
Flutter Mitts, 54–56
Flutter Toque, 31–32
Flying Gulls Cowl, 180–81
Foster, Diana, 27, 126, 285

G

Gabriella Bracelet and Choker, 257–58
Galvez Socks, 68–70
garter stitch, 292
Gildersleeve, Mary C., 242, 285
gloves. *See* mitts, gloves & cuffs
Granny's Little Diamond Lace Blankie, 122–23, **123**
Grapevine Shawl, 218–23, **219–23**
guide to yarn weights, **299**

H

hair accessories
 Drooping Elm Headband, 246–248, **247**
 Lace Headbands, 259–61, **261**
 Wavelet Hair Tie, 251–53, **252–53**
Hana, 109–111
Haru, 112–14, **114**
Harvey, Ellen, 8, 120, 285
hats and caps
 Alexandra Hat, 23–24, **24**
 Ellie's Orange Tam, 29–30, **30**

 Etta Hat, 10–11
 Flutter Toque, 31–32
 Hepatica Hats, 25–26, **26**
 Lace Liberty Wool Hat, 14–15, **15**
 Nicole's Angora Beanie, 27–28
 Pine Needle Toque, 16–17, **17**
 Tilting Ladders Hat, 33–35, **35**
 Tredegar Hat, 12–13, **13**
 Twig Lace Cap, 21–23, **22**
 Very Pretty Lace Beret, 18–21, **20**
Haymark, Debbie, 8, 68, 286
Hepatica Hats, 25–26, **26**
Herzfeld, Naomi, 79, 286
Hobart, Marianne, 136, 286
home dec projects
 Alka Dishcloth Set, The, 273–75, **274**
 Circular Magic Trivet Set, 281–82, **282**
 Firefly Table Mat, 275–77, **276**
 Iloise Lace Bath Set, The, 266–69, **268–69**
 Lace Bottle Cozy, 270–72, **272**
 New Wave Sachets, 277–78
 Tilting Blocks Pillow, 279–80
Hood, Sarah Jean, 33, 48, 286
House, Gina, 174, 286

I

I Heart You Dress, 115–19, **117**
I-cord, making and binding off, 292
Iloise Lace Bath Set, The, 266–69, **268–69**
increase, 1 into 3 and 3 into 9, 214
Indian Paintbrush Shawl, 204–6, **206**
Islandwood Cowl, 183–85, **185**
Isobel Shawl, 193–99, **196–99**

J

Jade Sapphire Cowl, 177–79, **179**

Johanson, Kirsti, 248, 286
Judy's magic cast on, 292–93, *292–93*
Julep's Beaded Shawl, 207–10, **208–9**

K

Kaya Baby Sweater, 95–99, **96, 99**
Kent, Molly, 183, 286
Kitchener stitch, 293–94, *294*
Knit Picks Design Team, 286
knitted-on cast on, 294, *294*
knitwise, 294

L

LT (left twist), 74, 141
Lace Baby Top, 100–102
Lace Bottle Cozy, 270–72, **272**
Lace Headbands, 259–61, **261**
Lace Liberty Wool Hat, 14–15, **15**
Lacy Hand Warmers, 39–42
Lacy Legs!, 256–57, **257**
Lacy Pig Buddy, 124–26
Lake Effect Scarf, 148–49
Lang, Brigitte, 187, 286
Lattice Frost Purse, 261–64
left decreasing twist, 22
leg warmers
 Lacy Legs!, 256–57, **257**
 Little Leg Warmers, 92–94, **94**
Linen Lace Belt, 254–55, **255**
Lewchuk, Lindsay, 158, 286
Little Leg Warmers, 92–94, **94**
long-tail cast on, 294–95, *294–95*
Lucy Steele's Fancywork Bags, 248–51, **250**
Luxe Möbius Scarf, 139–40, **140**

M

M1 (make 1) increase, 295
M1L (left slant, knit), 295, *295*
M1LP (left slant, purl), 295, *295*
M1R (right slant, knit), 295, *295*
M1RP (right slant, purl), 295, *295*

Magenta Mohair Lace Stole, 240–41, **241**
magic loop, 295–96, *295–96*
Markkanen, Henna, 8, 169, 286
Mary's Shawl, 192–93
mattress stitch, 296, *296*
McClure, Ann, 43, 287
Meg's Doll Ensemble, 126–28
Melchior, Marin, 130, 287
Melifera Shawl, 226–29, **228–29**
Menat Scarf, **150**, 150–51
Mercier, Rebecca, 8, 60, 74, 141, 155, 287
Mezzaluna Scarf, 136–39, **138**
Miller, Nancy, 257, 287
Mirabel Shawl, 188–91, **191**
Miser, Lorna, 100, 287
mitts, gloves & cuffs
    Damask Lace Gloves, **56**, 56–59
    Flutter Mitts, 54–56
    Lacy Hand Warmers, 39–42
    Pine Needle Mittens, 51–53, **53**
    Spicy Lace Cuffs, 60–61, **61**
    Sweet Pea Mitts, 36–38, **38**
    Travel-Worthy Mitts, 48–50, **50**
    Trellis Mitts, 43–45, **45**
    Vine Lace Fingerless Gloves, 46–47
möbius cast on, 296–97, *296–97*
Moores, Michaela, 12, 287
Moreno, Jillian, 23, 287
Morgan-Oakes, Melissa, 62, 287
Moss & Leaves Stole, 233–39, **235–37, 239**
Myers, Angela, 200, 287
Myers, Meg, 8, 14, 207, 275, 287

N

New Wave Sachets, 277–78
Nicole's Angora Beanie, 27–28
Nields, Liz, 8, 103, 240, 287
Nissley, Christine, 134, 287
Nitta, Kendra, 270, 288

O

Oberle, Cheryl, 8, 109, 112, 288
Ohmay Designs, 46, 288
Orry, Marina, 192, 256, 288
Ostrich Plumes Scarf, 166–67
Ouchi, Izumi, 176, 288

P

Paper Lanterns Scarf, 154–55
Papoojian, Paula, 164, 288
Parmeter, Sarah-Hope, 139, 154, 288
Patipa, Brenda, 64, 95, 288
pick up and knit, 297, *297*
pick up and purl, 297
pick up dropped yarnovers, 226
picot (crochet), 211, 225
picot bind off, 86
Pine Needle Mittens, 51–53, **53**
Pine Needle Toque, 16–17, **17**
Pitched Cowl, 186–87, **187**
place bead, 134, 149, 207, 233, 249
point shell (crochet), 225
provisional cast on
    crochet chain, 297, *297*
    crochet over needle, 298, *298*
purlwise, 298

R

RC (right cross), 194
RT (right twist), 74, 141
Raindrops Scarf, 152–53
Red Sky at Night Capelet, 242–44, **243–44**
Reid, Jenise, 8, 16, 31, 51, 54, 166, 251, 288
right decreasing twist, 22
River Rapids, 143–44, **144**
Robinson, Karlie, 8, 157, 288
Rush, Hélène, 71, 288

S

Sakurai, Yumiko, 56, 288
Sanon, Vera, 8, 18, 204, 288

scarves
    Beaded Lace Scarf, 134–36, **136**
    Broomstick Lace Scarf, 157–58
    Butterflies Are Free, 145–47, **147**
    Chantilly Lace Scarf, 155–56, **156**
    Choose Your Look Scarf, 167–68
    Christine's Alpaca Lace Scarf, 132–34, **133**
    Cleopatra Scarf, 158–63, **160–62**
    Emerald Lace Scarf, 141–42, **142**
    Lake Effect Scarf, 148–49
    Luxe Möbius Scarf, 139–140, **140**
    Menat Scarf, **150**, 150–51
    Mezzaluna Scarf, 136–39, **138**
    Ostrich Plumes Scarf, 166–67
    Paper Lanterns Scarf, 154–55
    Raindrops Scarf, 152–53
    River Rapids, 143–44, **144**
    Spray of Lace, A, **164**, 164–65
    Spring Leaves Scarf, 130–31, **131**
    Symmetria Scarf, 169–72, **170–72**
Sea Mist Baby Hat, 88–89
sewn bind off, 298, *298*
Shank, Kerri, 233, 289
shawls and stoles
    Cortona Kerchief, 211–13
    Crashing Waves Shawl, 200–203, **202–3**
    Grapevine Shawl, 218–23, **219–23**
    Indian Paintbrush Shawl, 204–6, **206**
    Isobel Shawl, 193–99, **196–99**
    Julep's Beaded Shawl, 207–10, **208–9**
    Magenta Mohair Lace Stole, 240–41, **241**
    Mary's Shawl, 192–93
    Melifera Shawl, 226–29, **228–29**
    Mirabel Shawl, 188–91, **191**

Moss & Leaves Stole, 233–39, **235–37, 239**

Red Sky at Night Capelet, 242–44, **243–44**

Simply Sweet Shawl, 224–26

Snowdrop Shawlette, 214–17, **216–17**

Trellis Leaf Stole, **230**, 230–32

Silver Lamé Cowl, 176–77, **177**

Simply Sweet Shawl, 224–26

single crochet, 298

single crochet around handle, 262

slender bobble (crochet), 262

slip stitch crochet, 298

Small Falls Socks, 82–84, **84**

Snowdrop Shawlette, 214–17, **216–17**

socks

    Buckhorn Socks, 71–73, **72**

    Downey Buffalo Socks, 62–64, **63**

    Flemish Lace Socks, 79–81, **81**

    Galvez Socks, 68–70

    Small Falls Socks, 82–84, **84**

    Tribute Socks, 64–67, **67**

    Vesta Socks, 74–78, **78**

Sorsdahl, Carol J., 105, 289

Spicy Lace Cuffs, 60–61, **61**

Spray of Lace, A, **164**, 164–65

Spring Leaves Scarf, 130–31, **131**

sssk (slip, slip, slip, knit), 39

Stahman, Myrna A. I., 122, 132, 266, 273, 281, 289

Steege, Gwen, 92, 279, 289

stitch cluster, 194

stockinette stitch, 298

stoles. *See* shawls and stoles

Strong, Meg, 173, 289

Swanson, Lisa, 8, 36, 289

Sweet Pea Mitts, 36–38, **38**

Symmetria Scarf, 169–72, **170–72**

T

Three-Button Baby Sweater, 105–8

three-needle bind off, 299, *299*

Tilting Blocks Pillow, 279–80

Tilting Ladders Hat, 33–35, **35**

tips for lace knitting

    blocking wires and pins, 232

    blocking, the magic of, 175

    casting on and binding off, 241

    casting on lots of stitches, 101

    following charts, 163

    joining new yarn, 119

    lifeline, ripping without, 146

    lifelines, using, 210

    linings, 264

    picking up missed yarnover, 153

    pointy needles, 142

    stitch markers, 108

toddler. *See* baby and toddler wear

toys

    Lacy Pig Buddy, 124–26

    Meg's Doll Ensemble, 126–28

Travel-Worthy Mitts, 48–50, **50**

treble cluster (crochet), 225

Tredegar Hat, 12–13, **13**

Trellis Leaf Stole, **230**, 230–31

Trellis Mitts, 43–45, **45**

Tribute Socks, 64–67, **67**

tubular cast on, 299

Turnbull, Laura H., 254, 289

Twig Lace Cap, 21–23, **22**

twist, LT and RT, 74

V

V-stitch (crochet), 225

Vasil, Mindy, 25, 167, 289

Vaughan, Katherine, 186, 289

Very Pretty Lace Beret, 18–21, **20**

Vesta Socks, 74–78, **78**

Vine Lace Fingerless Gloves, 46–47

Violeta Cowl, 181–82, **182**

W

Wavelet Hair Tie, 251–53, **252–53**

Welcome Home Baby Blanket, 120–21, **121**

Whelan, Kim, 8, 10, 289

Wilson, Lynn M., 177, 289

WL (work lifted strand), 39

wrap 3, 43

wrap and turn, 74, 207

Wright, Jill, 90, 289

Y

yarn weights, guide to, **299**

yarnovers, dropped 226

{ *Tips for Lace Knitting* }

blocking wires and pins . . 232

blocking, the magic of. . . 175

casting on and binding off 241

casting on lots of stitches 101

following charts 163

joining new yarn 119

lifeline, ripping without . . 146

lifelines, using. 210

linings 264

picking up missed yarnover. 153

pointy needles 142

stitch markers. 108

Welcome to the World of One-Skein Wonders

Judith Durant's best-selling One-Skein Wonders books each come with 101 unique projects for using those spare skeins or giving you a reason to buy more! From scarves and shawls to home dec accessories and outfits for baby, there are so many fabulous projects in each book, you'll want to buy them all!

One-Skein Wonders
240 pages. Paper.
ISBN 978-1-58017-645-3.

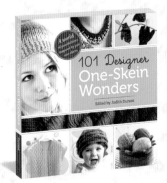

101 Designer One-Skein Wonders
256 pages. Paper.
ISBN 978-1-58017-688-0.

Luxury Yarn One-Skein Wonder
272 pages. Paper.
ISBN 978-1-60342-079-2.

Sock Yarn One-Skein Wonders
288 pages. Paper.
ISBN 978-1-60342-579-7.

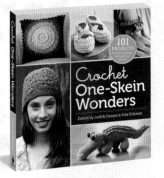

Crochet One-Skein Wonders
Edited by Judith Durant and Edie Eckman
288 pages. Paper. ISBN 978-1-61212-042-3.

These and other books from Storey Publishing are available wherever quality books are sold or by calling 1-800-441-5700. Visit us at *www.storey.com* or sign up for our newsletter at *www.storey.com/signup*.